# VENOMOUS SNAKES OF THE WORLD

## A CHECKLIST

# VENOMOUS SNAKES OF THE WORLD

## A CHECKLIST

By

**KEITH A. HARDING**
and
**KENNETH R. G. WELCH**

**PERGAMON PRESS**

OXFORD · NEW YORK · TORONTO · SYDNEY · PARIS · FRANKFURT

| U.K. | Pergamon Press Ltd., Headington Hill Hall, Oxford OX3 0BW, England |
|---|---|
| U.S.A. | Pergamon Press Inc., Maxwell House, Fairview Park, Elmsford, New York 10523, U.S.A. |
| CANADA | Pergamon of Canada, Suite 104, 150 Consumers Road, Willowdale, Ontario M2J 1P9, Canada |
| AUSTRALIA | Pergamon Press (Aust.) Pty. Ltd., P.O. Box 544, Potts Point, N.S.W. 2011, Australia |
| FRANCE | Pergamon Press SARL, 24 rue des Ecoles, 75240 Paris, Cedex 05, France |
| FEDERAL REPUBLIC OF GERMANY | Pergamon Press GmbH, 6242 Kronberg-Taunus, Pferdstrasse 1, Federal Republic of Germany |

First edition 1980

**British Library Cataloguing in Publication Data**

Harding, Keith A
Venomous snakes of the world.
1. Poisonous snakes
I. Title  II. Welch, Kenneth R G
598.1'2'0469      QL666.06      80-40162
ISBN 0-08-025495-0


Published as Supplement No. 1 (1980) to the
journal *Toxicon*.

*In order to make this volume available as economically and as rapidly as possible the author's typescript has been reproduced in its original form. This method has its typographical limitations but it is hoped that they in no way distract the reader.*

*Printed and bound in Great Britain by*
*William Clowes (Beccles) Limited, Beccles and London.*

# CONTENTS

# *PREFACE AND ACKNOWLEDGEMENTS*

Because of their medical importance, venomous snakes have in general attracted more attention from researchers than their harmless allies.  However, only one world checklist of species has previously been published (Klemmer, 1963).  This work, which we have not seen, appeared in a German publication sixteen years ago, since when many important revisions have taken place at all levels and several new forms have been described.  The need for an up-to-date summary has prompted us to compile this book, which is not intended as a treatise on venomous snakes, but merely as a simple and concise guide to present nomenclature and distribution.  Because of its wide scope and the somewhat unstable state of snake classification, it will rapidly become outdated, but every effort will be made to ensure that future editions keep abreast of developments.  Comments and criticisms, as well as new material for inclusion in the next edition, will be most gratefully received by us in care of the Publishing Manager (Life Sciences) at Pergamon Press, Headington Hill Hall, Oxford, OX3 OBW, England.

We wish to thank C.J. McCarthy of the Department of Zoology, British Museum (Natural History) for supplying citations and type details for twelve forms, Martin J. Richardson of Pergamon Press for many helpful discussions, and Jenny Drummond for re-typing the manuscript.

Keith A. Harding
Kenneth R. G. Welch


13th August, 1979

# INTRODUCTION

This checklist is divided into two sections: the first dealing with basic
taxonomy, and the second with geographical distribution. The taxonomic section is
arranged phylogenetically by families, subfamilies and tribes, with genera and
species listed in alphabetical order. Classification (see Table 1) follows Smith,
Smith and Sawin (1977), with three families (Elapidae, Hydrophiidae and Viperidae)
consisting entirely of venomous snakes, and three subfamilies (Natricinae,
Dispholidinae and Atractaspidinae) containing species capable of causing life-
threatening envenomation in man from the predominantly harmless Colubridae. Other
less dangerous, though technically venomous Colubrids, including members of the
subfamily Aparallactinae, have been omitted.

In Section 1, information given is restricted to the original description reference
and type species for genera, and the original description reference, original
citation (where necessary), type locality and brief details of present known
distribution for species and subspecies. Short taxonomic references are grouped
together at the end of Section 1 and all other references are listed in the main
Bibliography which follows Section 2. We have endeavoured to include all the
latest taxonomic revisions and range extensions. Synonymies, which are not included
in this checklist, may be found in the following important regional works: Broadley
(1968) for Africa, Hoge and Romano (1971) for Central and South America, Klemmer
(1968) for Europe and North Africa, Leviton (1968) for Asia and Indonesia, and
Klauber (1972) and Schmidt (1953) for North America.

Section 2 gives details of geographical distribution based on political boundaries.
A faunal list is given for each country or island group, to which recognized common
names have been added for those species which have them. Vernacular names have been
avoided due to their inconsistent usage. The sea snakes have been added to approp-
riate lists according to the shores off which they occur and not dealt with separ-
ately, by seas, as is sometimes the case. The final lists are arranged, as far as
possible, so that neighbouring countries appear in succession. Finally, references
to literature facilitating identification of species have been added to each faunal
list.

The Bibliography provides a useful guide to important literature on venomous snakes.

TABLE 1   Classification of Venomous Snakes

---

Class   REPTILIA   Reptiles
Order   SQUAMATA   Snakes and Lizards
Suborder   SERPENTES   Snakes
Infraorder   ALETHINOPHIDIA   Spectacled Snakes
Superfamily   COLUBROIDEA   Advanced Snakes


Family   COLUBRIDAE[1]   Colubrid Snakes
   Subfamilies   NATRICINAE[2]   Natricine Water Snakes
              DISPHOLIDINAE   African Rear-Fanged Snakes
              ATRACTASPIDINAE   Burrowing False Vipers


Series   PROTEROGLYPHA   Fixed Front-Fanged Snakes


Family   ELAPIDAE   Palatine Erectors
   Subfamily   BUNGARINAE   Cobras
     Tribes   BUNGARINI   Kraits
          NAJINI   Cobras, Mambas and African Coral Snakes

   Subfamily   ELAPINAE   Coral Snakes
     Tribes   ELAPINI   American and North Asiatic Coral Snakes
          MATICORINI   South Asiatic Coral Snakes
          LATICAUDINI   Sea Kraits


Family   HYDROPHIIDAE   Palatine Draggers
   Subfamily   OXYURANINAE   Australasian Venomous Snakes

   Subfamily   HYDROPHIINAE   True Sea Snakes
     Tribes   EPHALOPHINI   Ephalophine Sea Snakes
          HYDRELAPINI   Hydrelapine Sea Snakes
          AIPYSURINI   Aipysurine Sea Snakes
          HYDROPHIINI   Hydrophine Sea Snakes


Series   SOLENOGLYPHA   Movable Front-Fanged Snakes


Family   VIPERIDAE   Vipers
   Subfamily   VIPERINAE   Pitless Vipers
     Tribes   VIPERINI   True Vipers
          AZEMIOPINI   Fea's Viper
          CAUSINI   Night Adders

   Subfamily   CROTALINAE   Pit Vipers
     Tribes   LACHESINI   Bushmasters
          CROTALINI   Viviparous Pit Vipers

---

[1]Predominantly harmless family with three subfamilies containing venomous representatives.

[2]Predominantly harmless subfamily with two dangerous genera.

# SECTION 1
# *TAXONOMY*

# PART 1

# *Family COLUBRIDAE*

Subfamily NATRICINAE

Genus  BALANOPHIS  Smith 1938 p. 583.  Single species.
    Type species:  *Tropidonotus ceylonensis* Gunther

*Balanophis ceylonensis* (Gunther)
    *Tropidonotus chrysargus* var. *ceylonensis*  Gunther 1858 p. 71
    Type locality:  Ceylon
    Distribution:  Sri Lanka.

Genus  RHABDOPHIS  Fitzinger 1843 p. 27.  Twelve species.
    Type species:  *Rhabdophis subminiatus*  Fitzinger

*Rhabdophis auriculatus* (Gunther)
    *Tropidonotus auriculatus*  Gunther 1858 p. 80
    Type locality:  Philippine Islands
    Distribution:  Philippines.

*Rhabdophis callichroma* (Bourret)
    *Natrix chrysarga callichroma*  Bourret 1934 p. 155
    Type locality:  Ba-vi, Tong-King
    Distribution:  Vietnam.

*Rhabdophis chrysargoides* (Gunther)
    *Tropidonotus chrysargoides*  Gunther 1858 p. 71
    Type locality:  Sine patria
    Distribution:  Indonesia (Java and Sulawesi)

*Rhabdophis chrysargus* (Schlegel)
    *Tropidonotus chrysargus*  Schlegel 1837 p. 312
    Type locality:  Java
    Distribution:  Thailand, Malaya and Kampuchea.

*Rhabdophis himalayanus*  (Gunther)
   *Tropidonotus himalayanus*  Gunther 1864a p. 265
   Type locality:  Nepal
   Distribution:  Burma, India (Assam and Sikkim), Bhutan and Bangladesh.

*Rhabdophis murudensis*  (Smith)
   *Natrix murudensis*  Smith 1925 p. 5
   Type locality:  Mt. Murud, Borneo (5,500-6,000 ft)
   Distribution:  Borneo.

*Rhabdophis nigrocinctus*  (Blyth)
   *Tropidonotus nigrocinctus*  Blyth 1856 p. 717
   Type locality:  Pegu, Burma
   Distribution:  Burma.

*Rhabdophis nuchalis*  (Boulenger)
   *Tropidonotus nuchalis*  Boulenger 1891 p. 281
   Type locality:  Ichang, Upper Yangtse-Kiang
   Distribution:  Burma, western China, south-eastern Tibet and Vietnam.

*Rhabdophis spilogaster*  (Boie)
   *Tropidonotus spilogaster*  Boie 1827 p. 535
   Type locality:  Philippines
   Distribution:  Philippines.

*Rhabdophis subminiatus*  (Schlegel)
   *Tropidonotus subminiatus*  Schlegel 1837 p. 313
   Type locality:  Java
   Distribution:  India (Assam and Sikkim), Bhutan, Burma, Bangladesh, southern
        China, Thailand, Laos, Malaysia, Kampuchea, Vietnam, Taiwan and Indonesia.

*Rhabdophis swinhonis*  (Gunther)
   *Tropidonotus swinhonis*  Gunther 1868 p. 420
   Type locality:  Formosa
   Distribution:  Taiwan.

*Rhabdophis tigrinus*  (Boie)
   *Tropidonotus tigrinus*  Boie 1826 p. 205
   Type locality:  Japan
   Distribution:  China, Japan, Korea, Taiwan, Vietnam and Thailand.


                        Subfamily DISPHOLIDINAE


Genus  DISPHOLIDUS  Duvernoy 1832 p. 150.  Single species.
   Type species:  *Dispholidus lalandii*  Duvernoy


*Dispholidus typus typus*  (Smith)
   *Bucephalus typus*  Smith 1829 p. 441
   Type locality:  Old Latakoo, South Africa
   Distribution:  Africa south of the Sahara (Savannah areas).

*Dispholidus typus kivuensis*  Laurent 1955 p. 127
   Type locality:  Uvira, Lake Tanganyika, Kivu District, Ruanda-Urundi
   Distribution:  Zambia (Abercorn), Rwanda and Kenya (Eldoret and Subukia).

*Dispholidus typus punctatus* Laurent 1955 p. 129
    Type locality: Dundo, Angola
    Distribution: Angola, Zaire and Zambia.


Genus THELOTORNIS Smith 1849 p. 19. Single species.
    Type species: *Thelotornis capensis* Smith


*Thelotornis kirtlandi kirtlandi* (Hallowell)
    *Leptophis kirtlandii* Hallowell 1844 p. 62
    Type locality: Liberia
    Distribution: Somali Republic, Kenya, Tanzania, Uganda, Zaire, Angola, Congo,
        Gabon, Equatorial Guinea, Cameroun, Nigeria, Togo, Benin, Ghana, Ivory
        Coast, Liberia, Sierra Leone, Guinea and Guinea-Bissau.

*Thelotornis kirtlandi capensis* Smith 1849, p. 19
    Type locality: Kaffirland and the country toward Port Natal
    Distribution: Tanzania, Zambia (Abercorn), Malawi, Mozambique, southern
        Zimbabwe-Rhodesia, South Africa (north and east Transvaal, eastern Natal
        and northern Namibia) and southern Botswana.

*Thelotornis kirtlandi oatesi* (Gunther)
    *Dryiophis oatesi* Gunther 1881 p. 330
    Type locality: Matabeleland, Rhodesia
    Distribution: Angola, Zaire, northern Botswana and northern Zimbabwe-Rhodesia.


Subfamily ATRACTASPIDINAE


Genus ATRACTASPIS Smith 1849 p. 71. Fifteen species.
    Type species: *Atractaspis inornatus* Smith


*Atractaspis aterrima* Gunther 1863a p. 363
    Type locality: West Africa
    Distribution: Guinea, Guinea-Bissau, Ivory Coast, Ghana, Gabon, Zaire, Rwanda,
        Uganda and Tanzania.

*Atractaspis battersbyi* de Witte 1959 p. 350
    Type locality: Bolobo, Congo
    Distribution: Zaire.

*Atractaspis bibroni* Smith 1849 p. 51
    Type locality: Eastern districts of the Cape Colony
    Distribution: Kenya, Tanzania, Mozambique, Malawi, Zambia, Angola, South Africa,
        Botswana, Zimbabwe-Rhodesia and Swaziland.

*Atractaspis boulengeri boulengeri* Mocquard 1897 p. 16
    Type locality: Lambarene, Gabon
    Distribution: Gabon.

*Atractaspis boulengeri matschiensis* Werner 1897a p. 404
    Type locality: Cameroun
    Distribution: Cameroun.

*Atractaspis boulengeri mixta*  Laurent 1945 p. 332
  Type locality:  Mayombe, Lower Congo
  Distribution:  Zaire.

*Atractaspis boulengeri schmidti*  Laurent 1945 p. 333
  Type locality:  Route Aketi-Buta, Uele, Congo
  Distribution:  Zaire.

*Atractaspis boulengeri schultzei*  Sternfeld 1917 p. 489
  Type locality:  Mbio, Moyen-Congo
  Distribution:  Congo (Moyen-Congo).

*Atractaspis boulengeri vanderborghti*  Laurent 1956a p. 310
  Type locality:  Manguretshipa, Kivu, Congo
  Distribution:  Zaire (Kivu).

*Atractaspis coalescens*  Perret 1960 p. 130
  Type locality:  Bangwa, Cameroun
  Distribution:  Type locality only.

*Atractaspis congica congica*  Peters 1877 p. 616
  Type locality:  Chinchoxo, Cabinda
  Distribution:  Cameroun, northern Angola and Zaire.

*Atractaspis congica leleupi*  Laurent 1950a p. 351
  Type locality:  Kundelungu, Katanga, Congo
  Distribution:  Zaire (Kundelungu Mountains, eastern Katanga).

*Atractaspis congica orientalis*  Laurent 1945 p. 330
  Type locality:  Lualaba, Katanga, Congo
  Distribution:  Zaire (Katanga) and Zambia (Abercorn).

*Atractaspis corpulenta corpulenta* (Hallowell)
  *Brachycranion corpulentum*  Hallowell 1854 p. 99
  Type locality:  Liberia
  Distribution:  Cameroun, Gabon, Congo and Zaire.

*Atractaspis corpulenta kivuensis*  Laurent 1958 p. 127
  Type locality:  Bibugwa River, Kivu, Congo
  Distribution:  Zaire (Orientale and Kivu).

*Atractaspis corpulenta leucura*  Mocquard 1885 p. 15
  Type locality:  Assinie, Ivory Coast
  Distribution:  Ivory Coast and Ghana.

*Atractaspis dahomeyensis*  Bocage 1887 p. 196
  Type locality:  Zomai, Dahomey
  Distribution:  Guinea, Ivory Coast, Ghana, Benin, Nigeria and Cameroun.

*Atractaspis engaddensis*  Haas 1950 p. 52
  Type locality:  En-Geddi on the western side of the Dead Sea
  Distribution:  Israel, Egypt, Jordan and Lebanon.

*Atractaspis engdahli*  Lonnberg and Andersson 1913a p. 5
  Type locality:  Kismayu, Somalia
  Distribution:  Somali Republic.

*Atractaspis irregularis irregularis* (Reinhardt)
   *Elaps irregularis* Reinhardt 1843 p. 264
   Type locality: Gabon
   Distribution: Guinea, Liberia, Nigeria, Cameroun, Gabon, Sierra Leone, Ivory
         Coast, Ghana, Togo, Benin and Equatorial Guinea.

*Atractaspis irregularis angeli* Laurent 1950b p. 25
   Type locality: Mount Bizen, Eritrea
   Distribution: Ethiopia (Eritrea).

*Atractaspis irregularis bipostocularis* Boulenger 1905a p. 190
   Type locality: Fort Hall, near Mount Kenya, Kenya
   Distribution: Kenya, north-western Tanzania, Uganda, Rwanda and eastern Zaire.

*Atractaspis irregularis parkeri* Laurent 1945 p. 316
   Type locality: Kanungu, Congo
   Distribution: Cameroun, Zaire and northern Angola.

*Atractaspis irregularis uelensis* Laurent 1945 p. 320
   Type locality: Bambesa, Uele, Congo
   Distribution: Zaire (Uele), north-western Uganda and Sudan (Mongalla).

*Atractaspis leucomelas* Boulenger 1895a p. 16
   Type locality: Ogaden, Ethiopia
   Distribution: Ethiopia and the Somali Republic.

*Atractaspis microlepidota microlepidota* Gunther 1866 p. 29
   Type locality: Probably West Africa (in error)
   Distribution: Southern Sudan, Ethiopia, Kenya and Somali Republic.

*Atractaspis microlepidota andersoni* Boulenger 1905b p. 180
   Type locality: El Kubar, Aden
   Distribution: Yemen and South Yemen.

*Atractaspis microlepidota magrettii* Scortecci 1928 p. 308
   Type locality: Mandafena, Eritrea
   Distribution: Ethiopia (Eritrea) and southern Sudan.

*Atractaspis microlepidota micropholis* Gunther 1872a p. 36
   Type locality: Unknown
   Distribution: Mauritania, northern Nigeria, Mali and Niger.

*Atractaspis reticulata reticulata* Sjostedt 1896 p. 516
   Type locality: Ekundu, Cameroun
   Distribution: Cameroun.

*Atractaspis reticulata brieni* Laurent 1956b p. 256
   Type locality: Ipamu, Congo
   Distribution: Zaire.

*Atractaspis reticulata heterochilus* Boulenger 1901 p. 13
   Type locality: Albertville, Congo
   Distribution: Cameroun, Gabon, Equatorial Guinea and Congo.

*Atractaspis scorteccii* Parker 1949 p. 109
   Type locality: Haud, Somalia
   Distribution: Somali Republic.

# PART 2

# *Family ELAPIDAE*

Subfamily BUNGARINAE

Tribe BUNGARINI

Genus BUNGARUS Daudin 1803a p. 187. Twelve species.
   Type species: *Pseudoboa fasciata* Schneider

*Bungarus bungaroides* (Cantor)
   *Elaps bungaroides* Cantor 1839 p. 33
   Type locality: Cherra Pungi, Khasi Hills, Assam, India
   Distribution: Burma, India (Assam, Cachar and Sikkim).

*Bungarus caeruleus caeruleus* (Schneider)
   *Pseudoboa caerulea* Schneider 1801 p. 284
   Type locality: Vizagapatam, Andhra Pradesh, south India
   Distribution: Sri Lanka, India and Bangladesh.

*Bungarus caeruleus sindanus* Boulenger 1897 p. 73
   Type locality: Sind, West Pakistan
   Distribution: Pakistan (North-east Baluchistan and Sind) and India (Punjab and
      Bombay).

*Bungarus candidus* (Linnaeus)
   *Coluber candidus* Linnaeus 1758 p. 223
   Type locality: Habitat in Indiis
   Distribution: Vietnam, Malaysia, Indonesia (Bali, Sulawesi, Java and Sumatra)
      and south-eastern Thailand.

*Bungarus ceylonicus ceylonicus* Gunther 1864a p. 344
   Type locality: Ceylon
   Distribution: Sri Lanka (low elevations).

*Bungarus ceylonicus karavala* Deraniyagala 1955 p. 69
   Type locality: Gurutalava, near Valimada (C.P.)
   Distribution: Sri Lanka (above 2,500 ft).

7

*Bungarus fasciatus* (Schneider)
    *Pseudoboa fasciata* Schneider 1801 p. 283
    Type locality:  Bengal, India
    Distribution:  India, Burma, Thailand, Kampuchea, Laos, Vietnam, China, Malaysia
        and Indonesia (Sumatra, Java and Kalimantan).

*Bungarus flaviceps flaviceps* Reinhardt 1843 p. 267
    Type locality:  Java
    Distribution:  Thailand, Kampuchea, Malaysia and Indonesia (Kalimantan, Bangka,
        Sumatra, Java and Billiton).

*Bungarus flaviceps baluensis* Loveridge 1938 p. 44
    Type locality:  Kenokok River, near Kian, Mt. Kinabalu, North Borneo
    Distribution:  Type locality only.

*Bungarus javanicus* Kopstein 1932 p. 73
    Type locality:  Matanghadji, Soember, Cherobon, Western Java
    Distribution:  Indonesia (western Java).

*Bungarus lividus* Cantor 1839 p. 32
    Type locality:  Assam, India
    Distribution:  India (Bengal, Assam and Sikkim).

*Bungarus magnimaculatus* Wall and Evans 1901 p. 611
    Type locality:  Meiktila, Upper Burma
    Distribution:  Burma.

*Bungarus multicinctus multicinctus* Blyth 1861 p. 98
    Type locality:  Amoy
    Distribution:  China (Chekiang, Kiangsi, Hunan, Hupeh, Kwangsi and Hainan) and
        Taiwan.

*Bungarus multicinctus wanghoatingi* Pope 1928b p. 3
    Type locality:  Yuankiang, Yunnan, China
    Distribution:  Burma, China (Yunnan) and northern Laos.

*Bungarus niger* Wall 1908 p. 715
    Type locality:  Tindharia, eastern Himalayas, India
    Distribution:  India (Assam and Sikkim).

*Bungarus walli* Wall 1907 p. 608
    Type locality:  Fyzabad, Uttar Pradesh, India
    Distribution:  India (Bihar, West Bengal and Uttar Pradesh).

## Tribe NAJINI

Genus ASPIDELAPS Fitzinger 1843 p. 28.  Two species.
    Type species:  *Natrix lubrica* Laurenti

*Aspidelaps lubricus lubricus* (Laurenti)
    *Natrix lubrica* Laurenti 1768 p. 80
    Type locality:  Cape of Good Hope
    Distribution:  South Africa (west and central Cape Province and south Orange
        Free State).

*Aspidelaps lubricus cowlesi*  Bogert 1940 p. 94
    Type locality:  Munhino, Angola
    Distribution:  southern Angola.

*Aspidelaps lubricus infuscatus*  Mertens 1954 p. 215
    Type locality:  Farm Finkenstein, Windhoek, South West Africa
    Distribution:  South Africa (south-west).

*Aspidelaps scutatus scutatus*  (Smith)
    *Crytophis scutatus*  Smith 1849 p. 22
    Type locality:  Kaffirland and the country toward Natal
    Distribution:  South Africa, Botswana, Zimbabwe-Rhodesia and southern Mozambique.

*Aspidelaps scutatus intermedius*  Broadley 1968 p. 7
    Type locality:  Selati, Eastern Transvaal
    Distribution:  South Africa (eastern Transvaal).

*Aspidelaps scutatus fulafulus*  (Bianconi)
    *Naia fula-fula*  Bianconi 1849 p. 108
    Type locality:  Inhambane, Mozambique
    Distribution:  Southern Mozambique and south-eastern Zimbabwe-Rhodesia.


Genus BOULENGERINA  Dollo 1886 p. 159.  Two species.
    Type species:  *Boulengerina stormsi*  Dollo


*Boulengerina annulata annulata*  (Buchholz and Peters)
    *Naja annulata*  Buchholz and Peters 1877 p. 119
    Type locality:  Mbusu
    Distribution:  Cameroun, Gabon, Congo and Zaire.

*Boulengerina annulata stormsi*  Dollo 1886 p. 160
    Type locality:  Lake Tanganyika
    Distribution:  Zaire and Tanzania (borders of Lake Tanganyika).

*Boulengerina christyi*  Boulenger 1904, p. 14
    Type locality:  Leopoldville, Congo
    Distribution:  Congo.


Genus DENDROASPIS  Schlegel 1848 p. 5.  Four species.
    Type species:  *Elaps jamesonii*  Traill


*Dendroaspis angusticeps*  (Smith)
    *Naja angusticeps*  Smith 1849 p. 70
    Type locality:  Natal
    Distribution:  Kenya, Tanzania, Mozambique, Malawi, eastern Zimbabwe-Rhodesia
        and South Africa (Natal).

*Dendroaspis jamesoni jamesoni*  (Traill)
    *Elaps jamesonii*  Traill 1843 p. 179
    Type locality:  South America (in error)
    Distribution:  Guinea, Liberia, Ivory Coast, Ghana, Upper Volta, Nigeria, Togo,
        Benin, Cameroun, Central African Empire, Congo and Zaire.

*Dendroaspis jamesoni kaimosae*   (Loveridge)
  *Dendraspis jamesoni kaimosae*  Loveridge 1936 p. 64
  Type locality:  Kaimosi Forest, Kagamega, Kenya
  Distribution:  Zaire, Rwanda, Uganda and western Kenya.

*Dendroaspis polylepis polylepis*   (Gunther)
  *Dendraspis polylepis*  Gunther 1864b p. 310
  Type locality:  Zambezi River, Mozambique
  Distribution:  Southern Kenya, Zaire, Angola, Uganda, Rwanda, Tanzania, Zambia,
        Malawi, Mozambique, Botswana, South Africa, Zimbabwe-Rhodesia, Lesotho and
        Swaziland.

*Dendroaspis polylepis antinorii*   (Peters)
  *Dendraspis antinorii*  Peters 1873 p. 411
  Type locality:  Anseba, Eritrea
  Distribution:  Somali Republic, Ethiopia, north-east Uganda and northern Kenya.

*Dendroaspis viridis* (Hallowell)
  *Leptophis viridis*  Hallowell 1844 p. 172
  Type locality:  Liberia
  Distribution:  Senegal, The Gambia, Guinea, Guinea-Bissau, Liberia, Ivory Coast,
        Ghana and Sierra Leone.


Genus ELAPSOIDEA  Bocage 1866 p. 50.  Six species.
  Type species:  *Elapsoidea guntherii*  Bocage


*Elapsoidea guntheri*  Bocage 1866 p. 70
  Type locality:  Cabinda, Portugese Congo and Bissao, Portugese Guinea.
  Distribution:  Zaire, Angola, Zambia and Zimbabwe-Rhodesia.

*Elapsoidea laticincta* (Werner)
  *Elapechis laticinctus*  Werner 1919 p. 507
  Type locality:  Kadugli, Kordofan, Sudan
  Distribution:  Southern Ethiopia, Sudan, Zaire and the Central African Empire.

*Elapsoidea loveridgei loveridgei*  Parker 1949 p. 95
  Type locality:  Machakos, Kenya
  Distribution:  Kenya and northern Tanzania.

*Elapsoidea loveridgei colleti*  Laurent 1956a p. 281
  Type locality:  Astrida, Ruanda
  Distribution:  Zaire (Kivu), south-west Uganda and Rwanda.

*Elapsoidea loveridgei multicincta*  Laurent 1956a, p. 284
  Type locality:  Dramba, Uele, Congo
  Distribution:  Zaire (Kivu), Uganda, western Kenya and Tanzania.

*Elapsoidea loveridgei scalaris*  Laurent 1960, p. 60
  Type locality:  Luberizi, Kivu, Congo
  Distribution:  Zaire (Kivu).

*Elapsoidea nigra*  Gunther 1888 p. 322
  Type locality:  Ushambola
  Distribution:  Tanzania (Magrotto, Uluguru and Usambara Mountains).

*Elapsoidea semiannulata semiannulata*  Bocage 1882, p. 303
   Type locality:  Caconda, Angola
   Distribution:  Angola, south-western Zaire, western Zambia and north south-
      western South Africa.

*Elapsoidea semiannulata boulengeri*  Boettger 1895 p. 62
   Type locality:  Boroma, Mozambique
   Distribution:  Tanzania, Mozambique, Malawi, Zambia, Zimbabwe-Rhodesia, Botswana
      and South Africa.

*Elapsoidea semiannulata moebiusi*  Werner 1897a p. 400
   Type locality:  Kete, Togoland
   Distribution:  Senegal, southern Mauritania, Mali, Guinea-Bissau, Guinea, The
      Gambia, Sierra Leone, Liberia, Ivory Coast, Upper Volta, Ghana, Togo, Benin,
      Nigeria, Cameroun, Central African Empire, Congo and Zaire.

*Elapsoidea sundevalli sundevalli*  (Smith)
   *Elaps sundewallii*  Smith 1849 p. 66
   Type locality:  South Africa to the eastward of Cape Colony
   Distribution:  South Africa (Natal and Transvaal) and Swaziland.

*Elapsoidea sundevalli decosteri*  Boulenger 1888a p. 141
   Type locality:  Delagoa Bay, Mozambique
   Distribution:  Southern Mozambique, South Africa (Transvaal) and Swaziland.

*Elapsoidea sundevalli fitzsimonsi*  Loveridge  1944 p. 229
   Type locality:  Gomodimo Pan, Bechuanaland
   Distribution:  Western Botswana and South Africa (south-western and Cape
      Province).

*Elapsoidea sundevalli longicauda*  Broadley 1971 p. 617
   Type locality:  Malugwe Pan, southeastern Rhodesia
   Distribution:  South Africa (Northern Transvaal), south-eastern Zimbabwe-
      Rhodesia and Mozambique.

*Elapsoidea sundevalli media*  Broadley 1971 p. 615
   Type locality:  Edendale, Nr. Johannesburg, Transvaal
   Distribution:  South Africa (Transvaal, Orange Free State and northern Cape
      Province).


Genus HEMACHATUS  Fleming 1822 p. 295.  Single species.
   Type species:  *Hemachatus vulgaris*  Fleming


*Hemachatus haemachatus*  (Lacepede)
   *Coluber haemachata*  Lacepede 1789 p. 115
   Type locality:  Japon et Perse
   Distribution:  South Africa, Lesotho, Swaziland and Zimbabwe-Rhodesia.


Genus NAJA  Laurenti 1768 p. 90.  Six species.
   Type species:  *Coluber naja*  Linnaeus

*Naja haje haje*  (Linnaeus)
  *Coluber haje*  Linnaeus 1758 p. 225
  Type locality:  Lower Egypt
  Distribution:  Jordan, Egypt, Libya, Algeria, Tunisia, Morocco, Mauritania, Mali,
    Niger, Senegal, Upper Volta, Nigeria, Chad, Cameroun, Sudan, Ethiopia,
    Somali Republic, Tanzania, Kenya, Rwanda, Uganda, Zaire and the Central
    African Empire.

*Naja haje anchietae*  Bocage 1879 p. 89
  Type locality:  Caconda, Angola
  Distribution:  Angola, South Africa (south-western), Botswana, northern Zimbabwe-
    Rhodesia, Zambia and Zaire.

*Naja haje annulifera*  Peters 1854 p. 624
  Type locality:  Tete, Mozambique
  Distribution:  Zimbabwe-Rhodesia, South Africa (eastern Transvaal), Swaziland,
    Zambia, Malawi, Mozambique and eastern Botswana.

*Naja haje arabica*  Scortecci 1932 p. 47
  Type locality:  Sana, Yemen
  Distribution:  Saudi Arabia, Yemen and South Yemen.

*Naja melanoleuca*  Hallowell 1857 p. 61
  Type locality:  Gabon
  Distribution:  Senegal, Mali, Guinea-Bissau, Guinea, The Gambia, Sierra Leone,
    Liberia, Ivory Coast, Upper Volta, Ghana, Togo, Benin, Niger, Nigeria,
    Cameroun, Chad, Central African Empire, Sudan, Ethiopia, Somali Republic,
    Equatorial Guinea, Gabon, Congo, Zaire, Angola, Rwanda, Uganda, Kenya,
    Tanzania, Malawi, Mozambique, Zambia, Zimbabwe-Rhodesia and north-eastern
    South Africa.

*Naja mossambica mossambica*  Peters 1854 p. 625
  Type locality:  Sena and Tete, Mozambique
  Distribution:  Southern Tanzania, Malawi, Mozambique, southern Zambia, Botswana,
    Zimbabwe-Rhodesia, Swaziland and South Africa (Natal and Transvaal).

*Naja mossambica katiensis*  Angel 1922 p. 40
  Type locality:  Beledougou, Kati, Mali
  Distribution:  Mali, northern Nigeria and northern Ghana.

*Naja mossambica nigricincta*  Bogert 1940 p. 89
  Type locality:  Munhino, Angola
  Distribution:  North-western South Africa and south-western Angola.

*Naja mossambica pallida*  Boulenger 1896a p. 379
  Type locality:  Inland of Berbera, Somaliland
  Distribution:  Egypt, Sudan, Ethiopia, Somali Republic, Uganda, Kenya and
    northern Tanzania.

*Naja mossambica woodi*  Pringle 1955 p. 253
  Type locality:  Near Citrusdal, Cape Province
  Distribution:  South Africa (south-west and western Cape Province).

*Naja naja naja* (Linnaeus)
  *Coluber naja*  Linnaeus 1758 p. 221
  Type locality:  in India orientali
  Distribution:  Sri Lanka, India, Pakistan and Bangladesh.

*Naja naja atra*  Cantor 1842 p. 482
   Type locality:  Chusan Island, China
   Distribution:  South-eastern China, Taiwan and North Vietnam.

*Naja naja kaouthia*  Lesson 1831 p. 122
   Type locality:  Bengal
   Distribution:  India (Bengal and Assam), Bangladesh, Nepal, Sikkin, Burma,
      Thailand, Vietnam and south-west China.

*Naja naja miolepis*  (Boulenger)
   *Naia tripudians* var. *miolepis*  Boulenger 1896a p. 384
   Type locality:  Sarawak
   Distribution:  Philippines (Palawan) and Borneo.

*Naja naja oxiana*  (Eichwald)
   *Tomyris oxiana*  Eichwald 1831 p. 171
   Type locality:  Transcaspia
   Distribution:  Afghanistan, India (Kashmir and Punjab) and U.S.S.R. (Transcaspia).

*Naja naja philippinensis*  Taylor 1922 p. 265
   Type locality:  Manila, Luzon Island
   Distribution:  Philippines.

*Naja naja sagittifera*  Wall 1913 p. 248
   Type locality:  Andaman Islands
   Distribution:  Andaman Islands.

*Naja naja samarensis*  Peters 1861 p. 690
   Type locality:  Loquilocum, Samar Island
   Distribution:  Philippines (Bohol, Leyte, Mindanao and Samar).

*Naja naja sputatrix*  Boie 1827 p. 557
   Type locality:  Java
   Distribution:  Indonesia (Bangka, Bali, Sulawesi, Flores, Java, Komodo, Lombok
      and Sumbawa), Riou Archipelago and Malaya.

*Naja naja sumatrana*  Muller 1890 p. 277
   Type locality:  Solok, Sumatra
   Distribution:  Indonesia (Sumatra).

*Naja nigricollis*  Reinhardt 1843 p. 369
   Type locality:  Guinea
   Distribution:  Southern Mauritania, southern Mali, southern Niger, southern
      Egypt, Senegal, The Gambia, Guinea, Guinea-Bissau, Ivory Coast, Ghana,
      Upper Volta, Central African Empire, Sudan, Ethiopia, Somali Republic,
      Congo, Zaire, Rwanda, Uganda, Kenya, Tanzania, Zambia and northern Angola.

*Naja nivea*  (Linnaeus)
   *Coluber niveus*  Linnaeus 1758 p. 223
   Type locality:  Africa
   Distribution:  South Africa, Botswana and Lesotho.


Genus OPHIOPHAGUS  Gunther 1864a, p. 341.  Single species.
   Type species:  *Ophiophagus elaps*  Gunther

*Ophiophagus hannah*  (Cantor)
   *Hamadryas hannah*  Cantor 1836 p. 87
   Type locality:  Sandarbans, Near Calcutta, India
   Distribution:  India, Bangladesh, Burma, Thailand, Kampuchea, Laos, Vietnam,
       China (Fukien, Kwangtung and Kwangsi), Malaysia, Indonesia (Sumatra, Java,
       Kalimantan, Sulawesi and smaller islands in the western archipelago) and
       the Philippines (Balabac, Jolo, Luzon, Mindanao, Mindoro, Negros and Palawan).


Genus PARANAJA  Loveridge 1944 p. 231.  Single species.
   Type species:  *Naja anomala*  Sternfeld


*Paranaja multifasciata multifasciata*  (Werner)
   *Naia multifasciata*  Werner 1902 p. 347
   Type locality:  Upper Maringa River, Congo
   Distribution:  Zaire.

*Paranaja multifasciata anomala* (Sternfeld)
   *Naia anomala*  Sternfeld 1917 p. 482
   Type locality:  Assobam Forest region, Cameroun
   Distribution:  Cameroun.


Genus PSEUDOHAJE  Gunther 1858 p. 222.  Two species.
   Type species:  *Pseudohaje nigra*  Gunther


*Pseudohaje goldii*  (Boulenger)
   *Naia goldii*  Boulenger 1895b p. 34
   Type locality:  Near Asaba, Nigeria
   Distribution:  Ghana, Nigeria, Togo, Benin, Cameroun, Central African Empire,
       Gabon, Equatorial Guinea, Congo, Zaire, Rwanda, Uganda, Angola, Zambia and
       South Africa (north south-western).

*Pseudohaje nigra*  Gunther 1858 p. 222
   Type locality:  Sine patria
   Distribution:  Sierra Leone, Liberia, Ivory Coast, Ghana, Togo, Benin and
       Nigeria.


Genus WALTERINNESIA  Lataste 1887 p. 411.  Single species.
   Type species:  *Walterinnesia aegyptia*  Lataste


*Walterinnesia aegyptia*  Lataste 1887 p. 411
   Type locality:  Vicinity of Cairo
   Distribution:  Egypt, Israel, Syria, Lebanon, Jordan, Iraq, Iran, Kuwait and
       Saudi Arabia.

Subfamily ELAPINAE


Tribe ELAPINI


Genus CALLIOPHIS   Gray 1834 vol. 2, p. 86.   Ten species.
     Type species:  *Calliophis gracilis*  Gray


*Calliophis beddomei*   Smith 1943 p. 423
     Type locality:  Shevaroy Hills, Southern India
     Distribution:  India (Mysore).

*Calliophis bibroni*   (Jan)
     *Elaps bibroni*   Jan 1858 p. 526
     Type locality:  India
     Distribution:  India (western Ghats).

*Calliophis calligaster calligaster*   (Wiegmann)
     *Elaps calligaster*   Wiegmann 1834 p. 253
     Type locality:  Manila, Luzon Island
     Distribution:  Philippines (Luzon).

*Calliophis calligaster gemianulis*   (Peters)
     *Hemibungarus gemianulis*   Peters 1872 p. 587
     Type locality:  Philippine Islands
     Distribution:  Philippines (Cebu, Negros and Panay).

*Calliophis calligaster mcclungi*   (Taylor)
     *Hemibungarus mcclungi*   Taylor 1922 p. 272
     Type locality:  Polillo Island, Philippine Islands
     Distribution:  Philippines (Polillo).

*Calliophis gracilis*   Gray 1834 vol. 2, p. 86
     Type locality:  Unknown
     Distribution:  Malaya and Indonesia (Sumatra).

*Calliophis japonicus japonicus*   Gunther 1868 p. 428
     Type locality:  Nagasaki (in error)
     Distribution:  Ryukyu Islands (Amami Oshima).

*Calliophis japonicus boettgeri*   Fritze 1894 p. 861
     Type locality:  Tokuchimura, Okinawa shima, Ryukyu Islands
     Distribution:  Ryukyu Islands (Okinawa).

*Calliophis japonicus sauteri*   (Steindachner)
     *Oligodon sauteri*   Steindachner 1913 p. 219
     Type locality:  Formosa
     Distribution:  Taiwan.

*Calliophis kelloggi*   (Pope)
     *Hemibungarus kelloggi*   Pope 1928a p. 6
     Type locality:  Chungan Hsien, Fukien, China
     Distribution:  China (Fukien and Kwangsi) and northern Laos.

*Calliophis macclellandi macclellandi*  (Reinhardt)
    *Elaps macclellandii*  Reinhardt 1844 p. 532
    Type locality:  Assam, India
    Distribution:  India (Assam and Sikkim), northern Burma, Vietnam and China
        (Hainan).

*Calliophis macclellandi iwasakii*  Maki 1935 p. 216
    Type locality:  Banna-san, Ishigaki shima, Ryukyu Islands
    Distribution:  Ryukyu Islands (Ishigaki).

*Calliophis macclellandi swinhoei*  Van Denburgh 1912 p. 8
    Type locality:  Suishako, Formosa
    Distribution:  Taiwan.

*Calliophis macclellandi univirgatus*  (Gunther)
    *Elaps univirgatus*  Gunther 1858 p. 231
    Type locality:  Nepal
    Distribution:  India (Sikkim) and Nepal.

*Calliophis maculiceps maculiceps* (Gunther)
    *Elaps maculiceps*  Gunther 1858 p. 232
    Type locality:  East Indies
    Distribution:  Southern Burma, Thailand and northern Malaya.

*Calliophis maculiceps atrofrontalis*  (Sauvage)
    *Elaps atrofrontalis*  Sauvage 1877 p. 111
    Type locality:  Cochin-China
    Distribution:  South Vietnam and Kampuchea.

*Calliophis maculiceps hughi*  Cochran 1927 p. 190
    Type locality:  Tao Island, Gulf of Siam
    Distribution:  Type locality only.

*Calliophis maculiceps michaelis*  Deuve 1961 p. 377
    Type locality:  Mekong, Laos
    Distribution:  Laos.

*Calliophis maculiceps smithi*  Klemmer 1963 p. 285
    Type locality:  Nong Kai Ploi, Thailand
    Distribution:  Thailand.

*Calliophis melanurus melanurus*  (Shaw)
    *Coluber melanurus*  Shaw 1802a p. 552
    Type locality:  Nerva, Bengal, India
    Distribution:  India (Bombay, Madras and Mysore).

*Calliophis melanurus sinhaleyus*  Deraniyagala 1951 p. 147
    Type locality:  Ceylon
    Distribution:  Sri Lanka.

*Calliophis nigrescens*  Gunther 1862 p. 131
    Type locality:  India
    Distribution:  India (south and west).


Genus LEPTOMICRURUS  Schmidt 1937 p. 363.  Three species.
    Type species:  *Elaps collaris*  Schlegel

*Leptomicrurus collaris*  (Schlegel)
  *Elaps collaris*  Schlegel 1837 p. 448
  Type locality:  Not given
  Distribution:  South-eastern Venezuela, Guyana, Surinam, French Guiana and
      Brazil (Para).

*Leptomicrurus narduccii*  (Jan)
  *Elaps narduccii*  Jan 1863 p. 222
  Type locality:  Bolivia and Peru
  Distribution:  Eastern Peru, Ecuador, Colombia, Bolivia and Brazil (Acre).

*Leptomicrurus schmidti*  Hoge and Romano 1966 p. 1
  Type locality:  Tapurucuara, Amazonas, Brazil
  Distribution:  Type locality only.


Genus MICRUROIDES  Schmidt 1928 p. 63.  Single species.
  Type species:  *Elaps euryxanthus*  Kennicott


*Micruroides euryxanthus euryxanthus*  (Kennicott)
  *Elaps euryxanthus*  Kennicott 1860 p. 337
  Type locality:  Sonora, Mexico
  Distribution:  U.S.A. (Arizona, New Mexico and Texas) and Mexico (Chihuahua and
      Sonora).

*Micruroides euryxanthus australis*  Zweifel and Norris 1955 p. 230
  Type locality:  Guirocoba, Sonora, Mexico
  Distribution:  Type locality only.

*Micruroides euryxanthus neglectus*  Roze 1967 p. 4
  Type locality:  Sixteen and three-tenths miles north-northwest of Mazatlan,
      Sinaloa, Mexico
  Distribution:  Mexico (North of Mazatlan, Sinaloa).


Genus MICRURUS  Wagler 1824 p. 48.  Forty-eight species.
  Type species:  *Micrurus spixii*  Wagler

*Micrurus albicinctus*  Amaral 1926a p. 26
  Type locality:  Northern and central Mato Grosso, Brazil
  Distribution:  Brazil (type locality and Sao Paulo de Olivenca, Amazonas).

*Micrurus alleni alleni*  Schmidt 1936a p. 209
  Type locality:  Rio Mico, 7 miles above Rama, Siquia District, Nicaragua
  Distribution:  Eastern Nicaragua, Costa Rica and north-west Panama.

*Micrurus alleni yatesi*  Dunn 1942 p. 8
  Type locality:  Farm Two, Chiriqui Land Co., near Puerto Armuelles, Chiriqui,
      Panama
  Distribution:  South-eastern Costa Rica and south-western Panama.

*Micrurus ancoralis ancoralis*  (Jan)
  *Elaps marcgravii* var. *ancoralis*  Jan 1872 p. 4
  Type locality:  Ecuador
  Distribution:  Ecuador.

*Micrurus ancoralis jani*  Schmidt 1936a p. 197
    Type locality:  Andagoya, Choco, Colombia
    Distribution:  Colombia and Panama (Choco Region).

*Micrurus annellatus annellatus* (Peters)
    *Elaps annellatus*  Peters 1871 p. 402
    Type locality:  Pozuzu, Peru
    Distribution:  North-eastern Peru and south-eastern Ecuador.

*Micrurus annellatus balzani*  (Boulenger)
    *Elaps balzani*  Boulenger 1898a p. 130
    Type locality:  Yungas, Bolivia
    Distribution:  Bolivia (Amazon drainage).

*Micrurus annellatus bolivianus*  Roze 1967 p. 7
    Type locality:  Charobamba River, about 50 km northeast of Zudanez, Chuquisaca,
        Bolivia
    Distribution:  Bolivia (type locality and Yungas de Cochabamba).

*Micrurus annellatus montanus* Schmidt 1954 p. 322
    Type locality:  Camp 4, about 10 km north of Santo Domingo Mine, Puno, Peru
    Distribution:  South-eastern Peru and Bolivia.

*Micrurus averyi*  Schmidt 1939 p. 45
    Type locality:  Courantyne District, near Brazilian border, at latitude 1° 40' N,
        longitude 58° W, British Guiana.
    Distribution:  Guyana (type locality only).

*Micrurus bernardi*  (Cope)
    *Elaps bernardi*  Cope 1887 p. 87
    Type locality:  Zacualtipan, Hidalgo, Mexico
    Distribution:  Mexico (western Hidalgo and northern Puebla).

*Micrurus bocourti bocourti*  (Jan)
    *Elaps bocourti*  Jan 1872 p. 6
    Type locality:  Unknown
    Distribution:  Ecuador (coastal area).

*Micrurus bocourti sangilensis*  Niceforo Maria 1942 p. 98
    Type locality:  San Gil, Santander, Colombia
    Distribution:  Northern Colombia.

*Micrurus bogerti*  Roze 1967 p. 9
    Type locality:  Tangola-Tangola (Tangolunda), east of Puerto Angel, Oaxaca,
        Mexico
    Distribution:  Mexico (extreme southern Oaxaca).

*Micrurus browni browni*  Schmidt and Smith 1943 p. 29
    Type locality:  Chilpancingo, Guerrero, Mexico
    Distribution:  Mexico and western Guatemala.

*Micrurus browni importunus*  Roze 1967 p. 11
    Type locality:  Duenas, about 25 km west-southwest of Guatemala City in the
        Antigua Basin, Sacatepequez, Guatemala
    Distribution:  Type locality only.

*Micrurus browni taylori*  Schmidt and Smith 1943 p. 30
    Type locality:  Acapulco, Guerrero, Mexico
    Distribution:  Mexico (Guerrero).

*Micrurus clarki*  Schmidt 1936a p. 211
    Type locality:  Yavisa, Darien, Panama
    Distribution:  Eastern Costa Rica, Panama and Colombia.

*Micrurus corallinus*  (Merrem)
    *Elaps corallinus*  Merrem 1820 p. 144
    Type locality:  Rio de Janeiro, Cabo Frio, Brazil
    Distribution:  Eastern Brazil and Northern Argentina.

*Micrurus decoratus*  (Jan)
    *Elaps decoratus*  Jan 1858 p. 525
    Type locality:  Mexico (in error)
    Distribution:  Brazil (Rio de Janeiro to Santa Catarina).

*Micrurus diastema*  (Dumeril, Bibron and Dumeril)
    *Elaps diastema*  Dumeril, Bibron and Dumeril 1854 p. 1222
    Type locality:  Mexico
    Distribution:  Mexico, Honduras, Guatemala and Belize.

*Micrurus dissoleucus dissoleucus*  (Cope)
    *Elaps dissoleucus*  Cope 1859 p. 345
    Type locality:  Maracaibo, Venezuela
    Distribution:  North-eastern Colombia and north-eastern Venezuela.

*Micrurus dissoleucus dunni*  Barbour 1923 p. 15
    Type locality:  Ancon, Canal Zone, Panama
    Distribution:  Panama.

*Micrurus dissoleucus melanogenys* (Cope)
    *Elaps melanogenys*  Cope 1860 p. 72
    Type locality:  South America
    Distribution:  Colombia (Santa Marta Region).

*Micrurus dissoleucus nigrirostris*  Schmidt 1955 p. 355
    Type locality:  Barranquilla, Colombia
    Distribution:  Colombia.

*Micrurus distans distans* (Kennicott)
    *Elaps distans*  Kennicott 1860 p. 338
    Type locality:  Batosegachie, Chihuahua, Mexico
    Distribution:  Mexico.

*Micrurus distans michoacanensis*  (Duges)
    *Elaps distans* var. *michoacanensis*  Duges 1891 p. 487
    Type locality:  Michoacan, Mexico
    Distribution:  Mexico (Michoacan and Guerrero).

*Micrurus distans oliveri*  Roze 1967 p. 18
    Type locality:  Periquillo, Colima, Mexico
    Distribution:  Mexico (Colima).

*Micrurus distans zweifeli*  Roze 1967 p. 21
    Type locality:  Laguna Santa Maria, Nayarit, Mexico, between elevations of
        2000 and 4000 feet
    Distribution:  Mexico (Nayarit and Jalisco).

*Micrurus dumerili dumerili*  (Jan)
   *Elaps dumerilii*  Jan 1858 p. 522
   Type locality:  Cartagena, Colombia
   Distribution:  Colombia (Cartagena to Santa Marta and southward to Nontander
      Santander).

*Micrurus dumerili antioquiensis*  Schmidt 1936a p. 195
   Type locality:  Santa Rita, north of Medellin, Colombia
   Distribution:  Colombia (Cauca Valley).

*Micrurus dumerili carinicauda*  Schmidt 1936a p. 194
   Type locality:  Orope, Zulia, Venezuela
   Distribution:  North-west Venezuela and Colombia.

*Micrurus dumerili colombianus*  (Griffin)
   *Elaps colombianus*  Griffin 1916 p. 216
   Type locality:  Minca, Colombia
   Distribution:  Northern Colombia.

*Micrurus dumerili transandinus*  Schmidt 1936a p. 195
   Type locality:  Andagoya, Choco, Colombia
   Distribution:  Colombia (Choco) and Ecuador.

*Micrurus elegans elegans*  (Jan)
   *Elaps elegans*  Jan 1858 p. 524
   Type locality:  Mexico
   Distribution:  Mexico (Vera Cruz and eastern Oaxaca to western Tabasco).

*Micrurus elegans veraepacis*  Schmidt 1933 p. 32
   Type locality:  Campur, Alta Verapaz, Guatemala
   Distribution:  Mexico (Southern Tabasco and Chiapas) and Guatemala.

*Micrurus ephippifer*  (Cope)
   *Elaps ephippifer*  Cope 1886 p. 281
   Type locality:  Pacific side of the Isthmus of Tehuantepec
   Distribution:  Mexico (Oaxaca).

*Micrurus filiformis filiformis*  (Gunther)
   *Elaps filiformis*  Gunther 1859 p. 86
   Type locality:  Para, Brazil
   Distribution:  Northern Brazil, southern Colombia and northern Peru.

*Micrurus filiformis subtilis*  Roze 1967 p. 22
   Type locality:  Cararu, Rio Vaupes, Colombia-Brazil boundary
   Distribution:  Colombia-Brazil border.

*Micrurus fitzingeri*  (Jan)
   *Elaps fitzingeri*  Jan 1858 p. 521
   Type locality:  Mexico
   Distribution:  Mexico (Distrito Federal and Morelos).

*Micrurus frontalis frontalis*  (Dumeril, Bibron and Dumeril)
   *Elaps frontalis*  Dumeril, Bibron and Dumeril 1854 p. 1223
   Type locality:  Corrientes and Missiones, Argentina
   Distribution:  Southern Brazil, southern Paraguay and north-eastern Argentina.

*Micrurus frontalis altirostris*  (Cope)
  *Elaps altirostris*  Cope 1859 p. 345
  Type locality:  South America
  Distribution:  Southern Brazil, Uruguay and north-eastern Argentina.

*Micrurus frontalis brasiliensis*  Roze 1967 p. 25
  Type locality:  Barreiras, Bahia, Brazil
  Distribution:  Brazil (Bahia, Minas Gerais and Goias).

*Micrurus frontalis mesopotamicus*  Barrio and Miranda 1968 p. 872
  Type locality:  Villa Federal, Entre Rios, Argentina
  Distribution:  Argentina (Entre Rios, Corrientes and south-west Missiones).

*Micrurus frontalis pyrrhocryptus*  (Cope)
  *Elaps pyrrhocryptus*  Cope 1862 p. 347
  Type locality:  Vermejo River, Argentine Choco
  Distribution:  Brazil (south-west Mato Grosso), Bolivia, Paraguay and Argentina.

*Micrurus fulvius fulvius*  (Linnaeus)
  *Coluber fulvius*  Linnaeus 1766 p. 381
  Type locality:  Carolina
  Distribution:  U.S.A. (North Carolina south along the Atlantic and Gulf Plain
     to Mississippi).

*Micrurus fulvius maculatus*  Roze 1967 p. 27
  Type locality:  Tampico, Tamaulipas, Mexico
  Distribution:  Type locality only.

*Micrurus fulvius macrogalbineus*  Brown and Smith 1942 p. 63
  Type locality:  Seven kilometers south of Antigo Morelos, Tamaulipas, Mexico
  Distribution:  Mexico (Tamaulipas and San Luis Potosi).

*Micrurus fulvius tenere*  (Baird and Girard)
  *Elaps tenere*  Baird and Girard 1853 p. 22
  Type locality:  San Pedro of Rio Grande and New Braunfels, Texas, United States
  Distribution:  U.S.A. (west of the Mississippi Valley) and northern Mexico.

*Micrurus hemprichi hemprichi*  (Jan)
  *Elaps hemprichi*  Jan 1858 p. 523
  Type locality:  Colombia
  Distribution:  Eastern Colombia, Venezuela, Guyana, Surinam and French Guiana.

*Micrurus hemprichi ortoni*  Schmidt 1953 p. 166
  Type locality:  Pebas, Peru
  Distribution:  Ecuador, Peru, Bolivia and Brazil (Para).

*Micrurus hippocrepis*  (Peters)
  *Elaps hippocrepis*  Peters 1862 p. 925
  Type locality:  Santo Tomas, Guatemala
  Distribution:  Eastern Belize and northern Guatemala

*Micrurus ibiboboca*  (Merrem)
  *Elaps ibiboboca*  Merrem 1820 p. 142
  Type locality:  Brazil
  Distribution:  North-eastern Brazil.

*Micrurus isozonus* (Cope)
   *Elaps isozonus*  Cope 1860 p. 73
   Type locality:  South America
   Distribution:  Northern Venezuela

*Micrurus langsdorffi langsdorffi*  Wagler 1824 p. 10
   Type locality:  Rio Japura, Amazonas
   Distribution:  Southern Colombia, north-western Brazil, northern Peru and
      Ecuador.

*Micrurus langsdorffi ornatissimus* (Jan)
   *Elaps ornatissimus*  Jan 1858 p. 521
   Type locality:  Mexico (in error)
   Distribution:  Eastern Ecuador and northern Peru.

*Micrurus laticollaris laticollaris* (Peters)
   *Elaps marcgravii* var. *laticollaris*  Peters 1869 p. 877
   Type locality:  Southern Mexico, probably Puebla
   Distribution:  Mexico (Michoacan, Guerrero, Puebla and Morelos).

*Micrurus laticollaris maculirostris*  Roze 1967 p. 31
   Type locality:  Vicinity of Colima, Colima, Mexico
   Distribution:  Mexico (Colima and Jalisco).

*Micrurus latifasciatus*  Schmidt 1933 p. 35
   Type locality:  Finca El Cipres, Volcan Zunil, Suchitepequez, Guatemala
   Distribution:  Mexico (Chiapas) and western Guatemala.

*Micrurus lemniscatus lemniscatus* (Linnaeus)
   *Coluber lemniscatus*  Linnaeus 1758 p. 224
   Type locality:  Asia (in error)
   Distribution:  Brazil (Amapa), Guyana, Surinam and French Guiana.

*Micrurus lemniscatus carvalhoi*  Roze 1967 p. 33
   Type locality:  Catanduva, Sao Paulo, Brazil
   Distribution:  Brazil.

*Micrurus lemniscatus diutius*  Burger 1955 p. 8
   Type locality:  Tunapuna, Trinidad
   Distribution:  Trinidad, Venezuela, Guyana, Surinam and French Guiana.

*Micrurus lemniscatus frontifasciatus* (Werner)
   *Elaps frontifasciatus*  Werner 1927 p. 250
   Type locality:  Bolivia
   Distribution:  Bolivia (eastern slopes of the Andes).

*Micrurus lemniscatus helleri*  Schmidt and Schmidt 1925 p. 129
   Type locality:  Pozuzo, Huanuco, Peru
   Distribution:  Northern Brazil, southern Venezuela, Colombia, Ecuador, Peru and
      Bolivia.

*Micrurus limbatus*  Fraser 1964 p. 570
   Type locality:  Southern slope of Volcan San Martin, 7 airline miles north of
      San Andres Tuxtla, Veracruz, Mexico
   Distribution:  Mexico (southern Verz Cruz).

*Micrurus margaritiferus*  Roze 1967 p. 35
   Type locality:  Boca Rio Santiago-Rio Maranon, Peru
   Distribution:  Type locality only.

*Micrurus mertensi* Schmidt 1936a p. 192
  Type locality: Pacasmayo, Peru
  Distribution: Peru and south-eastern Ecuador.

*Micrurus mipartitus mipartitus* (Dumeril, Bibron and Dumeril)
  *Elaps mipartitus* Dumeril, Bibron and Dumeril 1854 p. 1220
  Type locality: Rio Sucio or Senio, Colombia
  Distribution: Eastern Panama and Colombia.

*Micrurus mipartitus anomalus* (Boulenger)
  *Elaps anomalus* Boulenger 1896a p. 417
  Type locality: Colombia
  Distribution: Colombia and western Venezuela.

*Micrurus mipartitus decussatus* (Dumeril, Bibron and Dumeril)
  *Elaps decussatus* Dumeril, Bibron and Dumeril 1854 p. 1221
  Type locality: Probably New Granada
  Distribution: Colombia and western Ecuador.

*Micrurus mipartitus hertwigi* (Werner)
  *Elaps hertwigi* Werner 1897b p. 354
  Type locality: Central America
  Distribution: Nicaragua, Costa Rica and north-western Panama.

*Micrurus mipartitus multifasciatus* (Jan)
  *Elaps multifasciatus* Jan 1858 p. 521
  Type locality: Central America
  Distribution: Panama.

*Micrurus mipartitus semipartitus* (Jan)
  *Elaps semipartitus* Jan 1858 p. 516
  Type locality: Cayenne
  Distribution: Venezuela (Cordillera de la Costa).

*Micrurus nigrocinctus nigrocinctus* (Girard)
  *Elaps nigrocinctus* Girard 1854 p. 226
  Type locality: Taboga Island, Bay of Panama
  Distribution: South-eastern Costa Rica, Panama and northern Colombia.

*Micrurus nigrocinctus babaspul* Roze 1967 p. 38
  Type locality: Little Hill, Great Corn Island (Isla del Maiz Grande), in the
      Caribbean Sea, about 55 kilometers east-northeast of Bluefields, Nicaragua
  Distribution: Nicaragua (Great Corn Island).

*Micrurus nigrocinctus coibensis* Schmidt 1936a p. 208
  Type locality: Coiba Island, Panama
  Distribution: Type locality only.

*Micrurus nigrocinctus divaricatus* (Hallowell)
  *Elaps divaricatus* Hallowell 1855 p. 36
  Type locality: Honduras
  Distribution: Honduras.

*Micrurus nigrocinctus melanocephalus* (Hallowell)
  *Elaps melanocephalus* Hallowell 1860 p. 226
  Type locality: Ometepec, Nicaragua
  Distribution: Nicaragua and south-western Costa Rica.

*Micrurus nigrocinctus mosquitensis*  Schmidt 1933 p. 33
    Type locality:  Limon, Costa Rica
    Distribution:  Nicaragua, Costa Rica and north-western Panama.

*Micrurus nigrocinctus zunilensis*  Schmidt 1932 p. 266
    Type locality:  Finca El Cipres, Volcan Zunil, Suchitepequez, Guatemala.
    Distribution:  Mexico (Chiapas), Guatemala, El Salvador and southern Honduras.

*Micrurus nuchalis*  Schmidt 1933 p. 35
    Type locality:  Tapanatepec, Oaxaca, Mexico
    Distribution:  Mexico (Tehuantepec).

*Micrurus peruvianus*  Schmidt 1936a p. 193
    Type locality:  Perico, Department of Cajamarca, Peru
    Distribution:  North-west Peru.

*Micrurus proximans*  Smith and Chrapliwy 1958 p. 270
    Type locality:  Four miles north of San Blas, Nayarit, Mexico
    Distribution:  Mexico (Nayarit).

*Micrurus psyches psyches*  (Daudin)
    *Vipera psyches*  Daudin 1803b, vol. 8, p. 320
    Type locality:  Surinam
    Distribution:  Surinam, Guyana, French Guiana, southern Venezuela and southern
        Colombia.

*Micrurus psyches circinalis*  (Dumeril, Bibron and Dumeril)
    *Elaps circinalis*  Dumeril, Bibron and Dumeril 1854 p. 1210
    Type locality:  Martinique (in error)
    Distribution:  Trinidad and north-eastern Venezuela.

*Micrurus psyches medemi*  Roze 1967 p. 41
    Type locality:  Villavicencio, Meta, Colombia
    Distribution:  Type locality only.

*Micrurus putumayensis*  Lancini 1962 p. 1
    Type locality:  Puerto Socorro, 270 kilometers northeast of Iquitos, Rio Putumayo,
        Departamento de Loreto, Peru
    Distribution:  Type locality only.

*Micrurus ruatanus*  (Gunther)
    *Elaps ruatanus*  Gunther 1895 p. 185
    Type locality:  Ruatan Island, Honduras
    Distribution:  Honduras (Ruatan and the adjacent mainland).

*Micrurus spixi spixi*  Wagler 1824 p. 48
    Type locality:  At the Rio Solimoes, Brazil
    Distribution:  Brazil (Amazonas).

*Micrurus spixi martiusi*  Schmidt 1953 p. 175
    Type locality:  Santarem, Para, Brazil
    Distribution:  Brazil (Para and Mato Grosso).

*Micrurus spixi obscurus*  (Jan)
    *Elaps corallinus* var. *obscura*  Jan 1872 p. 6
    Type locality:  Lima (in error)
    Distribution:  Colombia, Ecuador, Peru and Venezuela.

*Micrurus spixi princeps*  (Boulenger)
  *Elaps princeps*  Boulenger 1905a p. 456
  Type locality:  Province Sara, Santa Cruz de la Sierra, Bolivia
  Distribution:  Bolivia.

*Micrurus spurrelli*  (Boulenger)
  *Elaps spurrelli*  Boulenger 1914a p. 817
  Type locality:  Penna Lisa, Condoto River, Colombia
  Distribution:  Colombia.

*Micrurus steindachneri steindachneri*  (Werner)
  *Elaps steindachneri*  Werner 1901a p. 599
  Type locality:  Ecuador
  Distribution:  Ecuador (Macas-Mendez).

*Micrurus steindachneri orcesi*  Roze 1967 p. 43
  Type locality:  Meta trail, Banos, Ecuador, 1200 meters
  Distribution:  Ecuador (Rio Pastaza Valley).

*Micrurus steindachneri petersi*  Roze 1967 p. 45
  Type locality:  One mile south of Plan de Milagro on the trail to Pan de Azucar,
      Morona-Santiago Province, Ecuador, 5600 feet
  Distribution:  Type locality only.

*Micrurus stewarti*  Barbour and Amaral 1928 p. 100
  Type locality:  Sierra de la Bruja, Panama
  Distribution:  Panama.

*Micrurus stuarti*  Roze 1967 p. 47
  Type locality:  Finca La Paz, San Marcos, Guatemala, 1345 meters
  Distribution:  Guatemala (San Marcos and Suchitepequez).

*Micrurus surinamensis surinamensis*  (Cuvier)
  *Elaps surinamensis*  Cuvier 1817 p. 84
  Type locality:  Surinam
  Distribution:  Guyana, French Guiana, Brazil, Ecuador, Colombia, Surinam, Bolivia
      and Venezuela.

*Micrurus surinamensis nattereri*  Schmidt 1952 p. 27
  Type locality:  Between Guaramoca and San Fernando, Venezuela
  Distribution:  Venezuela (Upper Orinoco) and Brazil (Rio Negro).

*Micrurus tschudii tschudii*  (Jan)
  *Elaps tschudii*  Jan 1858 p. 524
  Type locality:  Peru
  Distribution:  Peru

*Micrurus tschudii olssoni*  Schmidt and Schmidt 1925 p. 130
  Type locality:  Negritos, Piura, Peru
  Distribution:  North-western Peru and south-western Ecuador.


Tribe MATICORINI


Genus MATICORA  Gray 1834, vol. 2, p. 86.  Two species
  Type species:  *Maticora lineata*  Gray

*Maticora bivirgata bivirgata* (Boie)
   *Elaps birvirgatus* Boie 1827 p. 556
   Type locality: Java
   Distribution: Indonesia (Java).

*Maticora bivirgata flaviceps* (Cantor)
   *Elaps flaviceps* Cantor 1839 p. 33
   Type locality: Penang Island
   Distribution: Indonesia (Nias, Mentawai, Sumatra, Batam, Bintan and Bangka),
      Malaysia, Thailand and Kampuchea.

*Maticora bivirgata tetrataenia* (Bleeker)
   *Elaps tetrataenia* Bleeker 1859 p. 201
   Type locality: Sintang, West Borneo
   Distribution: Borneo.

*Maticora intestinalis intestinalis* (Laurenti)
   *Aspis intestinalis* Laurenti 1768 p. 106
   Type locality: In Africa (in error)
   Distribution: Indonesia (Java and eastern Sumatra).

*Maticora intestinalis bilineata* (Peters)
   *Callophis bilineatus* Peters 1881 p. 109
   Type locality: Palawan Island, Philippines
   Distribution: Philippines (Balabac, Busuanga, Palawan and Culion).

*Maticora intestinalis everetti* (Boulenger)
   *Doliophis intestinalis everetti* Boulenger 1896a p. 404
   Type locality: Kina Balu, N. Borneo
   Distribution: Malaysia (Mount Kinabalu, North Borneo).

*Maticora intestinalis lineata* Gray 1834 vol. 2, p. 86
   Type locality: Pinang, Malaya
   Distribution: Malaya, Singapore, Riou Archipelago, Thailand and Indonesia
      (western Sumatra).

*Maticora intestinalis nigrotaeniatus* (Peters)
   *Callophis furcates* var. *nigrotaeniatus* Peters 1863 p. 404
   Type locality: Kepahiang, Benkulen, Sumatra
   Distribution: Indonesia (Borneo, Sumatra and Sulawesi).

*Maticora intestinalis philippina* (Gunther)
   *Callophis intestinalis* var. *philippina* Gunther 1864a p. 349
   Type locality: Philippines
   Distribution: Philippines (Luzon, Mindanao and Samar).

*Maticora intestinalis suluensis* (Steindachner)
   *Callophis intestinalis suluensis* Steindachner 1891 p. 295
   Type locality: Sulu Archipelago, Philippines
   Distribution: Philippines (Jolo).


Genus PARAPISTOCALAMUS  Roux 1934 p. 77.  Single species.
   Type species:  *Parapistocalamus hedigeri*  Roux

*Parapistocalamus hedigeri*  Roux 1934 p. 77
    Type locality:  Buin District, Bougainville
    Distribution:  Papua New Guinea and the Solomon Islands (Bougainville).


Tribe LATICAUDINI


Genus LATICAUDA  Laurenti 1768 p. 109.  Five species.
    Type species:  *Laticauda scutata*  Laurenti


*Laticauda colubrina*  (Schneider)
    *Hydrus colubrinus*  Schneider 1799 p. 238
    Type locality:  Unknown
    Distribution:  East India, Sri Lanka, Burma, Malaya, Gulf of Thailand, Japan,
        Sumatra, Philippines, New Guinea, Australia, Melanesia and Polynesia.

*Laticauda crockeri*  Slevin 1934 p. 186
    Type locality:  Lake Tungano, Rennell Island, Solomon Islands
    Distribution:  Solomon Islands (type locality only).

*Laticauda laticaudata*  (Linnaeus)
    *Coluber laticaudatus*  Linnaeus 1754 p. 31
    Type locality:  India
    Distribution:  East India, Sri Lanka, China, Taiwan, Japan, Indonesia (Sumatra
        and Java), Philippines, New Guinea, Australia, Melanesia and Polynesia.

*Laticauda semifasciata*  (Reinhardt)
    *Platurus semifasciatus*  Reinhardt 1837 p. 516
    Type locality:  Moluccas
    Distribution:  China, Taiwan, Japan and the Philippines.

*Laticauda schistorhynchus*  (Gunther)
    *Platurus schistorhynchus*  Gunther 1874 p. 297
    Type locality:  Savage Island
    Distribution:  New Guinea, Melanesia and Polynesia.

# PART 3

# *Family HYDROPHIIDAE*

## Subfamily OXYURANINAE

Genus ACANTHOPHIS  Daudin 1803b, vol. 5, p. 287.  Two species.
    Type species:  *Acanthophis cerastinus*  Daudin

*Acanthophis antarcticus antarcticus*  (Shaw)
    *Boa antarctica*  Shaw 1794a p. 535
    Type locality:  Australia
    Distribution:  Australia and New Guinea.

*Acanthophis antarcticus laevis*  Macleay 1878 p. 40
    Type locality:  Near Katow River
    Distribution:  Eastern Australia.

*Acanthophis pyrrhus*  Boulenger 1898b p. 75
    Type locality:  Charlotte Waters
    Distribution:  Central and western Australia.


Genus ASPIDOMORPHUS  Fitzinger 1843 p. 28.  Three species.
    Type species:  *Elaps muelleri*  Schlegel

*Aspidomorphus lineaticollis*  (Werner)
    *Pseudelaps muelleri* var. *lineaticollis* Werner 1903 p. 251
    Type locality:  New Guinea
    Distribution:  Papua New Guinea (including d'Entrecasteaux Archipelago and
        Trobriand, Woodlark, Misima and Sudest Islands).

*Aspidomorphus muelleri*  (Schlegel)
    *Elaps muelleri*  Schlegel 1837 p. 452
    Type locality:  Lobo, Triton Bay, New Guinea
    Distribution:  Papua New Guinea (including New Britain, Duke of York Island and
        New Ireland).

29

*Aspidomorphus schlegeli*  (Gunther)
  *Diemenia schlegeli*  Gunther 1872a p. 35
  Type locality:  N. Ceram
  Distribution:  Indonesia (Irian Jaya) and Papua New Guinea (Sepik).


Genus AUSTRELAPS  Worrell 1963a p. 1.  Single species.
  Type species:  *Hoplocephalus superbus*  Gunther


*Austrelaps superbus*  (Gunther)
  *Hoplocephalus superbus*  Gunther 1858 p. 217
  Type locality:  Not given
  Distribution:  South-eastern Australia.


Genus BRACHYUROPHIS  Gunther 1863b, p. 21.  Single species.
  Type species:  *Rhynchelaps woodjonesii*  Thomson


*Brachyurophis woodjonesi*  (Thomson)
  *Rhynchelaps woodjonesii*  Thomson 1934 p. 529
  Type locality:  Lower Archer River, Gulf of Carpentaria
  Distribution:  Australia (Cape York Peninsula).


Genus CACOPHIS  Gunther 1863a, p. 361.  Three species.
  Type species:  *Cacophis kreffti*  Gunther


*Cacophis harriettae*  Krefft 1869a p. 319
  Type locality:  Gayndah
  Distribution:  Australia (Queensland).

*Cacophis kreffti*  Gunther 1863a p. 361
  Type locality:  North of the Clarence River
  Distribution:  Australia (Queensland and New South Wales).

*Cacophis squamulosus*  (Dumeril, Bibron and Dumeril)
  *Pseudelaps squamulosus*  Dumeril, Bibron and Dumeril 1854 p. 1235
  Type locality:  New South Wales
  Distribution:  Australia (Queensland and New South Wales).


Genus CRYPTOPHIS  Worrell 1961 p. 18.  Two species.
  Type species:  *Hoplocephalus nigrescens*  Gunther


*Cryptophis nigrescens*  (Gunther)
  *Hoplocephalus nigrescens*  Gunther 1862 p. 131
  Type locality:  Sydney
  Distribution:  Eastern Australia.

*Cryptophis pallidiceps*  (Gunther)
  *Hoplocephalus pallidiceps*  Gunther 1858 p. 214
  Type locality:  Port Essington
  Distribution:  Northern Australia.


Genus DEMANSIA  Gray 1842 p. 54.  Four species.
  Type species:  *Elaps psammophis*  Schlegel


*Demansia atra*  (Macleay)
  *Diemenia atra*  Macleay 1884 p. 549
  Type locality:  Ripple Creek, Ingham, in Northern Queensland
  Distribution:  North and north-eastern Australia and southern Papua New Guinea.

*Demansia olivacea*  (Gray)
  *Lycodon olivaceus*  Gray 1842 p. 54
  Type locality:  North-eastern Australia
  Distribution:  Northern Australia.

*Demansia psammophis*  (Schlegel)
  *Elaps psammophis*  Schlegel 1837 p. 455
  Type locality:  Australia
  Distribution:  Australia.

*Demansia torquatus*  Gunther 1862 p. 130
  Type locality:  Percy Island
  Distribution:  North-eastern Australia.


Genus DENISONIA  Krefft 1869a p. 321.  Four species.
  Type species:  *Denisonia ornata*  Krefft


*Denisonia devisi*  Waite and Longman 1920 p. 173
  Type locality:  Surat, Queensland
  Distribution:  Australia (Queensland and New South Wales).

*Denisonia fasciata*  Rosen 1905 p. 179
  Type locality:  Western Australia
  Distribution:  Western Australia.

*Denisonia maculata*  (Steindachner)
  *Hoplocephalus maculatus*  Steindachner 1867 p. 81
  Type locality:  Rockhampton
  Distribution:  Australia (eastern-central Queensland).

*Denisonia punctata*  Boulenger 1896a p. 341
  Type locality:  Port Walcott
  Distribution:  Australia.


Genus DRYSDALIA  Worrell 1961 p. 18.  Three species.
  Type species:  *Drysdalia coronoides*  Worrell

*Drysdalia coronata*  (Schlegel)
  *Elaps coronatus*  Schlegel 1837 p. 454
  Type locality:  Australia
  Distribution:  South-eastern Australia.

*Drysdalia coronoides*  (Gunther)
  *Hoplocephalus coronoides*  Gunther 1858 p. 215
  Type locality:  Van Diemen's Land
  Distribution:  South-eastern Australia and Tasmania.

*Drysdalia mastersi*  (Krefft)
  *Hoplocephalus mastersi*  Krefft 1866 p. 370
  Type locality:  Flinders Range, South Australia
  Distribution:  Southern Australia.


Genus ECHIOPSIS  Fitzinger 1843 p. 28.  Single species.
  Type species:  *Naja curta*  Schlegel


*Echiopsis curta*  (Schlegel)
  *Naja curta*  Schlegel 1837 p. 486
  Type locality:  Australia
  Distribution:  South-western Australia.


Genus ELAPOGNATHUS  Boulenger 1896a p. 356.  Single species.
  Type species:  *Hoplocephalus minor*  Gunther


*Elapognathus minor*  (Gunther)
  *Hoplocephalus minor*  Gunther 1863a p. 362
  Type locality:  Swan River
  Distribution:  South-western Australia.


Genus FURINA  Dumeril, Bibron and Dumeril 1854 p. 1236.  Single species.
  Type species:  *Furina diadema*  Dumeril, Bibron and Dumeril


*Furina diadema*  (Schlegel)
  *Calamaria diadema*  Schlegel 1837 p. 32
  Type locality:  Australia
  Distribution:  Southern Australia.


Genus GLYPHODON  Gunther 1858 p. 210.  Three species.
  Type species:  *Glyphodon tristis*  Gunther


*Glyphodon barnardi*  Kinghorn 1939 p. 258
  Type locality:  Duaringa, Southern Queensland
  Distribution:  Australia (Queensland).

*Glyphodon dunmalli*  Worrell 1955 p. 41
    Type locality:  Gayndah and Glenmorgan
    Distribution:  Australia (Queensland).

*Glyphodon tristis*  Gunther 1858 p. 210
    Type locality:  N.E. Coast of Australia
    Distribution:  South-eastern Papua New Guinea and Australia (Cape York).


Genus HEMIASPIS  Fitzinger 1861 p. 410.  Two species.
    Type species:  *Alecto signata*  Jan


*Hemiaspis daemelii*  (Gunther)
    *Hoplocephalus daemelii*  Gunther 1876 p. 46
    Type locality:  Peak Downs
    Distribution:  Australia (central New South Wales and south-eastern Queensland).

*Hemiaspis signata*  (Jan)
    *Alecto signata*  Jan 1859 p. 128
    Type locality:  Australia
    Distribution:  Eastern Australia.


Genus HOPLOCEPHALUS  Cuvier 1832 p. 143.  Three species.
    Type species:  *Naja bungaroides*  Boie


*Hoplocephalus bitorquatus*  (Jan)
    *Alecto bitorquata*  Jan 1859 p. 128
    Type locality:  Australia
    Distribution:  Australia (New South Wales and Queensland).

*Hoplocephalus bungaroides*  (Boie)
    *Naja bungaroides*  Boie 1828 p. 1034
    Type locality:  Australia
    Distribution:  Australia (southern Queensland and northern New South Wales).

*Hoplocephalus stephensi*  Krefft 1869b p. 58
    Type locality:  Port Macquarie, New South Wales
    Distribution:  Australia (southern Queensland and northern New South Wales).


Genus LOVERIDGELAPS  McDowell 1970 p. 170.  Single species.
    Type species:  *Hoplocephalus elapoides*  Boulenger


*Loveridgelaps elapoides*  (Boulenger)
    *Hoplocephalus elapoides*  Boulenger 1890 p. 30
    Type locality:  Florida Island
    Distribution:  Solomon Islands (Gizo, Guadalcanal, Florida, Malaita and Santa
        Isabel).

Genus MICROPECHIS  Boulenger 1896a p. 346.  Single species.
  Type species:  *Micropechis ikaheka*  Boulenger


*Micropechis ikaheka*  (Lesson)
  *Coluber ikaheka*  Lesson 1830 p. 54
  Type locality:  New Guinea
  Distribution:  Papua New Guinea and Indonesia (Irian Jaya).


Genus NEELAPS  Gunther 1863b p. 24.  Two species.
  Type species:  *Neelaps calonotus*  Gunther


*Neelaps bimaculata*  (Dumeril, Bibron and Dumeril)
  *Furina bimaculata*  Dumeril, Bibron and Dumeril 1854 p. 1240
  Type locality:  Tasmania (in error)
  Distribution:  Southern Australia.

*Neelaps calonotus*  (Dumeril, Bibron and Dumeril)
  *Furina calonotos*  Dumeril, Bibron and Dumeril 1854 p. 1241
  Type locality:  Tasmania (in error)
  Distribution:  Australia (south-west coast).


Genus NOTECHIS  Boulenger 1896a p. 351.  Two species.
  Type species:  *Notechis scutatus*  Boulenger


*Notechis ater ater*  (Krefft)
  *Hoplocephalus ater*  Krefft 1866 p. 373
  Type locality:  Tasmania
  Distribution:  Southern Australia.

*Notechis ater humphreysi*  Worrell 1963b p. 1
  Type locality:  King Island
  Distribution:  Australia (King and adjacent islands).

*Notechis ater niger*  Kinghorn 1921 p. 143
  Type locality:  Kangaroo Island
  Distribution:  Australia (Kangaroo Island and the Sir Joseph Banks Group).

*Notechis ater serventyi*  Worrell 1963b p. 1
  Type locality:  Chappell Island
  Distribution:  Australia (Chappell and Badger Islands, Furneaux Group).

*Notechis scutatus scutatus*  (Peters)
  *Naja (Hamadryas) scutata*  Peters 1861 p. 690
  Type locality:  Java (in error)
  Distribution:  South-eastern Australia.

*Notechis scutatus occidentalis*  Glauert 1948 p. 139
  Type locality:  South West Australia
  Distribution:  South-western Australia.

Genus OGMODON   Peters 1864 p. 274.   Single species.
    Type species:  *Ogmodon vitianus*  Peters


*Ogmodon vitianus*  Peters 1864 p. 275
    Type locality:  Der Fidji-Insel Viti-Levu
    Distribution:  Fiji Islands.



Genus OXYURANUS   Kinghorn 1923 p. 42.   Single species.
    Type species:  *Pseudechis scutellatus*  Peters


*Oxyuranus scutellatus scutellatus* (Peters)
    *Pseudechis scutellatus*  Peters 1867 p. 710
    Type locality:  Rockhampton
    Distribution:  North-eastern Australia.

*Oxyuranus scutellatus cani*  Slater 1956 p. 202
    Type locality:  Napa Napa, Port Moresby
    Distribution:  Papua New Guinea (south coast).



Genus PSEUDECHIS   Wagler 1830 p. 171.   Five species.
    Type species:  *Pseudechis porphyriacus*  Wagler


*Pseudechis australis*  (Gray)
    *Naja australis*  Gray 1842 p. 55
    Type locality:  N.E. Australia
    Distribution:  Australia.

*Pseudechis colletti*  Boulenger 1902 p. 494
    Type locality:  Queensland
    Distribution:  Australia (Queensland).

*Pseudechis guttatus*  De Vis 1905 p. 49
    Type locality:  Cecil Plains, Queensland
    Distribution:  Australia (Queensland and New South Wales).

*Pseudechis papuanus*  Peters and Doria 1878 p. 409
    Type locality:  Near Yule Island
    Distribution:  Eastern Papua New Guinea.

*Pseudechis porphyriacus*  (Shaw)
    *Coluber porphyriacus*  Shaw 1794b p. 27
    Type locality:  Australia
    Distribution:  Australia (Queensland, New South Wales and Victoria).



Genus PSEUDONAJA   Gunther 1858 p. 227.   Six species.
    Type species:  *Pseudonaja nuchalis*  Gunther

*Pseudonaja affinis*  Gunther 1872a p. 35
   Type locality:  Australia
   Distribution:  South-western Australia.

*Pseudonaja guttata*  (Parker)
   *Demansia guttata*  Parker 1926 p. 668
   Type locality:  Winton, Queensland, 22° 19' S, 143° 4' E.
   Distribution:  Australia (Queensland)

*Pseudonaja ingrami*  (Boulenger)
   *Diemenia ingrami*  Boulenger 1908 p. 334
   Type locality:  Alexandria, northern Territory of the colony of South Australia
   Distribution:  Australia (Queensland and Northern Territory).

*Pseudonaja modesta*  (Gunther)
   *Cacophis modesta*  Gunther 1872a p. 35
   Type locality:  Perth
   Distribution:  Australia.

*Pseudonaja nuchalis*  Gunther 1858 p. 227
   Type locality:  N.W. Australia
   Distribution:  Australia.

*Pseudonaja textilis*  (Dumeril, Bibron and Dumeril)
   *Furina textilis*  Dumeril, Bibron and Dumeril 1854 p. 1242
   Type locality:  New South Wales
   Distribution:  Eastern Australia.


Genus RHINOPLOCEPHALUS  Muller 1885 p. 690.  Single species.
   Type species:  *Rhinoplocephalus bicolor*  Muller


*Rhinoplocephalus bicolor*  Muller 1885 p. 690
   Type locality:  Australia
   Distribution:  Western Australia.


Genus SALOMONELAPS  McDowell 1970 p. 151.  Single species.
   Type species:  *Hoplocephalus par*  Boulenger


*Salomonelaps par*  (Boulenger)
   *Hoplocephalus par*  Boulenger 1884 p. 210
   Type locality:  Faro Island
   Distribution:  Solomon Islands.


Genus SIMOSELAPS  Jan 1859 p. 123.  Six species.
   Type species:  *Simoselaps bertholdi*  Jan


*Simoselaps australis*  (Krefft)
   *Simotes australis*  Krefft 1864 p. 180
   Type locality:  Port Curtis
   Distribution:  Eastern Australia.

*Simoselaps bertholdi* (Jan)
  *Elaps bertholdi* Jan 1859 p. 123
  Type locality: Australia
  Distribution: Australia.

*Simoselaps fasciolatus* (Gunther)
  *Rhinelaps fasciolatus* Gunther 1872a p. 34
  Type locality: Perth
  Distribution: South-western Australia.

*Simoselaps incinctus* (Storr)
  *Vermicella semifasciata incincta* Storr 1967 p. 89
  Type locality: Near Alice Springs, Northern Territory, 23° 46' S, 133° 53' E.
  Distribution: Australia (Northern Territory).

*Simoselaps semifasciata* (Gunther)
  *Brachyurophis semifasciata* Gunther 1863b p. 21
  Type locality: West Australia
  Distribution: Southern and western Australia.

*Simoselaps warro* (De Vis)
  *Cacophis warro* De Vis 1884 p. 139
  Type locality: Warro Station near Port Curtis
  Distribution: Australia (Eastern Queensland).


Genus SUTA Worrell 1961 p. 18. Single species.
  Type species: *Hoplocephalus sutus* Peters


*Suta suta* (Peters)
  *Hoplocephalus sutus* Peters 1863 p. 234
  Type locality: Adelaide, South Australia
  Distribution: Australia.


Genus TOXICOCALAMUS Boulenger 1896b p. 152. Nine species.
  Type species: *Toxicocalamus longissimus* Boulenger


*Toxicocalamus buergersi* (Sternfeld)
  *Ultrocalamus buergersi* Sternfeld 1913 p. 388
  Type locality: German New Guinea
  Distribution: Papua New Guinea (Toricelli and Prince Alexander Mountains).

*Toxicocalamus grandis* (Boulenger)
  *Apistocalamus grandis* Boulenger 1914b p. 265
  Type locality: Launch Camp, Setekwa River, West Irian
  Distribution: Indonesia (type locality only, Irian Jaya).

*Toxicocalamus holopelturus* McDowell 1969 p. 467
  Type locality: Mount Rossel at 700m, Rossel Island, Territory of Papua
  Distribution: Papua New Guinea (type locality only).

*Toxicocalamus longissimus* Boulenger 1896b p. 152
  Type locality: Woodlark Island
  Distribution: Papua New Guinea (Woodlark and Furgusson Islands).

*Toxicocalamus loriae*  (Boulenger)
  *Apistocalamus loriae*  Boulenger 1898c p. 705
  Type locality:  Haveri, British New Guinea
  Distribution:  Indonesia (West Irian Jaya) and Papua New Guinea.

*Toxicocalamus misimae*  McDowell 1969 p. 470
  Type locality:  Misima Island, Milne Bay Division, Territory of Papua
  Distribution:  Papua New Guinea (type locality only).

*Toxicocalamus preussi*  (Sternfeld)
  *Ultrocalamus preussi*  Sternfeld 1913 p. 388
  Type locality:  Seleo Island
  Distribution:  Indonesia (north coast of Irian Jaya) and Papua New Guinea (north
     coast).

*Toxicocalamus spilolepidotus*  McDowell 1969 p. 464
  Type locality:  Purosa, (near Okapa) Eastern Highlands Division, Territory of
  Distribution:  Type locality only.                                New Guinea

*Toxicocalamus stanleyanus*  Boulenger 1903a p. 128
  Type locality:  Dinawa, Owen Stanley Mountains at 4000 ft.
  Distribution:  Indonesia (southern Irian Jaya) and Papua New Guinea.


Genus TROPIDECHIS  Gunther 1863a p. 363.  Single species.
  Type species:  *Tropidechis carinata*  Gunther


*Tropidechis carinata*  (Krefft)
  *Hoplocephalus carinatus*  Krefft 1863 p. 86
  Type locality:  Clarence River
  Distribution:  Australia (Queensland and New South Wales).


Genus UNECHIS  Worrell 1961 p. 18.  Seven species.
  Type species:  *Unechis carpentariae*  Worrell


*Unechis boschmai*  (Brongersma and Knaap-Van Meeuwen)
  *Denisonia boschmai*  Brongersma and Knaap-Van Meeuwen 1964 p. 550
  Type locality:  Merauke, New Guinea
  Distribution:  Type locality only.

*Unechis brevicaudus*  (Mitchell)
  *Denisonia nigrostriata brevicauda*  Mitchell 1951 p. 550
  Type locality:  Fowler's Bay
  Distribution:  Southern Australia.

*Unechis carpentariae*  (Macleay)
  *Hoplocephalus carpentariae*  Macleay 1887 p. 403
  Type locality:  Peak Downs
  Distribution:  Australia (Queensland).

*Unechis flagellum*  (McCoy)
  *Hoplocephalus flagellum*  McCoy 1878 p. 7.
  Type locality:  Victoria
  Distribution:  South-eastern Australia.

*Unechis gouldi* (Gray)
 *Elaps gouldi* Gray 1841 p. 444
 Type locality: W. Australia
 Distribution: South-eastern Australia.

*Unechis monachus* (Storr)
 *Denisonia monachus* Storr 1964 p. 89
 Type locality: Kalgoorlie, Western Australia, Lat. 30° 43' S., Long. 121° 27' E.
 Distribution: South-western Australia.

*Unechis nigrostriatus* (Krefft)
 *Hoplocephalus nigrostriatus* Krefft 1864 p. 181
 Type locality: Rockhampton, Queensland
 Distribution: North-eastern Australia.


Genus VERMICELLA  Gunther 1858 p. 236.  Two species.
 Type species: *Vermicella annulata*  Gunther


*Vermicella annulata* (Gray)
 *Calamaria annulata* Gray 1849
 Type locality: Australia
 Distribution: Australia.

*Vermicella multifasciata* (Longman)
 *Furina multifasciata* Longman 1915 p. 30
 Type locality: Port Darwin, Northern Territory
 Distribution: Northern and western Australia.


Subfamily HYDROPHIINAE


Tribe EPHALOPHINI


Genus EPHALOPHIS  Smith 1931a p. 397.  Single species.
 Type species: *Ephalophis greyi*  Smith


*Ephalophis greyi*  Smith 1931a p. 397
 Type locality: Broome, N. Australia
 Distribution: Type locality only.


Genus PARAHYDROPHIS  Burger and Natsuno 1975 p. 65.  Single species.
 Type species: *Disteira mertoni*  Roux


*Parahydrophis mertoni* (Roux)
 *Disteira mertoni*  Roux 1910 p. 222
 Type locality: Aru Islands
 Distribution: New Guinea and Australia (Arafura Sea).

## Tribe HYDRELAPINI

Genus HYDRELAPS  Boulenger 1896a p. 270.  Single species.
      Type species:  *Hydrelaps darwiniensis*  Boulenger


*Hydrelaps darwiniensis*  Boulenger 1896a p. 270
      Type locality:  Port Darwin
      Distribution:  Australia.


## Tribe AIPYSURINI

Genus AIPYSURUS  Lacepede 1804 p. 197.  Seven species.
      Type species:  *Aipysurus laevis*  Lacepede


*Aipysurus apraefrontalis*  Smith 1926 p. 24
      Type locality:  Ashmore Reefs, Timor Sea
      Distribution:  Indonesia (Java).

*Aipysurus duboisi*  Bavay 1869 p. 33
      Type locality:  New Caledonia
      Distribution:  New Guinea, Australia and Melanesia.

*Aipysurus eydouxi*  (Gray)
      *Tomogaster eydouxii*  Gray 1849 p. 59.
      Type locality:  Indian Ocean
      Distribution:  Malaysia, Gulf of Thailand, Vietnam, Indonesia (Java and
            Kalimantan), New Guinea and Australia.

*Aipysurus foliosquama*  Smith 1926 p. 22
      Type locality:  Ashmore Reefs, Timor Sea
      Distribution:  Indonesia (Java).

*Aipysurus fuscus*  (Tschudi)
      *Stephanohydra fusca*  Tschudi 1837 p. 331
      Type locality:  Celebes
      Distribution:  Indonesia (Java) and New Guinea.

*Aipysurus laevis*  Lacepede 1804 p. 197
      Type locality:  Arafura Sea
      Distribution:  New Guinea, Australia and Melanesia.

*Aipysurus tenuis*  Lonnberg and Andersson 1913b p. 13
      Type locality:  Near Broome on the north-west coast of Australia
      Distribution:  Australia.


Genus EMYDOCEPHALUS  Krefft 1869a p. 321.  Two species.
      Type species:  *Emydocephalus annulatus*  Krefft

*Emydocephalus annulatus*  Krefft 1869a p. 322
   Type locality:  Loyalty Islands
   Distribution:  Indonesia (Java) and Melanesia.

*Emydocephalus ijimae*  Stejneger 1898 p. 223
   Type locality:  Loo Chao Island
   Distribution:  China, Taiwan and Japan.


## Tribe HYDROPHIINI


Genus ACALYPTOPHIS  Boulenger 1896a p. 269.  Single species.
   Type species:  *Acalyptus peronii*  Dumeril, Bibron and Dumeril


*Acalyptophis peroni*  (Dumeril, Bibron and Dumeril)
   *Acalyptus peronii*  Dumeril, Bibron and Dumeril 1854 p. 1339
   Type locality:  Western Tropical Pacific
   Distribution:  China, Taiwan and Australia.


Genus DISTEIRA  Lacepede 1804 p. 210.  Three species.
   Type species:  *Disteira doliata*  Lacepede


*Disteira kingi*  (Boulenger)
   *Hydrophis kingii*  Boulenger 1896a p. 276
   Type locality:  N. Australia
   Distribution:  Australia.

*Disteira major*  (Shaw)
   *Hydrus major*  Shaw 1802a p. 558
   Type locality:  Indian Ocean
   Distribution:  Australia.

*Disteira stokesi*  (Gray)
   *Hydrus stokesii*  Gray 1846 p. 502
   Type locality:  Australian Seas
   Distribution:  India, Sri Lanka, Malaya and Australia.


Genus ENHYDRINA  Gray 1849 p. 47.  Single species.
   Type species:  *Enhydrina valakadyen*  Gray


*Enhydrina schistosa*  (Daudin)
   *Hydrophis schistosus*  Daudin 1803b vol. 7, p. 386
   Type locality:  Tranquebar
   Distribution:  India, Sri Lanka, Burma, Malaysia, Gulf of Thailand, Vietnam,
         Indonesia (Sumatra, Java and Kalimantan), New Guinea and Australia.

Genus HYDROPHIS  Latreille 1802 p. 193.  Twenty-four species.
    Type species:  *Hydrophis fasciatus*  Schneider


*Hydrophis belcheri*  (Gray)
    *Aturia belcheri*  Gray 1849 p. 46
    Type locality:  New Guinea
    Distribution:  Philippines, New Guinea and Melanesia.

*Hydrophis bituberculatus*  Peters 1872 p. 855
    Type locality:  Colombo
    Distribution:  Sri Lanka (known only from the type specimen).

*Hydrophis brooki*  Gunther 1872b p. 597
    Type locality:  Sarawak, Borneo
    Distribution:  Malaysia, Gulf of Thailand, Vietnam and Indonesia (Sumatra, Java
        and Kalimantan).

*Hydrophis caerulescens*  (Shaw)
    *Hydrus caerulescens*  Shaw 1802a p. 561
    Type locality:  Indian Ocean
    Distribution:  India, Malaysia, Sri Lanka, Burma, Gulf of Thailand, and
        Indonesia (Sumatra, Java and Kalimantan).

*Hydrophis cantoris*  Gunther 1864a p. 374
    Type locality:  Penang
    Distribution:  India, Sri Lanka, Burma and Malaya.

*Hydrophis cyanocinctus*  Daudin 1803b vol. 7, p. 383
    Type locality:  Sandarbans
    Distribution:  Persian Gulf, India, Sri Lanka, Malaysia, Gulf of Thailand,
        Vietnam, China, Taiwan, Japan, Indonesia (Sumatra, Java and Kalimantan)
        and the Philippines.

*Hydrophis elegans*  (Gray)
    *Aturia elegans*  Gray 1842 p. 63
    Type locality:  Port Essington
    Distribution:  Australia.

*Hydrophis fasciatus fasciatus*  (Schneider)
    *Hydrus fasciatus*  Schneider 1799 p. 240
    Type locality:  East Indies
    Distribution:  East India, Sri Lanka, Burma, Malaya, Indonesia (Java and Sumatra),
        Gulf of Thailand, Vietnam, the Philippines, New Guinea and Australia.

*Hydrophis fasciatus atriceps*  Gunther 1864a p. 371
    Type locality:  Siam
    Distribution:  Gulf of Thailand, Vietnam, Indonesia (Java), Philippines,
        New Guinea and Australia.

*Hydrophis gracilis*  (Shaw)
    *Hydrus gracilis*  Shaw 1802a p. 560
    Type locality:  Unknown
    Distribution:  Persian Gulf, India, Sri Lanka, Burma, Malaya, Gulf of Thailand,
        Vietnam, China, Taiwan, Indonesia (Sumatra and Java), Australia and
        Melanesia.

*Hydrophis inornatus*  (Gray)
  *Chitulia inornata*  Gray 1849 p. 56
  Type locality:  Indian Ocean
  Distribution:  Philippines and Australia.

*Hydrophis klossi*  Boulenger 1912 p. 190
  Type locality:  Coast of Selangor, Malay Peninsula
  Distribution:  Malaya, Gulf of Thailand and Indonesia (Sumatra).

*Hydrophis lapemoides*  (Gray)
  *Aturia lapemoides*  Gray 1849 p. 46
  Type locality:  Ceylon, Madras
  Distribution:  Persian Gulf, India and Sri Lanka.

*Hydrophis mamillaris*  (Daudin)
  *Anguis mamillaris*  Daudin 1803b vol. 7, p. 340
  Type locality:  Vizagapatam
  Distribution:  India and Sri Lanka.

*Hydrophis melanocephalus*  Gray 1849 p. 53
  Type locality:  Indian Ocean
  Distribution:  China, Taiwan and Japan.

*Hydrophis melanosoma*  Gunther 1864a p. 367
  Type locality:  Not given
  Distribution:  Malaysia and Indonesia (Sumatra, Java and Kalimantan).

*Hydrophis nigrocinctus*  Daudin 1803b vol. 7, p. 380
  Type locality:  Sunderbunds, Bengal
  Distribution:  East India, Sri Lanka and Burma.

*Hydrophis obscurus*  Daudin 1803b vol. 7, p. 375
  Type locality:  Sunderbunds, Bengal
  Distribution:  East India, Sri Lanka and Burma.

*Hydrophis ornatus ornatus*  (Gray)
  *Aturia ornata*  Gray 1842 p. 61
  Type locality:  Indian Ocean
  Distribution:  Persian Gulf, India, Sri Lanka, Burma, Malaya, Gulf of Thailand,
      Vietnam, China, Taiwan, Indonesia (Sumatra and Java), New Guinea and
      Australia).

*Hydrophis ornatus ocellatus*  Gray 1849 p. 53
  Type locality:  Australia
  Distribution:  New Guinea.

*Hydrophis pacificus*  Boulenger 1896a p. 278
  Type locality:  New Britian
  Distribution:  New Guinea and Australia.

*Hydrophis parviceps*  Smith 1935 p. 5
  Type locality:  Coast of Cochin, China
  Distribution:  Type locality only.

*Hydrophis semperi*  Garman 1881 p. 85
  Type locality:  Lake Taal, Luzon
  Distribution:  Philippines (type locality only).

*Hydrophis spiralis*  (Shaw)
    *Hydrus spiralis*  Shaw 1802a p. 564
    Type locality:  Indian Ocean
    Distribution:  Persian Gulf, India, Sri Lanka, Burma, Malaysia, Indonesia
          (Sumatra, Java and Kalimantan) and the Philippines.

*Hydrophis stricticollis*  Gunther 1864a p. 376
    Type locality:  India
    Distribution:  East India, Sri Lanka and Burma.

*Hydrophis torquatus torquatus*  Gunther 1864a p. 369
    Type locality:  Penang
    Distribution:  Malaya and Indonesia (Sumatra).

*Hydrophis torquatus aagaardi*  Smith 1920 p. 149
    Type locality:  Bangnara, Patani
    Distribution:  Malaysia.

*Hydrophis torquatus diadema*  Gunther 1864a p. 373
    Type locality:  Unknown
    Distribution:  Gulf of Thailand.


Genus KERILIA  Gray 1849 p. 57.  Single species.
    Type species:  *Kerilia jerdoni*  Gray


*Kerilia jerdoni jerdoni*  Gray 1849 p. 57
    Type locality:  Madras
    Distribution:  East India, Sri Lanka, Burma, Malaya and Indonesia (Sumatra).

*Kerilia jerdoni siamensis*  Smith 1926 p. 32
    Type locality:  Patani Bay
    Distribution:  Gulf of Thailand and Vietnam.


Genus KOLPOPHIS  Smith 1926 p. 106.  Single species.
    Type species:  *Kolpophis annandalei*  Smith


*Kolpophis annandalei*  (Laidlaw)
    *Distira annandalei*  Laidlaw 1901 p. 579
    Type locality:  Patani Bay
    Distribution:  Malaya, Vietnam and Indonesia (Java).


Genus LAPEMIS  Gray 1835 vol. 2, p. 87.  Two species.
    Type species:  *Lapemis curtus*  Gray


*Lapemis curtus*  (Shaw)
    *Hydrus curtus*  Shaw 1802a p. 562
    Type locality:  Unknown
    Distribution:  Persian Gulf and western India.

*Lapemis hardwicki*  Gray 1835 vol. 2, p. 87
    Type locality:  Penang
    Distribution:  East India, Sri Lanka, Burma, Malaya, Vietnam, Gulf of Thailand,
        China, Taiwan, Japan, Indonesia (Sumatra and Java), Philippines, New Guinea
        and Australia.


Genus THALASSOPHIS  Schmidt 1852 p. 75.  Two species.
    Type species:  *Thalassophis anomalus*  Schmidt


*Thalassophis anomalus*  Schmidt 1852 p. 81
    Type locality:  Java
    Distribution:  Gulf of Thailand, Malaysia (North Borneo) and Indonesia (Sumatra,
        Java and Kalimantan).

*Thalassophis viperinus*  Schmidt 1852 p. 79
    Type locality:  Java
    Distribution:  Persian Gulf, India, Sri Lanka, Burma, Malaysia, Gulf of Thailand,
        Vietnam, China, Taiwan and Indonesia (Sumatra, Java and Kalimantan).


Genus PELAMIS  Daudin 1803b vol. 7, p. 361.  Single species.
    Type species:  *Pelamis platurus*  Daudin


*Pelamis platurus*  (Linnaeus)
    *Anguis platurus*  Linnaeus 1766 p. 391
    Type locality:  Not given
    Distribution:  East Africa, Persian Gulf, India, Sri Lanka, Burma, Malaysia,
        Gulf of Thailand, Vietnam, China, Taiwan, Japan, Indonesia (Sumatra, Java
        and Kalimantan), Philippines, New Guinea, Australia, Melanesia, Polynesia
        and the Pacific coast of Central America.

# PART 4

# *Family VIPERIDAE*

Subfamily VIPERINAE

Tribe VIPERINI

Genus ADENORHINOS  Marx and Rabb 1965 p. 186.  Single species.
   Type species:  *Atheris barbouri*  Loveridge

*Adenorhinos barbouri*  (Loveridge)
   *Atheris barbouri*  Loveridge 1930 p. 107
   Type locality:  Dabaga, Uzungwe Mountains, Tanganyika
   Distribution:  Tanzania (Uzungwe and Ukinga Mountains).

Genus ATHERIS  Cope 1862 p. 337.  Eight species.
   Type species:  *Vipera chloroechis*  Schlegel

*Atheris ceratophorus*  Werner 1895 p. 194
   Type locality:  Usambara Mountains, Tanganyika
   Distribution:  Tanzania (Usambara Mountains).

*Atheris desaixi*  Ashe 1968 p. 53
   Type locality:  Near Chuka, Lat. 0° 20' S, Long. 37° 35' E. in rain forest at
      an altitude of c. 1600 meters.
   Distribution:  Kenya.

*Atheris hindii*  (Boulenger)
   *Vipera hindii*  Boulenger 1910 p. 513
   Type locality:  Fort Hall, Kenya
   Distribution:  Kenya (Kinangop and Aberdare Mountains).

*Atheris hispidus*  Laurent 1955 p. 138
   Type locality:  Lutungura, Kivu, Congo
   Distribution:  Zaire, south-western Uganda and western Kenya.

47

*Atheris katangensis*  de Witte 1953 p. 301
    Type locality:  Mubale-Munte, Upemba, Katanga, Congo
    Distribution:  Zaire (Katanga).

*Atheris nitschei nitschei*  Tornier 1902 p. 589
    Type locality:  Mpororo Swamp, Tanganyika
    Distribution:  Uganda, western Tanzania, Rwanda and Zaire (Kivu and Katanga).

*Atheris nitschei rungweensis*  Bogert 1940 p. 104
    Type locality:  Rungwe Mountain, Tanganyika
    Distribution:  South-western Tanzania, north-eastern Zambia, and northern Malawi.

*Atheris squamiger squamiger*  (Hallowell)
    *Echis squamiger*  Hallowell 1854 p. 193
    Type locality:  Gabon river
    Distribution:  Cameroun, Zaire, Uganda, western Kenya and Angola.

*Atheris squamiger anisolepis*  Mocquard 1887 p. 89
    Type locality:  Alima, Leketi, French Cameroun.
    Distribution:  Southern Congo and Angola.

*Atheris squamiger chloroechis*  (Schlegel)
    *Vipera chloroechis*  Schlegel 1855 p. 317
    Type locality:  Guinea
    Distribution:  Guinea, Guinea-Bissau, Sierra Leone, Liberia, Ivory Coast, Ghana,
        Togo, Benin, Nigeria, Cameroun, Gabon and Equatorial Guinea.

*Atheris squamiger robustus*  Laurent 1956a p. 332
    Type locality:  Nioka, Ituri, Congo
    Distribution:  Zaire (Ituri Forest, Orientale).

*Atheris superciliaris*  (Peters)
    *Vipera superciliaris*  Peters 1854 p. 625
    Type locality:  Mainland opposite Querimba Island, Cape Delgado, Mozambique.
    Distribution:  Mozambique, Malawi and southern Tanzania.


Genus BITIS  Gray 1842 p. 69.  Twelve species.
    Type species:  *Bitis arietans*  Merrem


*Bitis arientans arietans*  (Merrem)
    *Vipera (Echidna) arietans*  Merrem 1820 p. 152
    Type locality:  Cape of Good Hope
    Distribution:  Central and southern Africa.

*Bitis arietans somalica*  Parker 1949 p. 101
    Type locality:  Bohodle, British Somaliland
    Distribution:  Somali Republic and northern Kenya.

*Bitis atropos atropos*  (Linnaeus)
    *Coluber atropos*  Linnaeus 1758 p. 216
    Type locality:  In America (in error)
    Distribution:  Lesotho, South Africa (coastal areas of eastern Cape Province
        and mountains of the eastern escarpment), Transkei and Zimbabwe-Rhodesia
        (Chimanimani Mountains to Inyanga).

*Bitis atropos unicolor*  FitzSimons 1959 p. 409
   Type locality:  Doornkop, E. Transvaal
   Distribution:  South Africa (south-eastern Transvaal north of Belfast).

*Bitis caudalis caudalis*  (Smith)
   *Vipera (Cerastes) caudalis*  Smith 1849 p. 7
   Type locality:  Sandy districts north of Cape Colony
   Distribution:  Angola, South Africa, Botswana amd south-western Zimbabwe-Rhodesia.

*Bitis caudalis paucisquamata*  Mertens 1954 p. 218
   Type locality:  Little Namaqualand
   Distribution:  South Africa (coastal strip of Little Namaqualand).

*Bitis cornuta cornuta*  (Daudin)
   *Vipera cornuta*  Daudin 1803b, vol. 6, p. 188
   Type locality:  Cape of Good Hope
   Distribution:  South Africa (south-west).

*Bitis cornuta albanica*  Hewitt 1937 p. 76
   Type locality:  The dene, Port Elizabeth;  Addo;  Braakkloof;  Springvale and
      Kleinpoort, Albany District, Cape Province.
   Distribution:  South Africa (south-eastern Cape Province).

*Bitis gabonica gabonica*  (Dumeril, Bibron and Dumeril)
   *Echidna gabonica*  Dumeril, Bibron and Dumeril 1854 p. 1428
   Type locality:  Gabon
   Distribution:  Southern Sudan, Uganda, Tanzania, Congo, Zaire, Gabon, Angola,
      Zambia, eastern Zimbabwe-Rhodesia, Mozambique and South Africa (Zululand).

*Bitis gabonica rhinoceros*  (Schlegel)
   *Vipera rhinoceros*  Schlegel 1855 p. 316
   Type locality:  Gold Coast
   Distribution:  Guinea, Guinea-Bissau, Liberia, Sierra Leone, Ivory Coast, Ghana
      and Togo.

*Bitis heraldica*  (Bocage)
   *Vipera heraldica*  Bocage 1889 p. 127
   Type locality:  Calai River, Caconda, Angola
   Distribution:  Central Angola.

*Bitis inornata*  (Smith)
   *Echidna inornata*  Smith 1849 p. 4
   Type locality:  Sneeuwbergen, near Graaf-Reinet, Cape Province, South Africa
   Distribution:  South Africa (south-eastern Cape Province).

*Bitis nasicornis*  (Shaw)
   *Coluber nasicornis*  Shaw 1802b p. 94
   Type locality:  Interior of Africa
   Distribution:  Southern Sudan, western Kenya, Uganda, Rwanda, Zaire (Kivu,
      Leopoldville, Equateur and Orientale), Angola, Congo, Gabon, Equatorial
      Guinea, Cameroun, Ghana, Ivory Coast, Liberia, Guinea and Guinea-Bissau.

*Bitis peringueyi*  (Boulenger)
   *Vipera peringueyi*  Boulenger 1888a p. 141
   Type locality:  10 miles east of Walvis Bay, South West Africa
   Distribution:  South Africa (Namib Desert) and southern Angola.

*Bitis schneideri* (Boettger)
  *Vipera schneideri* Boettger 1886 p. 8
  Type locality: Luderitzbucht
  Distribution: South Africa (Orange River).

*Bitis worthingtoni* Parker 1932 p. 221
  Type locality: Lake Naivasha, Kenya
  Distribution: Kenya.

*Bitis xeropaga* Haacke 1975 p. 116
  Type locality: Dreikammberg on north bank of Orange River, Luderitz district,
      South West Africa (16° 52' E, 28° 05' S, alt. about 300 m)
  Distribution: South Africa (Orange River).


Genus CERASTES Laurenti 1768 p. 18. Two species.
  Type species: *Coluber cerastes* Linnaeus

*Cerastes cerastes cerastes* (Linnaeus)
  *Coluber cerastes* Linnaeus 1758 p. 217
  Type locality: In Oriente
  Distribution: Egypt, Libya, Algeria, Tunisia, Morocco, Mauritania, Mali and
      Niger.

*Cerastes cerastes gasperettii* Leviton and Anderson 1967 p. 157
  Type locality: Beda, Azan, Abu Dhabi
  Distribution: Jordan, Israel, Lebanon, Iraq, Kuwait and Saudi Arabia.

*Cerastes vipera* (Linnaeus)
  *Coluber vipera* Linnaeus 1758 p. 216
  Type locality: Egypt
  Distribution: Egypt, Libya, Algeria, Tunisia, Morocco, Mauritania, Mali, Niger,
      Israel and Lebanon.


Genus ECHIS Merrem 1820 p. 149. Two species.
  Type species: *Pseudoboa carinata* Schneider


*Echis carinatus carinatus* (Schneider)
  *Pseudoboa carinata* Schneider 1801 p. 285
  Type locality: Arni, Madras, India
  Distribution: Peninsular India.

*Echis carinatus leakeyi* Stemmler and Sochurek 1969 p. 1
  Type locality: Campi ya Samaka, W. of L. Baringo, Kenya
  Distribution: Kenya, southern Ethiopia and the Somali Republic.

*Echis carinatus ocellatus* Stemmler 1970 p. 1
  Type locality: Haute Volta, Garango  048°N, 033°W.
  Distribution: West Africa.

*Echis carinatus pyramidium* (Geoffroy Saint Hilaire)
  *Scythale pyramidium* Geoffroy Saint Hilaire 1827 p. 152
  Type locality: Egypt
  Distribution: North Africa, Afghanistan, Russia (Turkestan), Iran, Iraq and
      the Arabian Peninsula.

*Echis carinatus sinhaleyus*  Deraniyagala 1951 p. 148
   Type locality:  Shavakacheri, N.P.
   Distribution:  Sri Lanka.

*Echis carinatus sochureki*  Stemmler 1969 p. 1
   Type locality:  Pishin, W. Pakistan
   Distribution:  Northern India, Pakistan and Bangladesh.

*Echis coloratus*  Gunther 1878 p. 978
   Type locality:  Jebel Sharr, Midian, Arabia
   Distribution:  South-eastern Egypt, the Arabian Peninsula and Sokotra Island.


Genus ERISTOCOPHIS  Alcock and Finn 1897 p. 564.  Single species.
   Type species:  *Eristocophis macmahoni*  Alcock and Finn


*Eristocophis macmahoni*  Alcock and Finn 1897 p. 564
   Type locality:  Desert south of the Helmand River, Baluchistan
   Distribution:  Iran, Afghanistan and Pakistan.


Genus PSEUDOCERASTES  Boulenger 1896a p. 501.  Single species.
   Type species:  *Cerastes persicus*  Dumeril, Bibron and Dumeril


*Pseudocerastes persicus persicus*  (Dumeril, Bibron and Dumeril)
   *Cerastes persicus*  Dumeril, Bibron and Dumeril 1854 p. 1443
   Type locality:  Persia
   Distribution:  Iraq, Kuwait, Saudi Arabia, Iran, Afghanistan and Pakistan.

*Pseudocerastes persicus fieldi*  Schmidt 1930 p. 227
   Type locality:  Bair Wells, Jordan
   Distribution:  Jordan, Israel and Lebanon.


Genus VIPERA  Laurenti 1768 p. 99.  Twelve species.
   Type species:  *Vipera francisci redi*  Laurenti


*Vipera ammodytes ammodytes*  (Linnaeus)
   *Coluber ammodytes*  Linnaeus 1758 p. 216
   Type locality:  Zadar, Yugoslavia
   Distribution:  Austria, northern Italy, southern Czechoslovakia, western Hungary,
      Yugoslavia, south-western Romania and north-western Bulgaria.

*Vipera ammodytes meridionalis*  Boulenger 1903a p. 185
   Type locality:  Athens, Greece
   Distribution:  Albania, Greece, Cyclade Islands, Turkey and Syria.

*Vipera ammodytes montandoni*  Boulenger 1904 p. 134
   Type locality:  Greci, District of Macin, Dobruja, Romania
   Distribution:  Romania (east of the Danube) and Bulgaria.

*Vipera ammodytes transcaucasiana*  Boulenger 1913 p. 284
   Type locality:  Borzom, District of Gori, Privince of Tiflis, Azerbaidshan
   Distribution:  U.S.S.R. (Transcaucasia).

*Vipera aspis aspis*  (Linnaeus)
   *Coluber aspis*  Linnaeus 1758 p. 218
   Type locality:  Poitou, France
   Distribution:  France, Switzerland, southern Austria, Germany, Italian Peninsula
      (except Calabria), Elba Island and north-western Yugoslavia.

*Vipera aspis atra*  Meisner 1820 p. 93
   Type locality:  Kandersteg, Switzerland
   Distribution:  Switzerland.

*Vipera aspis francisciredi*  Laurenti 1768 p. 99
   Type locality:  Italy
   Distribution:  Italy.

*Vipera aspis hugyi*  Schinz 1833 p. 179
   Type locality:  Etna, Sicily
   Distribution:  Italy (Calabria) and Sicily.

*Vipera aspis montecristi*  Mertens 1956 p. 222
   Type locality:  Montecristo Island, Italy
   Distribution:  Type locality only.

*Vipera aspis zinnikeri*  Kramer 1958 p. 323
   Type locality:  Auch, Department Gers, France
   Distribution:  South-western France (Gascony).

*Vipera berus berus*  (Linnaeus)
   *Coluber berus*  Linnaeus 1758 p. 217
   Type locality:  Uppsala, Sweden
   Distribution:  Northern and central Europe as far north as the Arctic Circle
      and south to the Pyrenees, and Asia east to the Amur River.

*Vipera berus bosniensis*  Boettger 1889 p. 272
   Type locality:  Trebinj, Yugoslavia
   Distribution:  Mountains of Yugoslavia and Bulgaria.

*Vipera berus sachalinensis*  Zarevsky 1917 p. 37
   Type locality:  Sakhalin Island, U.S.S.R.
   Distribution:  Type locality only.

*Vipera berus seoanei*  Lataste 1879 p. 132
   Type locality:  Cabanas, Province of La Coruna, Spain
   Distribution:  Northern Portugal and north-west Spain.

*Vipera bornmulleri*  Werner 1898
   Type locality:  Libanon-Gebirge (1800-2200 m hoch) und Kar Boghaz (Bulgar Dagh,
      2500 m hoch)
   Distribution:  Lebanon, Israel and Jordan.

*Vipera kaznakovi*  Nikolsky 1909 p. 174
   Type locality:  Suchumi District, Grusinia
   Distribution:  U.S.S.R. (western Caucasus) and Turkey (north-eastern Anatolia).

*Vipera latastei latastei*  Bosca 1878 p. 121
    Type locality:  Valencia, Spain
    Distribution:  Spain (south of the Ebro River), Portugal, northern Tunisia,
        northern Algeria and Morocco (north of the Atlas Mountains).

*Vipera latastei monticola*  Saint Girons 1954 p. 475
    Type locality:  Massif de Toubkal, High Atlas Mountains, Morocco
    Distribution:  Morocco (Atlas Mountains).

*Vipera latifii*  Mertens, Darevsky and Klemmer 1967 p. 161
    Type locality:  Albors Mountains, Iran
    Distribution:  Type locality only.

*Vipera lebetina lebetina*  (Linnaeus)
    *Coluber lebetinus*  Linnaeus 1758 p. 216
    Type locality:  Cyprus
    Distribution:  Cyprus.

*Vipera lebetina deserti*  Anderson 1892 p. 20
    Type locality:  Douirat, Tunisia
    Distribution:  Algeria (south of the Atlas Mountains), Tunisia and Libya.

*Vipera lebetina euphratica*  Martin 1838 p. 82
    Type locality:  Birejik, Euphrates Valley
    Distribution:  Iraq.

*Vipera lebetina mauritanica*  (Gray)
    *Clotho mauritanica*  Gray 1849 p. 27
    Type locality:  Algeria
    Distribution:  Morocco and coastal area of Algeria and Tunisia.

*Vipera lebetina obtusa*  Dvigubsky 1832 p. 30
    Type locality:  Elisavetpol, Transcaucasia
    Distribution:  Turkey, Iraq, Afghanistan, U.S.S.R. (Caucasus), Syria, Israel,
        Lebanon, Iran and Pakistan.

*Vipera lebetina schweizeri*  Werner 1935 p. 117
    Type locality:  Milos Island, Cyclade Archipelago, Greece
    Distribution:  Cyclades (Milos, Kinalos, Polyagos and Siphnos).

*Vipera lebetina turanica*  Chernov 1940 p. 163
    Type locality:  Turan, U.S.S.R.
    Distribution:  U.S.S.R. (Turkmenistan and Uzbek), north-eastern Iran,
        Afghanistan, northern Pakistan and Kashmir.

*Vipera palaestinae*  Werner 1938 p. 316
    Type locality:  Haifa, Israel
    Distribution:  Syria, Jordan, Israel and Lebanon.

*Vipera russelli russelli*  (Shaw)
    *Coluber russelli*  Shaw 1797 p. 291
    Type locality:  Coromandel Coast, India
    Distribution:  India, Pakistan and Bangladesh.

*Vipera russelli formosensis*  Maki 1931 p. 197
    Type locality:  Choshu, Formosa
    Distribution:  Taiwan.

*Vipera russelli limitis*  Mertens 1927 p. 183
    Type locality:  Endeh Island (near Flores)
    Distribution:  Indonesia (Eastern Java, Komodo, Flores and Lomblen).

*Vipera russelli pulchella*  (Gray)
    *Daboia pulchella*  Gray 1842 p. 69
    Type locality:  Ceylon
    Distribution:  Sri Lanka.

*Vipera russelli siamensis*  Smith 1917 p. 223
    Type locality:  Samkok, about 60 km north of Bangkok, Siam
    Distribution:  Burma, China (Kwangtung) and Thailand.

*Vipera ursinii ursinii*  (Bonaparte)
    *Pelias ursinii*  Bonaparte 1835
    Type locality:  Abruzzi Mountains, Province of Ascoli, Italy
    Distribution:  Type locality only.

*Vipera ursinii macrops*  Mehely 1911 p. 9
    Type locality:  Korito, Hercegovina
    Distribution:  Southern and western Yugoslavia (including Krk Island) and
        northern Albania.

*Vipera ursinii rakosiensis*  Mehely 1894 p. 190
    Type locality:  Rakos Fields, near Budapest, Hungary
    Distribution:  Eastern Austria, Hungary, northern Yugoslavia, southern Romania
        and northern Bulgaria.

*Vipera ursinii renardi*  (Cristoph)
    *Pelias renardi*  Cristoph 1861 p. 599
    Type locality:  Sarepte on Lower Volga River, U.S.S.R.
    Distribution:  North-eastern Romania, U.S.S.R. (southern plains, Kirziz Steppes,
        Altai Mountains and Turkmenistan), north-eastern Turkey and north-western
        Iran).

*Vipera ursinii wettsteini*  Knoeppfler and Sochurek 1955 p. 187
    Type locality:  Montagne de Lure, Basses Alpes, Sudost-Frankreich
    Distribution:  South-eastern France (type locality only).

*Vipera xanthina xanthina*  (Gray)
    *Daboia xanthina*  Gray 1849 p. 24
    Type locality:  Xanthos, Turkey
    Distribution:  Western Turkey.

*Vipera xanthina raddei*  Boettger 1890 p. 62
    Type locality:  Kasikoparan, Armenia
    Distribution:  Eastern Turkey (Armenia) and U.S.S.R. (Armenia).


Tribe AZEMIOPINI


Genus AZEMIOPS  Boulenger 1888b p. 602.  Single species.
    Type species:  *Azemiops feae*  Boulenger

*Azemiops feae*  Boulenger 1888b p. 602
   Type locality:  Kakhyen Hills, Burma
   Distribution:  Burma, China (Kiangsi, Szechwan and south-eastern Tibet) and
      Tonkin.


Tribe CAUSINI


Genus CAUSUS  Wagler 1830 p. 172.  Six species.
   Type species:  *Sepedon rhombeata*  Lichtenstein


*Causus bilineatus*  Boulenger 1905b p. 114
   Type locality:  Between Benguella and Bihe, Angola
   Distribution:  Angola, Zambia (North West Province), Zaire (Katanga) and Rwanda.

*Causus defilippii*  (Jan)
   *Heterodon De Filippii*  Jan 1862 p. 225
   Type locality:  Africa
   Distribution:  Tanzania, Zanzibar, Mozambique, Malawi, Zambia, Zimbabwe-
      Rhodesia and South Africa (northern Transvaal and Natal).

*Causus lichtensteini*  (Jan)
   *Aspidelaps lichtensteini*  Jan 1859 p. 551
   Type locality:  Gold Coast
   Distribution:  Guinea, Guinea-Bissau, Liberia, Ghana, Benin, Nigeria, Cameroun,
      Zaire, Uganda, Kenya and Angola.

*Causus maculatus*  (Hallowell)
   *Distichurus maculatus*  Hallowell 1842 p. 337
   Type locality:  Liberia
   Distribution:  Senegal, The Gambia, Guinea, Guinea-Bissau, Sierra Leone,
      Liberia, Mali, Ivory Coast, Ghana, Togo, Benin, Nigeria, Upper Volta, Chad,
      Cameroun, Gabon, Zaire and northern Angola.

*Causus resimus*  (Peters)
   *Heterophis resimus*  Peters 1862 p. 277
   Type locality:  Jebel Ghule, Sennar, Sudan
   Distribution:  Sudan, Somali Repbulic, Uganda, Kenya, Tanzania, northern
      Mozambique, Rwanda, Chad, Cameroun and Zaire (Orientale and Kivu).

*Causus rhombeatus*  (Lichtenstein)
   *Sepedon rhombeata*  Lichtenstein 1823 p. 106
   Type locality:  Not given
   Distribution:  Africa south of the Sahara (except Eritrea, West Africa, south-
      western South Africa, western Botswana and north-eastern Cape Province).

Subfamily CROTALINAE


Tribe LACHESINI


Genus LACHESIS   Daudin 1803b, vol. 5, p. 351.   Single species.
    Type species:  *Crotalus mutus*  Linnaeus


*Lachesis muta muta*  (Linnaeus)
    *Crotalus mutus*  Linnaeus 1766 p. 373
    Type locality:  Surinam
    Distribution:  Brazil (north of the Amazon Basin), Guyana, Surinam, French
        Guiana, Venezuela, Trinidad, Bolivia, Peru, Ecuador and Colombia.

*Lachesis muta noctivaga*  Hoge 1966 p. 162
    Type locality:  Vitoria, Espirito Santo, Brazil
    Distribution:  Brazil (Atlantic States from Alagoas to Rio de Janeiro).

*Lachesis muta stenophrys*  Cope 1876 p. 152
    Type locality:  Sipurio, Costa Rica
    Distribution:  Costa Rica and Panama.


Tribe CROTALINI


Genus AGKISTRODON   Beauvois 1799 p. 381.   Twelve species.
    Type species:  *Agkistrodon mokasen*  Beauvois

*Agkistrodon acutus*  (Gunther)
    *Halys acutus*  Gunther 1888 p. 171
    Type locality:  Wusueh, Hupeh, China
    Distribution:  China (Hupeh, Hunan, Chekiang, Fukien and Kwangtung), Taiwan and
        North Vietnam.

*Agkistrodon bilineatus bilineatus*  (Gunther)
    *Ancistrodon bilineatus*  Gunther 1863a p. 364
    Type locality:  Pacific coast of Guatemala
    Distribution:  Southern Mexico, Guatemala, El Salvador, Belize, Honduras and
        Nicaragua.

*Agkistrodon bilineatus russeolus*  Gloyd 1972 p. 557
    Type locality:  11.7 km north of Piste, Yucatan, Mexico
    Distribution:  Mexico (Yucatan Peninsula)

*Agkistrodon bilineatus taylori*  Burger and Robertson 1951 p. 213
    Type locality:  21 km north of Villagran, Tamaulipas, Mexico
    Distribution:  Mexico (Tamaulipas and Nuero Leon).

*Agkistrodon blomhoffi blomhoffi*  (Boie)
    *Trigonocephalus blomhoffi*  Boie 1826 p. 214
    Type locality:  Japan
    Distribution:  Japan (Bonin Islands).

*Agkistrodon blomhoffi affinis*  (Gray)
  *Trigonocephalus affinis*  Gray 1849 p. 14
  Type locality:  Unknown
  Distribution:  Ryukyu Islands (Yaeyama Group).

*Agkistrodon blomhoffi brevicaudus*  Stejneger 1907 p. 463
  Type locality:  Fusan, Korea
  Distribution:  Taiwan, Pescadores Islands, Korea and eastern China.

*Agkistrodon caliginosus*  Gloyd 1972 p. 557
  Type locality:  Vicinty of Seoul, South Korea
  Distribution:  South Korea.

*Agkistrodon contortrix contortrix*  (Linnaeus)
  *Boa contortrix*  Linnaeus 1766 p. 373
  Type locality:  Carolina
  Distribution:  U.S.A. (East and north Carolina to the Florida Pahandle and west
      to eastern Texas and eastern Oklahoma, north in the Mississippi Valley to
      southern Illinois and southern Missouri).

*Agkistrodon cortortrix laticinctus*  Gloyd and Conant 1934 p. 2
  Type locality:  26 miles northwest of San Antonio, Bexar County, Texas
  Distribution:  U.S.A. (southern Kansas south through Oklahoma to southern and
      central Texas).

*Agkistrodon cortortrix mokasen*  Beauvois 1799 p. 370
  Type locality:  North America
  Distribution:  U-S.A. (Massachusetts to Illinois and western Tennessee, south
      in the uplands to Georgia and Alabama).

*Agkistrodon contortrix phaeogaster*  Gloyd 1969 p. 219
  Type locality:  Jefferson County, Kansas
  Distribution:  U.S.A. (eastern Kansas and central Missouri).

*Agkistrodon cortortix pictigaster*  Gloyd and Conant 1943 p. 56
  Type locality:  Maple Canyon (Chisos Mountains), Brewster County, Texas, U.S.A.
  Distribution:  U.S.A. (western Texas from Crockett and Val Verde Counties through
      the Big Bend Region and the Davis Mountains).

*Agkistrodon halys halys*  (Pallas)
  *Coluber halys*  Pallas 1776 p. 703
  Type locality:  Am oberen Jenissei, bei dem Salzseen unweit des Lugaskoi Sawod
  Distribution:  U.S.S.R. (southern Siberia) and Mongolia.

*Agkistrodon halys caraganus*  (Eichwald)
  *Trigonocephalus caraganus*  Eichwald 1831 p. 170
  Type locality:  Karagan, east of the Caspian Sea
  Distribution:  U.S.S.R. (mouth of the Volga River east to eastern Kazakhstan).

*Agkistrodon halys caucasicus*  Nikolsky 1916 p. 274
  Type locality:  Lenkovan, south-west coast of the Caspian Sea
  Distribution:  U.S.S.R. (eastern Transcaucasia) and Iran.

*Agkistrodon halys intermedius*  (Strauch)
  *Trigonocephalus intermedius*  Strauch 1868 p. 294
  Type locality:  Irkutsk, Eastern Siberia
  Distribution:  U.S.S.R. (southern Siberia and eastern Turkestan) and Mongolia.

*Agkistrodon halys ussuriensis*  Emelianov 1929 p. 123
   Type locality:  Suchan River
   Distribution:  Northern China (to the mouth of the Amur River).

*Agkistrodon himalayanus*  (Gunther)
   *Halys himalayanus*  Gunther 1864a p. 393
   Type locality:  Garhwal, northern West Pakistan
   Distribution:  Pakistan (Chitral), India (Kashmir, Punjab and Sikkim) and Nepal.

*Agkistrodon monticola*  (Werner)
   *Ancistrodon blomhoffi monticola*  Werner 1922 p. 222
   Type locality:  Taoshan, Yunnan, China
   Distribution:  China (Yunnan).

*Agkistrodon piscivorus piscivorus*  (Lacepede)
   *Crotalus piscivorus*  Lacepede 1789 p. 130
   Type locality:  Carolina
   Distribution:  U.S.A. (south-eastern Virginia to eastern-central Alabama).

*Agkistrodon piscivorus conanti*  Gloyd 1969 p. 219
   Type locality:  Alachua County, Florida
   Distribution:  U.S.A. (Florida).

*Agkistrodon piscivorus leucostoma*  (Troost)
   *Acontias leucostoma*  Troost 1836 p. 176
   Type locality:  Western Tennessee
   Distribution:  U.S.A. (southern Illinois and western-central Kentucky to
      Alabama, and west to southern-central Oklahoma and central Texas.  Colony
      in northern-central Missouri).

*Agkistrodon rhodostoma*  (Boie)
   *Trigonocephalus rhodostoma*  Boie 1827 p. 561
   Type locality:  Java
   Distribution:  Thailand, Kampuchea, Laos, Vietnam, Malaya and Indonesia (Sumatra
      and Java).

*Agkistrodon saxatalis*  (Emelianov)
   *Ancistrodon saxatalis*  Emelianov 1937 p. 19
   Type locality:  Vladivostok River, U.S.S.R.
   Distribution:  Korea, China (extreme north-eastern) and U.S.S.R. (south of the
      Amur River mouth).

*Agkistrodon strauchi*  (Bedriaga)
   *Ancistrodon strauchi*   Bedriaga 1912 p. 728
   Type locality:  Tungngolo, Hsikang, China
   Distribution:  China (Hsikang and Szechwan).


Genus BOTHROPS  Wagler 1824 p. 50.  Sixty-two species.
   Type species:  *Bothrops megaera*  Wagler


*Bothrops albocarinatus*  Shreve 1934 p. 130
   Type locality:  Pastaza River, between Canelos and Maranon Rivers, Ecuador
   Distribution:  Ecuador (Pastaza River drainage).

*Bothrops alternatus*  Dumeril, Bibron and Dumeril 1854 p. 82
  Type locality:  South America, Argentina and Paraguay
  Distribution:  Argentina, Uruguay, Brazil and southern Paraguay.

*Bothrops alticolus*  Parker 1934 p. 272
  Type locality:  5 km east of Loja (9200 ft), Ecuador
  Distribution:  Type locality only.

*Bothrops ammodytoides*  Leybold 1873 p. 80
  Type locality:  Northern Argentina
  Distribution:  Argentina.

*Bothrops andianus*  Amaral 1923 p. 103
  Type locality:  Machu Pichu, Department of Cuzco, 9000 to 10000 ft., Peru
  Distribution:  Peru (Cuzco).

*Bothrops asper*  (Garman)
  *Trigonocephalus asper*  Garman 1883 p. 124
  Type locality:  Obispo, Isthmus of Darien, Panama
  Distribution:  Mexico, Guatemala, Costa Rica, Honduras, Nicaragua, Panama,
      Colombia and Ecuador.

*Bothrops atrox*  (Linnaeus)
  *Coluber atrox*  Linnaeus 1758 p. 222
  Type locality:  South America
  Distribution:  Colombia, Venezuela, Guyana, Surinam, French Guiana, Trinidad,
      Brazil, Peru, Ecuador and Bolivia.

*Bothrops barbouri*  (Dunn)
  *Lachesis barbouri*  Dunn 1919 p. 213
  Type locality:  Omilteme, Guerrero, Mexico
  Distribution:  Mexico (Sierra Madre del Sur and Guerrero).

*Bothrops barnetti*  Parker 1938 p. 47
  Type locality:  Between Lobitos and Talara, northern Peru
  Distribution:  Northern Peru.

*Bothrops bicolor*  Bocourt 1868 p. 202
  Type locality:  St. Augustin de Solola, Guatemala
  Distribution:  Guatemala (Pacific Foothills) and Mexico (Chicharas and Mount
      Orando in extreme south Chiapas).

*Bothrops bilineatus bilineatus*  (Wied)
  *Cophias bilineatus*  Wied 1821 p. 339
  Type locality:  Villa Vicosa on Peruhybe River, Brazil
  Distribution:  Venezuela, Guyana, Surinam, French Guiana and Brazil.

*Bothrops bilineatus smaragdinus*  Hoge 1966 p. 114
  Type locality:  Upper Purus, State of Amazonas, Brazil
  Distribution:  Ecuador, Peru, Bolivia and Brazil.

*Bothrops brazili*  Hoge 1953 p. 15
  Type locality:  Tome Assu on Acara Mirim River, State of Para, Brazil
  Distribution:  Venezuela, Guyana, Surinam, French Guiana, Colombia and Brazil
      (Para, Amazonas and extreme north Mato Grosso).

*Bothrops caribbaeus*  (Garman)
  *Trigonocephalus caribbaeus*  Garman 1887 p. 285
  Type locality:  Sainte Lucia Island
  Distribution:  St. Lucia

*Bothrops castelnaudi*  Dumeril, Bibron and Dumeril 1854 p. 1511
   Type locality:  Unknown
   Distribution:  Brazil, Ecuador and Peru.

*Bothrops colombiensis*  (Hallowell)
   *Trigonocephalus colombiensis*  Hallowell 1845 p. 241
   Type locality:  Republic of Colombia within 200 miles of Caracas
   Distribution:  Northern and north-west Venezuela and north-eastern Colombia.

*Bothrops cotiara*  (Gomes)
   *Lachesis cotiara*  Gomes 1913 p. 65
   Type locality:  Marechal Mallett, Parana, Brazil
   Distribution:  Argentina (Missiones) and Brazil.

*Bothrops dunni*  (Hartweg and Oliver)
   *Trimeresurus dunni*  Hartweg and Oliver 1938 p. 6
   Type locality:  Vicinity of Village of Tehuantepec, Oaxaca, Mexico
   Distribution:  Mexico (Pacific slopes of Oaxaca).

*Bothrops erythromelas*  Amaral 1923 p. 96
   Type locality:  Near Joazeiro, Bahia, Brazil
   Distribution:  Brazil (Ceara and Bahia).

*Bothrops fonsecai*  Hoge and Belluomini 1959 p. 195
   Type locality:  Santo Antonio do Capivary, State of Rio de Janeiro, Brazil
   Distribution:  Brazil (north-eastern Sao Paulo, southern Rio de Janeiro and
      extreme southern Minas Gerais).

*Bothrops godmanni*  (Gunther)
   *Bothriechis godmanni*  Gunther 1863a p. 364
   Type locality:  Duennas and other parts of the tableland of Guatemala
   Distribution:  Mexico (Chiapas), Guatemala, El Salvador, Honduras, Nicaragua,
      Costa Rica and Panama.

*Bothrops hesperus*  Campbell 1976 p. 151
   Type locality:  Foothills of Colima, Mexico
   Distribution:  Type locality only.

*Bothrops hyoprorus*  Amaral 1935 p. 222
   Type locality:  La Pedrera, Colombia
   Distribution:  Colombia, Ecuador, Peru and western Brazil.

*Bothrops inglesiasi*  Amaral 1923 p. 97
   Type locality:  Near Fazanda Grande on the right riverside of the Gurgueia
      River, State of Piaui, Brazil
   Distribution:  Brazil (northern Piaui).

*Bothrops insularis*  (Amaral)
   *Lachesis insularis*  Amaral 1921 p. 18
   Type locality:  Island Queimada Grande on the coast of the State of Sao Paulo,
      Brazil
   Distribution:  Type locality only.

*Bothrops itapetiningae*  (Boulenger)
   *Lachesis itapetiningae*  Boulenger 1907 p. 338
   Type locality:  Itapetininga, Sao Paulo, Brazil
   Distribution:  Brazil (north-eastern Parana, Sao Paulo, Minas Gerais, Distrito
      Federal and Mato Grosso).

*Bothrops jararaca*  (Wied)
  *Cophias jararaca*  Wied 1824 p. 8
  Type locality:  Espirito Santo, Brazil
  Distribution:  Northern Argentina, Paraguay and Brazil.

*Bothrops jararacussu*  Lacerda 1884 p. 8
  Type locality:  Province of Rio de Janeiro, Brazil
  Distribution:  Northern Argentina, Brazil, Paraguay and extreme southern Bolivia.

*Bothrops lanceolatus*  (Lacepede)
  *Coluber lanceolatus*  Lacepede 1789 p. 80
  Type locality:  Martinique
  Distribution:  Martinique.

*Bothrops lansbergi lansbergi*  (Schlegel)
  *Trigonocephalus lansbergii*  Schlegel 1841 p. 1
  Type locality:  Turbaco, Colombia
  Distribution:  Colombia (Costa del Caribe and Baja Magdalena).

*Bothrops lansbergi annectens*  (Schmidt)
  *Trimeresurus lansbergii annectens*  Schmidt 1936b p. 50
  Type locality:  Subirana-Tal, Yoro, Honduras
  Distribution:  Honduras.

*Bothrops lansbergi rozei*  Peters 1968 p. 320
  Type locality:  Carapito, Monagas, Venezuela
  Distribution:  Northern Venezuela.

*Bothrops lateralis*  (Peters)
  *Bothriechis lateralis*  Peters 1863 p. 674
  Type locality:  Veragua and Volcan Barbo, Costa Rica
  Distribution:  Costa Rica and Panama.

*Bothrops leucurus*  Wagler 1824 p. 50
  Type locality:  Bahia, Brazil
  Distribution:  Brazil.

*Bothrops lichenosus*  Roze 1958 p. 308
  Type locality:  Chimanta-Tepui, Estado Bolivar, Venezuela
  Distribution:  Type locality only.

*Bothrops lojanus*  Parker 1930 p. 568
  Type locality:  Loja, Ecuador
  Distribution:  Type locality only.

*Bothrops marajoensis*  Hoge 1966 p. 123
  Type locality:  Severino, Island of Marajo, State of Para, Brazil
  Distribution:  Brazil (Savannah of Marajo).

*Bothrops medusa*  (Sternfeld)
  *Lachesis medusa*  Sternfeld 1920 p. 180
  Type locality:  Caracas, Venezuela
  Distribution:  Venezuela (central Cordillera de la Costa).

*Bothrops melanurus*  (Muller)
  *Trimeresurus melanurus*  Muller 1924 p. 92
  Type locality:  Mexico
  Distribution:  Mexico (southern Puebla and northern Oaxaca).

*Bothrops microphthalmus microphthalmus*  Cope 1876 p. 182
   Type locality:  Between Balsas Puerto and Moyabamba, Peru
   Distribution:  Ecuador, Peru and Bolivia.

*Bothrops microphthalmus colombianus*  Rendahl and Vestergren 1940 p. 15
   Type locality:  La Costa, Cauca, Colombia
   Distribution:  Colombia.

*Bothrops moojeni*  Hoge 1966 p. 126
   Type locality:  Brasilia, Distrito Federal, Brazil
   Distribution:  Brazil (central savannah).

*Bothrops nasutus*  Bocourt 1868 p. 202
   Type locality:  Panzos, Rio Polochio, Guatemala
   Distribution:  Mexico (Verz Cruz), Guatemala, El Salvador, Honduras, Belize,
      Nicaragua, Costa Rica, Panama, Colombia and Ecuador.

*Bothrops neuwiedi neuwiedi*  Wagler 1824 p. 56
   Type locality:  Province of Bahia, Brazil
   Distribution:  Brazil (Southern Bahia).

*Bothrops neuwiedi bolivianus*  Amaral 1927 p. 6
   Type locality:  Buenavista, Province Sara, Department of Santa Cruz de la
      Sierra, Bolivia
   Distribution:  Bolivia and Brazil (extreme western Mato Grosso).

*Bothrops neuwiedi diporus*  Cope 1862 p. 347
   Type locality:  Vermejo River Region
   Distribution:  Argentina, Paraguay and Brazil.

*Bothrops neuwiedi goyazensis*  Amaral 1925 p. 58
   Type locality:  Ypomery, Goias, Brazil
   Distribution:  Brazil (Goias).

*Bothrops neuwiedi lutzi*  (Miranda-Ribeiro)
   *Lachesis lutzi*  Miranda-Ribeiro 1915 p. 4
   Type locality:  Sao Francisco River, Bahia, Brazil.
   Distribution:  Brazil (Bahia).

*Bothrops neuwiedi mattogrossensis*  Amaral 1925 p. 60
   Type locality:  Miranda, State of Mato Grosso, Brazil
   Distribution:  Brazil (southern Mato Grosso).

*Bothrops neuwiedi meridionalis*  Muller 1885 p. 669
   Type locality:  Andaray, State of Rio de Janeiro, Brazil
   Distribution:  Brazil (Rio de Janeiro, Guanabara and Espirito Santo).

*Bothrops neuwiedi paranaensis*  Amaral 1925 p. 61
   Type locality:  Castro, Parana, Brazil
   Distribution:  Brazil (Parana).

*Bothrops neuwiedi pauloensis*  Amaral 1925 p. 59
   Type locality:  Leme, Sao Paulo, Brazil
   Distribution:  Brazil (southern Sao Paulo).

*Bothrops neuwiedi piauhyensis*  Amaral 1925 p. 58
   Type locality:  Regeneracao, Piaui, Brazil
   Distribution:  Brazil (Piauhy, Pernambuco, Ceara and southern Marahao).

*Bothrops newwiedi pubescens* (Cope)
  *Trigonocephalus (Bothrops) pubescens*  Cope 1869 p. 157
  Type locality:  Rio Grande do Sul, Brazil
  Distribution:  Brazil (Rio Grande do Sul).

*Bothrops newwiedi urutu*  Lacerda 1884 p. 11
  Type locality:  Province de Minas Gerais
  Distribution:  Brazil (southern Minas Gerais and northern Sao Paulo).

*Bothrops nigroviridis nigroviridis*  (Peters)
  *Bothriechis nigroviridis*  Peters 1859 p. 278
  Type locality:  Vulcan Barbo, Costa Rica
  Distribution:  Costa Rica and Panama.

*Bothrops nigroviridis aurifer*  (Salvin)
  *Thamnocenchris aurifer*  Salvin 1860 p. 459
  Type locality:  Coban, Alto Verapaz, Guatemala
  Distribution:  Mexico (Chiapas) and Guatemala.

*Bothrops nigroviridis marchi*  Barbour and Loveridge 1929 p. 1
  Type locality:  Gold Mines near Quimistan, Honduras
  Distribution:  Honduras.

*Bothrops nummifer nummifer*  (Ruppel)
  *Atropos nummifer*  Ruppel 1845 p. 313
  Type locality:  Teapa, Tabasco, Mexico
  Distribution:  Mexico (Sao Luiz do Potosi south to Oaxaca).

*Bothrops nummifer mexicanus* (Dumeril, Bibron and Dumeril)
  *Atropos mexicanus*  Dumeril, Bibron and Dumeril 1854 p. 1521
  Type locality:  Coban, Verapaz, Guatemala
  Distribution:  Southern Mexico, Guatemala, El Salvador, Honduras, Belize,
      Nicaragua, Costa Rica and Panama.

*Bothrops nummifer occidduus*  Hoge 1966 p. 130
  Type locality:  San Augustin, on the west slope of the mountains, Guatemala, 610 m.
  Distribution:  El Salvador (Pacific slopes).

*Bothrops oligolepis*  (Werner)
  *Lachesis bilineatus* var. *oligolepis*  Werner 1901b p. 13
  Type locality:  Bolivia
  Distribution:  Bolivia and Peru.

*Bothrops ophryomegas*  Bocourt 1868 p. 201
  Type locality:  Occidental slopes of Escuntla Range, Guatemala
  Distribution:  Western Guatemala, El Salvador, Honduras, Nicaragua, Costa Rica
      and Panama.

*Bothrops peruvianus*  (Boulenger)
  *Lachesis peruvianus*  Boulenger 1903b p. 354
  Type locality:  La Oroya, Carabaya, South-eastern Peru
  Distribution:  South-eastern Peru.

*Bothrops pessoai*  Prado 1939 p. 2
  Type locality:  Rio Paraguay, Est. do Amazonas, Brasil
  Distribution:  Brazil (Amazonas).

*Bothrops picadoi*  (Dunn)
   *Trimeresurus nummifer picadoi*  Dunn 1939 p. 165
   Type locality:  La Palma, Costa Rica, 4500 ft.
   Distribution:  Costa Rica.

*Bothrops pictus*  (Tschudi)
   *Lachesis picta*  Tschudi 1845 p. 61
   Type locality:  The High Mountains of Peru
   Distribution:  Peru (coastal region).

*Bothrops pirajai*  Amaral 1923 p. 99
   Type locality:  Ilheos, State of Bahia, Brazil
   Distribution:  Southern Brazil.

*Bothrops pradoi*  (Hoge)
   *Trimeresurus pradoi*  Hoge 1948 p. 193
   Type locality:  Pau Gigante, State of Espirito Santo, Brazil
   Distribution:  Brazil (type locality north to southern Bahia).

*Bothrops pulcher*  (Peters)
   *Trigonocephalus pulcher*  Peters 1862 p. 672
   Type locality:  Quito, Ecuador
   Distribution:  Ecuador and Peru.

*Bothrops punctatus*  (Garcia)
   *Lachesis punctatus*  Garcia 1896 p. 31
   Type locality:  Las Montanhas del Dagua, Colombia
   Distribution:  Panama (Darien), Colombia and Ecuador (Chaco).

*Bothrops roedingeri*  Mertens 1942 p. 284
   Type locality:  Hacienda Huayri, southern Peru
   Distribution:  Peru (Pacific coast).

*Bothrops rowleyi*  Bogert 1968 p. 1
   Type locality:  5 miles west of Cerro Baul, Oaxaca, Mexico
   Distribution:  Mexico (southern Pacific coast).

*Bothrops santaecrucis*  Hoge 1966 p. 133
   Type locality:  Oromono, Rio Secure, Upper Beni, Bolivia
   Distribution:  Bolivia.

*Bothrops schlegeli*  (Berthold)
   *Trigonocephalus schlegeli*  Berthold 1846 p. 147
   Type locality:  Popayon
   Distribution:  Southern Mexico, Guatemala, El Salvador, Belize, Honduras,
       Nicaragua, Costa Rica, Panama, Colombia, Venezuela and Ecuador.

*Bothrops sphenophrys*  Smith 1960 p. 267
   Type locality:  La Soledad, Oaxaca, Mexico
   Distribution:  Mexico (southern Oaxaca).

*Bothrops supraciliaris*  Taylor 1954 p. 791
   Type locality:  Mountains near San Isidoro del General, San Jose Province,
       Costa Rica.
   Distribution:  Type locality only.

*Bothrops undulatus*  (Jan)
   *Trigonocephalus (Atropos) undulatus*  Jan 1859 p. 157
   Type locality:  Mexico
   Distribution:  Mexico.

*Bothrops venezuelensis*  Sandner Montilla 1952 p. 4
   Type locality:  Boca de Tigre, Serrania de El Avila, Distrito Federal al Norte
      de Caracas.
   Distribution:  Venezuela.

*Bothrops xantogrammus*  (Cope)
   *Trigonocephalus xantogrammus*  Cope 1868 p. 110
   Type locality:  Pallatanga, Ecuador
   Distribution:  Ecuador and Colombia.

*Bothrops yucatannicus* (Smith)
   *Trimeresurus yucatannicus* Smith 1941 p. 62
   Type locality:  Chichzen Itza, Yucatan, Mexico
   Distribution:  Mexico (north and north-eastern Yucatan).


Genus CROTALUS  Linnaeus 1758 p. 214.  Twenty-eight species.
   Type species:  *Crotalus horridus*  Linnaeus


*Crotalus adamanteus*  Beauvois 1799 p. 368
   Type locality:  United States
   Distribution:  U.S.A. (South-eastern and Gulf States, North Carolina to Louisiana).

*Crotalus atrox*  Baird and Girard 1853 p. 5
   Type locality:  Indianola, Texas
   Distribution:  U.S.A. and Mexico (Arkansas and Oklahoma, south to central Mexico
      and west to south-eastern California).

*Crotalus basiliscus basiliscus*  (Cope)
   *Caudisona basilisca*  Cope 1864 p. 166
   Type locality:  Near Colima, Colima, Mexico
   Distribution:  Mexico.

*Crotalus basiliscus oaxacus*  Gloyd 1948 p. 1
   Type locality:  Oaxaca, Mexico
   Distribution:  Mexico (central Oaxaca only).

*Crotalus catalinensis*  Cliff 1954 p. 80
   Type locality:  Santa Catalina Island, Gulf of California, Mexico
   Distribution:  Mexico (type locality only).

*Crotalus cerastes cerastes*  Hallowell 1854 p. 95
   Type locality:  Borders of the Mohave River and in the desert of Mohave
   Distribution:  U.S.A. (Mojave Desert)

*Crotalus cerastes cercobombus*  Savage and Cliff 1953 p. 2
   Type locality:  Near Gila Bend, Maricopa County, Arizona
   Distribution:  U.S.A. (Sonora Desert, Arizona) and Mexico (Sonora).

*Crotalus cerastes laterorepens*  Klauber 1944 p. 94
    Type locality:  The Narrows, San Diego County, California
    Distribution:  U.S.A. (Colorado Desert in south-eastern California and south-
        western Arizona) and north-western Mexico.

*Crotalus durissus durissus*  Linnaeus 1758 p. 214
    Type locality:  America
    Distribution:  South-eastern Mexico, Guatemala, Honduras, Belize, El Salvador,
        Nicaragua and Costa Rica.

*Crotalus durissus cascavella*  Wagler 1824 p. 60
    Type locality:  Mina Caraiba, State of Bahia, Brazil
    Distribution:  Brazil (States of Maranboa, Ceara, Piauhy, Pernambuco, Alagoas,
        Rio Grande do Norte and Bahia).

*Crotalus durissus collilineatus*  Amaral 1926b p. 90
    Type locality:  Central, south-eastern and southern Brazil, Argentina, Paraguay
        and probably Bolivia
    Distribution:  Brazil (south-eastern Mato Grosso, Goias, Distrito Federal,
        Minas Gerais and north-eastern Sao Paulo).

*Crotalus durissus culminatus*  Klauber 1952 p. 65
    Type locality:  Hacienda El Sabino, near Uruapan, Michoacan, Mexico
    Distribution:  Mexico (south-western Michoacan, southern and western Morelos,
        Guerrero and south-western Oaxaca).

*Crotalus durissus cumanensis*  Humboldt 1833 p. 6
    Type locality:  Cumana, Venezuela
    Distribution:  Venezuela and north-eastern Colombia.

*Crotalus durissus dryinus*  Linnaeus 1758 p. 214
    Type locality:  South America
    Distribution:  Guyana, Surinam and French Guiana.

*Crotalus durissus marajoensis*  Hoge 1966 p. 143
    Type locality:  Tuyuyu, Ilha do Marajo, State of Para, Brazil
    Distribution:  Brazil (Savannah of Marajo).

*Crotalus durissus rurima*  Hoge 1966 p. 145
    Type locality:  Paulo Camp, Mount Roraima, Venezuela
    Distribution:  Venezuela (Mount Roraima and Carinan Paru, Amazonas) and Brazil
        (Territorio Federal of Roraima).

*Crotalus durissus terrificus*  (Laurenti)
    *Caudisona terrifica*  Laurenti 1768 p. 93
    Type locality:  America below latitude 45° N.
    Distribution:  Southern Brazil, Uruguay, Argentina, Paraguay and Bolivia.

*Crotalus durissus totonacus*  Gloyd and Kauffeld 1940 p. 12
    Type locality:  Panaco Island, about 75 miles south of Tampico, Veracruz,
        Mexico, 12 miles inland fron Cabo Rojo
    Distribution:  Mexico (southern Tamaulipas, south-eastern San Luis Potosi and
        northern Verz Cruz).

*Crotalus durissus tzabcan*  Klauber 1952 p. 71
    Type locality:  Kantunil, Yucatan, Mexico
    Distribution:  Mexico (Yucatan southwards), Guatemala and northern Belize.

*Crotalus enyo enyo* (Cope)
   *Caudisona enyo* Cope 1861 p. 203
   Type locality: Lower California
   Distribution: Mexico (central and southern Baja California).

*Crotalus enyo cerralvensis* Cliff 1954 p. 82
   Type locality: Cerralvo Island, Gulf of California, Mexico
   Distribution: Type locality only.

*Crotalus enyo furvus* Lowe and Norris 1954 p. 52
   Type locality: 10.9 miles north of El Rosario, Baja California del Norte,
      Mexico
   Distribution: Mexico (north-western Baja California).

*Crotalus exsul* Garman 1883 p. 114
   Type locality: Cedros Island, west coast of Baja California, Mexico
   Distribution: Type locality only.

*Crotalus horridus horridus* Linnaeus 1758 p. 214
   Type locality: America
   Distribution: North-eastern and north-central U.S.A.

*Crotalus horridus atricaudatus* Latreille 1801 p. 209
   Type locality: Carolina
   Distribution: U.S.A. (South Atlantic and Gulf States and the Lower
      Mississippi Valley).

*Crotalus intermedius intermedius* Troschel 1865 p. 613
   Type locality: Mexico
   Distribution: Eastern-central Mexico.

*Crotalus intermedius gloydi* Taylor 1941 p. 130
   Type locality: Cerro San Felipe, elevation 10,000 ft, near Oaxaca de Juarez,
      Oaxaca, Mexico
   Distribution: Mexico (mountains of the south-west).

*Crotalus intermedius omiltemanus* Gunther 1895 p. 192
   Type locality: Omilteme, Guerrero, Mexico
   Distribution: Mexico (central Guerrero).

*Crotalus lannomi* Tanner 1966 p. 298
   Type locality: 1.8 miles west of the pass, Puerto Los Mazos, on Mexican Highway
      No. 80, Jalisco, Mexico
   Distribution: Type locality only.

*Crotalus lepidus lepidus* (Kennicott)
   *Caudisona lepida* Kennicott 1861 p. 206
   Type locality: Presidio del Norte and Eagle Pass, Texas
   Distribution: U.S.A. (southern Texas and New Mexico) and Mexico (north-east).

*Crotalus lepidus klauberi* Gloyd 1936a p. 2
   Type locality: Carr Canyon, Huachuca Mountains, Cochise County, Arizona
   Distribution: U.S.A. (south-eastern Arizona and south-western New Mexico) and
      north-western Mexico.

*Crotalus lepidus morulus* Klauber 1952 p. 52
   Type locality: 10 miles northwest of Gomez Farias on the trail to La Joya de
      Salas, Tamaulipas, Mexico
   Distribution: Mexico (Tamaulipas).

*Crotalus mitchelli mitchelli*  (Cope)
    *Caudisona mitchellii*  Cope 1861 p. 293
    Type locality:  Cape St. Lucas, Baja California, Mexico
    Distribution:  Mexico (southern Baja California and adjacent islands).

*Crotalus mitchelli angelensis*  Klauber 1963 p. 73
    Type locality:  Puerto Refugio, Angel de la Guarda Island, Gulf of California,
        Mexico
    Distribution:  Mexico (Angel de la Guarda Island, Gulf of California).

*Crotalus mitchelli muertensis*  Klauber 1949 p. 97
    Type locality:  El Muerto Island, Gulf of California, Mexico
    Distribution:  Type locality only.

*Crotalus mitchelli pyrrhus*  (Cope)
    *Caudisona pyrrha*  Cope 1866 p. 308
    Type locality:  Not given
    Distribution:  South-western U.S.A. and north-western Mexico.

*Crotalus mitchelli stephensi*  Klauber 1930 p. 108
    Type locality:  2 miles west of Jackass Springs, Panamint Mountains, altitude
        6,200 ft, Inyo County, California
    Distribution:  U.S.A. (eastern-central California and south-western Nevada).

*Crotalus molossus molossus*  Baird and Girard 1853 p. 10
    Type locality:  Fort Webster, Santa Rita del Cobre, New Mexico
    Distribution:  South-western U.S.A. and northern Mexico.

*Crotalus molossus estebanensis*  Klauber 1949 p. 104
    Type locality:  San Esteban Island, Gulf of California, Mexico
    Distribution:  Type locality only.

*Crotalus molossus nigrescens*  Gloyd 1936b p. 2
    Type locality:  4 miles west of La Colorada, Zacatecas, Mexico
    Distribution:  Mexico (from southern Sonora to Puebla).

*Crotalus polystictus*  (Cope)
    *Caudisona polysticta*  Cope 1865 p. 191
    Type locality:  Table land, Mexico
    Distribution:  Mexico (southern Zacatecas to central Vera Cruz).

*Crotalus pricei pricei*  Van Denburgh 1895 p. 856
    Type locality:  Huachuca Mountains, Arizona
    Distribution:  U.S.A. (mountains of south-eastern Arizona) and north-western
       Mexico.

*Crotalus pricei miquihuanus*  Gloyd 1940 p. 102
    Type locality:  Cerro Potosi, near Galeana, Nuevo Leon, Mexico
    Distribution:  Mexico (mountains of the north-east).

*Crotalus pusillus*  Klauber 1952 p. 34
    Type locality:  Tancitaro, Michoacan, altitude 5,000 ft, Mexico
    Distribution:  Mexico (mountains of Michoacan and Jalisco).

*Crotalus ruber ruber*  Cope 1892 p. 690
    Type locality:  Not given
    Distribution:  U.S.A. (southern California) and Mexico (northern Baja California
      and several adjacent islands).

*Crotalus ruber lorenzoensis*  Radcliffe and Maslin 1975 p. 490
    Type locality:  San Lorenzo Island in the Gulf of California, Baja California
       Norte, Mexico
    Distribution:  Type locality only.

*Crotalus ruber lucasensis*  Van Denburgh 1920 p. 29
    Type locality:  Agua Calienta, Cape region of Baja California
    Distribution:  Mexico (southern Baja California).

*Crotalus scutulatus scutulatus*  (Kennicott)
    *Caudisona scutulata*  Kennicott 1861 p. 207
    Type locality:  Not given
    Distribution:  U.S.A. (Mojave Desert of California) and southern-central Mexico.

*Crotalus scutulatus salvini*  Gunther 1895 p. 193
    Type locality:  Huamantla, Mexico, altitude 8,000 ft.
    Distribution:  Southern-central Mexico.

*Crotalus stejnegeri*  Dunn 1919 p. 214
    Type locality:  Plumosos, Sinaloa, Mexico
    Distribution:  Mexico (mountains of Sinaloa and Durango).

*Crotalus tigris*  Kennicott 1859 p. 14
    Type locality:  Sierra Verde and Pozo Verde
    Distribution:  U.S.A. (southern-central Arizona) and north-western Mexico.

*Crotalus tortugensis*  Van Denburgh and Slevin 1921 p. 398
    Type locality:  Tortuga Island, Gulf of California, Mexico
    Distribution:  Type locality only.

*Crotalus transversus*  Taylor 1944 p. 47
    Type locality:  Near Tres Marias, about 55 km southwest of Mexico, D.F., in
       Morelos, Mexico, elevation about 10,000 ft.
    Distribution:  Mexico (Distrito Federal and Morelos).

*Crotalus triseriatus triseriatus*  (Wagler)
    *Uropsophus triseriatus*  Wagler 1830 p. 176
    Type locality:  Mexico
    Distribution:  South-western Mexico.

*Crotalus triseriatus aquilus*  Klauber 1952 p. 24
    Type locality:  Near Alvarez, San Luis Potosi, Mexico
    Distribution:  Mexico (central mountains).

*Crotalus unicolor*  Van Lidth de Jeude 1887 p. 133
    Type locality:  Aruba Island, Netherlands West Indies
    Distribution:  Type locality only.

*Crotalus vegrandis*  Klauber 1941 p. 334
    Type locality:  Maturin Savannah, near Uracoa, Sotillo District, State of
       Monagas, Venezuela
    Distribution:  Venezuela (Monagas and Anzoateguy).

*Crotalus viridis viridis*  (Rafinesque)
    *Crotalinus viridis*  Rafinesque 1818 p. 41
    Type locality:  The Upper Missouri
    Distribution:  U.S.A. (The Great Plains from longitude 96° West to the Rocky
      Mountains).

*Crotalus viridis abyssus* Klauber 1930 p. 114
 Type locality: Tanner trail, 300 ft below the south rim of the Grand Canyon, Coconino County, Arizona
 Distribution: U.S.A. (Grand Canyon, Arizona).

*Crotalus viridis caliginis* Klauber 1949 p. 90
 Type locality: South Coronado Island, northwest coast of Baja California, Mexico
 Distribution: Type locality only.

*Crotalus viridis cerberus* (Coues)
 *Caudisona lucifer* var. *cerberus* Coues 1875 p. 606
 Type locality: San Francisco Mountains, Coconino County, Arizona
 Distribution: U.S.A. (mountains of northern and central Arizona).

*Crotalus viridis concolor* Woodbury 1929 p. 2
 Type locality: King's Ranch, at the base of the Henry Mountains, Garfield County, Utah
 Distribution: U.S.A. (south-western Wyoming, western Colorado and eastern Utah).

*Crotalus viridis helleri* Meek 1905 p. 7
 Type locality: San Jose, Baja California, Mexico
 Distribution: U.S.A. (southern California) and Mexico (northern Baja California).

*Crotalus viridis lutosus* Klauber 1930 p. 100
 Type locality: 10 miles northwest of Abraham on the road to Joy, Millard County, Utah
 Distribution: U.S.A. (The Great Basin).

*Crotalus viridis nuntius* Klauber 1935 p. 78
 Type locality: Canyon Diablo, Coconino County, Arizona
 Distribution: U.S.A. (north-east and north-central Arizona).

*Crotalus viridis oreganus* Holbrook 1840 p. 115
 Type locality: Banks of the Oregon or Columbia River
 Distribution: Canada and U.S.A. (Pacific slope east of the Cascades and west of the Sierra Nevada, from British Columbia south to central California).

*Crotalus willardi willardi* Meek 1905 p. 18
 Type locality: Above Hamburg, middle branch of Ramsey Canyon, Huachuca Mountains, altitude about 7,000 ft, Cochise County, Arizona
 Distribution: U.S.A. (mountains of southern Arizona) and Mexico (northern Sonora).

*Crotalus willardi amabilis* Anderson 1962 p. 160
 Type locality: Arroyo Mesteno, 8,500 ft, Sierra del Nido, Chihuahua, Mexico
 Distribution: Mexico (Sierra del Nido, north-central Chihuahua).

*Crotalus willardi meridionalis* Klauber 1949 p. 131
 Type locality: Coyotes, Durango, Mexico, altitude 8,000 ft.
 Distribution: Western-central Mexico.

*Crotalus willardi silus* Klauber 1949 p. 128
 Type locality: On the Rio Gavilan, 7 miles southwest of Pacheco, Chihuahua, Mexico, altitude 6,200 ft.
 Distribution: U.S.A. (south-western New Mexico) and Mexico (south-western Chihuahua).

Genus HYPNALE Fitzinger 1843 p. 28.  Three species.
   Type species:  *Trigonocephalus hypnale*  Schlegel


*Hypnale hypnale*  (Merrem)
   *Cophias hypnale*  Merrem 1820 p. 155
   Type locality:  Ceylon
   Distribution:  Sri Lanka and India (Kerala and Mysore).

*Hypnale nepa*  (Laurenti)
   *Coluber nepa*  Laurenti 1768 p. 97
   Type locality:  Madagascar (in error)
   Distribution:  Sri Lanka.

*Hypnale walli*  Gloyd 1977 p. 1002
   Type locality:  Sri Lanka
   Distribution:  Sri Lanka.


Genus SISTRURUS  Garman 1883 p. 110.  Three species.
   Type species:  *Crotalus miliarius*  Linnaeus


*Sistrurus catenatus catenatus*  (Rafinesque)
   *Crotalinus catenatus*  Rafinesque 1818 p. 41
   Type locality:  Prairies of the Upper Missouri
   Distribution:  U.S.A. (western New York to Nebraska and Kansas).

*Sistrurus catenatus edwardsi*  (Baird and Girard)
   *Crotalophorus edwardsii*  Baird and Girard 1853 p. 15
   Type locality:  Tamaulipas, Mexico
   Distribution:  U.S.A. (western Texas to south-eastern Arizona) and northern
      Mexico.

*Sistrurus catenatus tergeminus*  (Say)
   *Crotalus tergeminus*  Say 1823 p. 449
   Type locality:  Between the Mississippi River and the Rocky Mountains
   Distribution:  U.S.A. (south-western plains).

*Sistrurus miliarius miliarius*  (Linnaeus)
   *Crotalus miliarius*  Linnaeus 1766 p. 372
   Type locality:  Carolina
   Distribution:  U.S.A. (North Carolina to Georgia and Alabama).

*Sistrurus miliarius barbouri*  Gloyd 1935 p. 2
   Type locality:  Royal Palm Hammock, 12 miles west of Homestead, Dale County,
      Florida
   Distribution:  U.S.A. (South Carolina to Florida and south-eastern Mississippi).

*Sistrurus miliarius streckeri*  Gloyd 1935 p. 4
   Type locality:  Near Imboden, Lawrence County, Arkansas
   Distribution:  U.S.A. (Mississippi to south-western Tennessee and eastern Texas).

*Sistrurus ravus*  (Cope)
   *Crotalus ravus*  Cope 1865 p. 191
   Type locality:  Tableland of Mexico
   Distribution:  Mexico (central plateau).

Genus TRIMERESURUS  Lacepede 1804 p. 209.  Thirty-three species.
   Type species:  *Trimeresurus viridis*  Lacepede


*Trimeresurus albolabris*  Gray 1842 p. 48
   Type locality:  China
   Distribution:  India (Punjab and Bombay)., Nepal, Sikkim, Burma, Thailand,
      Kampuchea, Laos, Vietnam, China (Fukien, Hainan, Kwangtung and Kwangsi),
      Malaysia, Indonesia (Sumatra, Java, Lombok, Sumbawa, Sumba, Flores, Adonara,
      Alor, Roti, Semou, Timor, Wetar and Roma) and Taiwan.

*Trimeresurus cantori*  (Blyth)
   *Trigonocephalus cantori*  Blyth 1846 p. 377
   Type locality:  Nicobar Island
   Distribution:  Andaman and Nicobar Islands.

*Trimeresurus chaseni*  Smith 1931b p. 29
   Type locality:  Kiau, Mount Kinabalu, North Borneo
   Distribution:  Malaysia (Mount Kinabalu only).

*Trimeresurus convictus*  Stoliczka 1870 p. 224
   Type locality:  Western Hill, Penang, Malaya
   Distribution:  Malaya (south of the Isthmus of Kra).

*Trimeresurus cornutus*  Smith 1930 p. 682
   Type locality:  Fan-si-pan Mountains, North Vietnam
   Distribution:  North Vietnam

*Trimeresurus elegans*  (Gray)
   *Craspedocephalus elegans*  Gray 1849 p. 7
   Type locality:  West coast of North America (in error)
   Distribution:  Ryukyu Islands (Irimote, Ishigaki and Miyako).

*Trimeresurus erythrurus*  (Cantor)
   *Trigonocephalus erythrurus*  Cantor 1839 p. 31
   Type locality:  Ganges Delta, India
   Distribution:  India (West Bengal and Assam), Burma and Bangladesh.

*Trimeresurus flavomaculatus flavomaculatus*  (Gray)
   *Megaera flavomaculata*  Gray 1842 p. 49
   Type locality:  Philippine Islands
   Distribution:  Philippines (Camiguin, Jolo, Luzon and Mindanao).

*Trimeresurus flavomaculatus halieus*  Griffin 1910 p. 214
   Type locality:  Polillo Island
   Distribution:  Philippines (Polillo).

*Trimeresurus flavomaculatus mcgregori*  Taylor 1919 p. 110
   Type locality:  Batan Island, Batanes Group, Philippines
   Distribution:  Philippines (Batan).

*Trimeresurus flavoviridis flavoviridis*  (Hallowell)
   *Bothrops flavoviridis*  Hallowell 1860 p. 492
   Type locality:  Amakarima, Ryukyu Islands
   Distribution:  Ryukyu Islands (Okinawa and Amami Groups).

*Trimeresurus flavoviridis tinkhami*  Gloyd 1955 p. 123
   Type locality:  Kume Shima, Okinawa Group, Ryukyu Islands
   Distribution:  Type locality only.

*Trimeresurus gracilis*  Oshima 1920 p. 10
   Type locality:  Formosa
   Distribution:  Taiwan.

*Trimeresurus gramineus*  (Shaw)
   *Coluber gramineus*  Shaw 1802a p. 420
   Type locality:  Vizagapatam, India
   Distribution:  South and central India.

*Trimeresurus hageni*  (Van Lidth de Jeude)
   *Bothrops hageni*  Van Lidth de Jeude 1886 p. 53
   Type locality:  Beli, Sumatra
   Distribution:  Indonesia (Batu Group, Bangka, Mentawai Group, Nias, Simalur and
      Sumatra).

*Trimeresurus huttoni*  Smith 1949 p. 596
   Type locality:  High Wavy Mountains, Madura District, Southern India
   Distribution:  India (Madras).

*Trimeresurus jerdoni jerdoni*  Gunther 1875 p. 233
   Type locality:  Khasi Hills, Assam, India
   Distribution:  India (Assam), northern Burma, China (Yunnan) and the
      Burma-Tibet frontier.

*Trimeresurus jerdoni bourreti*  Klemmer 1963 p. 432
   Type locality:  Chapa, North Vietnam
   Distribution:  North Vietnam.

*Trimeresurus jerdoni xanthomelas*  Gunther 1889 p. 221
   Type locality:  Ichang, Hupeh, China
   Distribution:  China (Szechwan and Hupeh).

*Trimeresurus kanburiensis*  Smith 1943 p. 519
   Type locality:  Near Kanburi, south-western Siam
   Distribution:  Type locality only.

*Trimeresurus kaulbacki*  Smith 1940 p. 485
   Type locality:  North of the Triangle, Upper Burma
   Distribution:  Type locality only.

*Trimeresurus labialis*  Steindachner 1867 p. 86
   Type locality:  Nicobar Islands
   Distribution:  Andaman and Nicobar Islands.

*Trimeresurus macrolepis*  Beddome 1862 p. 2
   Type locality:  Anamallai Hills, India
   Distribution:  India (southern mountains).

*Trimeresurus malabaricus*  (Jerdon)
   *Trigonocephalus (Cophias) malabaricus*  Jerdon 1854 p. 523
   Type locality:  Western Ghats, India
   Distribution:  India (western and southern hills).

*Trimeresurus monticola monticola*  Gunther 1864a p. 388
   Type locality:  Nepal and Sikkim
   Distribution:  Nepal, India (Assam and Sikkim), Burma and China (Yunnan and
      Szechwan).

*Trimeresurus monticola makazayazaya*  Takahashi 1922 p. 4
　　Type locality:  Makazayazaya, Taiwan
　　Distribution:  Taiwan.

*Trimeresurus monticola meridionalis*  Bourret 1935 p. 13
　　Type locality:  Chapa, Vietnam
　　Distribution:  Kampuchea, Laos, Malaya, Thailand and Vietnam.

*Trimeresurus monticola orientalis*  Schmidt 1925b p. 3
　　Type locality:  Shaowu, Fukien, China
　　Distribution:  China (Chekiang and Fukien).

*Trimeresurus mucrosquamatus*  (Cantor)
　　*Trigonocephalus mucrosquamatus*  Cantor 1839 p. 32
　　Type locality:  Naga Hills, Assam, India
　　Distribution:  India (Assam and north-eastern Frontier Agency), Bangladesh,
　　　　China (Fukien, Kwangsi, Kwangtung and Szechwan), Taiwan and Vietnam.

*Trimeresurus okinavensis*  Boulenger 1892 p. 302
　　Type locality:  Okinawa, Ryukyu Islands
　　Distribution:  Ryukyu Islands (Okinawa and Amami).

*Trimeresurus popeorum*  Smith 1937 p. 730
　　Type locality:  Sikkim
　　Distribution:  India (Assam and Sikkim), Burma, Thailand, Malaysia and Indonesia
　　　　(Sumatra and Kalimantan).

*Trimeresurus puniceus*  (Boie)
　　*Cophias punincea*  Boie 1827 p. 561
　　Type locality:  Java
　　Distribution:  Peninsular Thailand, Malaysia and Indonesia (Java, Sumatra,
　　　　Kalimantan, Simalur and the Mentawai Islands).

*Trimeresurus purpureomaculatus purpureomaculatus*  (Gray)
　　*Trigonocephalus purpureomaculatus*  Gray 1830, Vol. 1, p. 81
　　Type locality:  Singapore
　　Distribution:  India (West Bengal and Assam), southern Burma, Malaya, Riou
　　　　Archipelago and Indonesia (Sumatra).

*Trimeresurus purpureomaculatus andersoni*  Theobald 1868 p. 75
　　Type locality:  Andaman Islands
　　Distribution:  Andaman and Nicobar Islands.

*Trimeresurus schultzei*  Griffin 1909 p. 601
　　Type locality:  Iwahig, Palawan Island
　　Distribution:  Philippines (Balabac and Palawan).

*Trimeresurus stejnegeri stejnegeri*  Schmidt 1925a p. 4
　　Type locality:  Shaowu, Fukien, China
　　Distribution:  China (Kwangsi, Kwangtung, Hainan, Fukien and Chekiang).

*Trimeresurus stejnegeri formosensis*  Maki 1931 p. 214
　　Type locality:  Taiwan
　　Distribution:  Type locality only.

*Trimeresurus stejnegeri kodairi*  Maki 1931 p. 216
　　Type locality:  Chikushiko, Taihoku, Taiwan
　　Distribution:  Taiwan (Mount Arisan and Mount Daiton).

*Trimeresurus stejnegeri yunnanensis*  Schmidt 1925a p. 4
    Type locality:  Tengyueh, Yunnan, China
    Distribution:  China (Yunnan), Nepal, India (Assam and Sikkim) and northern
        Burma.

*Trimesurus strigatus*  (Gray)
    *Trimeresurus strigatus*  Gray 1842 p. 49
    Type locality:  Madras, India
    Distribution:  India (southern hills).

*Trimeresurus sumatranus sumatranus*  (Raffles)
    *Coluber sumatranus*  Raffles 1822 p. 334
    Type locality:  Sumatra
    Distribution:  Malaysia and Indonesia (Mentawai Islands, Sumatra, Bangka,
        Billiton and Kalimantan).

*Trimeresurus sumatranus malcolmi*  Loveridge 1938 p. 45
    Type locality:  Sungii River, near Bundutuan, Mount Kinabalu, North Borneo
    Distribution:  Type locality only.

*Trimeresurus tokarensis*  Nagai 1928 p. 6
    Type locality:  Takara shima, Torara Group, Ryukyu Islands
    Distribution:  Ryukyu Islands (Takara).

*Trimeresurus tonkinensis*  Bourret 1934 p. 138
    Type locality:  Chapa, Vietnam
    Distribution:  Vietnam.

*Trimeresurus trigonocephalus*  (Sonnini and Latreille)
    *Vipera trigonocephala*  Sonnini and Latreille 1801 p. 332
    Type locality:  l'Ile S.-Eustace
    Distribution:  Sri Lanka.

*Trimeresurus wagleri*  (Schlegel)
    *Trigonocephalus wagleri*  Schlegel 1837 p. 542
    Type locality:  Sumatra
    Distribution:  Malaysia, Riou Archipelago, Indonesia (Nias, Mentawai Islands,
        Sumatra, Bangka, Billiton, Kalimantan, Karimata, Sulawesi, Sangihe Islands
        and Buton) and the Philippines (Balabac, Basilan, Jolo, Leyte, Luzon,
        Mindanao, Palawan and Samar).

# TAXONOMIC REFERENCES

Alcock, A. and Finn, F. (1897). *J. Asiat. Soc. Beng., 65.*
Amaral, A. do (1921). *Anex Mem. Inst. Butantan, Seccao Ofiologia, 1.*
Amaral, A. do (1923). *Proc. New Engl. zool. Club, 8.*
Amaral, A. do (1925). *Contr. Harv. Inst. trop. Biol. Med. (2).*
Amaral, A. do (1926a). *Comm. Linh. Telegr. Mato Grosso ao Amazonas*, publ. 84 (5).
Amaral, A. do (1926b). *Rev. Mus. Paul., 15.*
Amaral, A. do (1927). *Bull. Antiv. Inst. Am., 1.*
Amaral, A. do (1935). *Mem. Inst. Butantan, 9.*
Anderson, J.A. (1892). *Proc. zool. Soc. Lond.*
Anderson, J.D. (1962). *Copeia* (1).
Angel, F. (1922). *Bull. Mus. natn. Hist. nat., Paris, 28.*
Ashe, J. (1968). *Jl. E. Africa Nat. Hist. Soc., 27.*
Baird, S.F. and Girard, C. (1853). *Catalogue of North American Reptiles in the Museum of the Smithsonian Institution.* Part 1: Serpents. Washington, 172 pp.
Barbour, T. (1923). *Occ. Pap. Mus. zool., Univ. Mich. (129).*
Barbour, T. and Amaral, A. do (1928). *Bull. Antiv. Inst. Am., 1.*
Barbour, T. and Loveridge, A. (1929). *Bull. Antiv. Inst. Am., 3.*
Barrio, A. and Miranda, M.E. (1968). *Mem. Inst. Butantan, 33.*
Bavay, A. (1869). *Mem. Soc. Linn. Norm., 15.*
Beauvois, P. de (1799). *Trans. Am. Phil. Soc., 4.*
Beddome, R.H. (1862). *Madras Quart. J. Med. Sci., 5.*
Bedriaga, J. (1912). *Wiss. Res. Przewalski Cent.-Asien Reisen. Zool., 3.*
Berthold, A.A. (1846). *Nachr. Univ. Ges. Wiss. Guttingen.*
Bianconi, J.J. (1849). *Nuari Ann. Sci. Nat., 10.*
Bleeker, P. (1859). *Nat. Tijdschr. Ned. Ind., 20.*
Blyth, E. (1846). *J. Asiat. Soc. Beng., 15.*
Blyth, E. (1856). *J. Asiat. Soc. Beng., 24.*
Blyth, E. (1861). *J. Asiat. Soc. Beng., 29.*
Bocage, J.V.B. de (1866). *Journ. Sci., Lisboa, 1.*
Bocage, J.V.B. de (1879). *Journ. Sci., Lisboa, 7.*
Bocage, J.V.B. de (1882). *Journ. Sci., Lisboa, 8.*
Bocage, J.V.B. de (1887). *Journ. Sci., Lisboa, 11.*
Bocage, J.V.B. de (1889). *Journ. Sci., Lisboa (2), 2.*
Bocourt, M.-F. (1868). *Ann. Sci. Nat. zool. Paleont., Paris, 10.*
Boettger, O. (1886). *Ber. Senck. Ges.*
Boettger, O. (1889). In Mojsisovics, *Mitt. Naturw. Ver. Steiermark, Graz.*
Boettger, O. (1890). *Zool. Anz., Leipzig, 13.*
Boettger, O. (1895). *Zool. Anz., Leipzig, 18.*

Bogert, C.M. (1940). *Bull. Am. Mus. nat. Hist.*, *77*.
Bogert, C.M. (1968). *Am. Mus. Novit.* (2341).
Boie, F. (1827). *Isis Jena, 20*.
Boie, H. (1826). *Isis Jena, 19*.
Boie, H. (1828). *Isis Jena, 21*.
Bonaparte, C.L.J.L. (1835). *Icon. Faun. Ital.*, *2* (12).
Bosca, E. (1878). *Bull. Soc. zool. France, Paris, 3*.
Boulenger, G.A. (1884). *Proc. zool Soc. Lond.*
Boulenger, G.A. (1888a). *Ann. Mag. nat. Hist.* (6), *2*.
Boulenger, G.A. (1888b). *Ann. Mus. Civ. Stor. nat. Genova* (2), *6*.
Boulenger, G.A. (1890). *Proc. zool. Soc. Lond.*
Boulenger, G.A. (1891). *Ann. Mag. nat. Hist.* (6), *7*.
Boulenger, G.A. (1892). *Ann. Mag. nat. Hist.* (6), *10*.
Boulenger, G.A. (1895a). *Ann. Mus. Civ. Stor. nat. Genova* (2), *15*.
Boulenger, G.A. (1895b). *Ann. Mag. nat. Hist.* (6), *16*.
Boulenger, G.A. (1896a). *Catalogue of the Snakes in the British Museum (Natural History)*, *3*. London, 727 pp.
Boulenger, G.A. (1896b). *Ann. Mag. nat. Hist.* (6), *18*.
Boulenger, G.A. (1897). *J. Bombay nat. Hist. Soc.*, *18*.
Boulenger, G.A. (1898a). *Ann. Mus. Stor. nat. Genova* (2), *19*.
Boulenger, G.A. (1898b). *Ann. Mag. nat. Hist.* (7), *2*.
Boulenger, G.A. (1898c). *Ann. Mus. Stor. Nat.*, *38*.
Boulenger, G.A. (1901). *Annls. Mus. r. Congo Belge, zool.* (1), *2*.
Boulenger, G.A. (1902). *Ann. Mag. nat. Hist.* (7), *10*.
Boulenger, G.A. (1903a). *Proc. zool. Soc. Lond.*
Boulenger, G.A. (1903b). *Ann. Mag. nat. Hist.* (7), *12*.
Boulenger, G.A. (1904). *Ann. Mag. nat. Hist.* (7), *14*.
Boulenger, G.A. (1905a). *Ann. Mag. nat. Hist.* (7), *15*.
Boulenger, G.A. (1905b). *Ann. Mag. nat. Hist.* (7), *16*.
Boulenger, G.A. (1907). *Ann. Mag. nat. Hist.* (7), *20*.
Boulenger, G.A. (1908). *Ann. Mag. nat. Hist.* (8), *1*.
Boulenger, G.A. (1910). *Ann. Mag. nat. Hist.* (8), *5*.
Boulenger, G.A. (1912). *A Vertebrate Fauna of the Malay Peninsula from the Isthmus of Kra to Singapore including the Adjacent Islands.* London, 294 pp.
Boulenger, G.A. (1913). *Ann. Mag. nat. Hist.* (8), *11*.
Boulenger, G.A. (1914a). *Proc. zool. Soc. Lond.*
Boulenger, G.A. (1914b). *Trans. zool. Soc. Lond.*, *20*.
Bourret, R. (1934). *Bull. Gen. Instr. Publ., Hanoi*, Mar.
Bourret, R. (1935). *Bull. Gen. Instr. Publ., Hanoi* (9).
Broadley, D.G. (1968). *Arnoldia Rhodesia, 4*.
Broadley, D.G. (1971). *Occ. Pap. natl. Mus. Rhodesia, 4*.
Brongersma, L.D. and Knaap-Van Meeuwen, M.S. (1964). *Zool. Meded., Leiden, 39*.
Brown, B.C. and Smith, H.M. (1942). *Proc. biol. Soc. Wash.*, *55*.
Buchholz, W. and Peters, W. (1877). *Mber. k. preuss. Akad. Wiss.*
Burger, W.L. (1955). *Bol. Mus. Cien. nat., Caracas, 1*.
Burger, W.L. and Natsuno, T. (1975). *Snake, 6*.
Burger, W.L. and Robertson, W.B. (1951). *Kansas Univ. Sci. Bull.*, *34*.
Campbell, J.A. (1976). *J. Herpet.*, *10*.
Cantor, T.E. (1836). *Asiat. Reschs.*, *19*.
Cantor, T.E. (1839). *Proc. zool. Soc. Lond.*
Cantor, T.E. (1842). *Ann. Mag. nat. Hist.* (1), *9*.
Chernov, S.A. (1940). In P.V. Terentyev and S.A.Chernov, *Opredelitel Presmykayush-chikhsya i Zemnovodnykh.* Moscow.
Cliff, F.S. (1954). *Trans. San Diego Soc. nat. Hist.*, *12*.
Cochran, D.M. (1927). *Proc. biol. Soc. Wash.*, *40*.
Cope, E.D. (1859). *Proc. Acad. nat. Sci. Philad.*, *11*.
Cope, E.D. (1860). *Proc. Acad. nat. Sci. Philad.*, *12*.
Cope, E.D. (1861). *Proc. Acad. nat. Sci. Philad.*, *13*.
Cope, E.D. (1862). *Proc. Acad. nat. Sci. Philad.*, *14*.

Cope, E.D. (1864).  *Proc. Acad. nat. Sci. Philad.*, *16*.
Cope, E.D. (1865).  *Proc. Acad. nat. Sci. Philad.*, *17*.
Cope, E.D. (1866).  *Proc. Acad. nat. Sci. Philad.*, *18*.
Cope, E.D. (1868).  *Proc. Acad. nat. Sci. Philad.*, *20*.
Cope, E.D. (1869).  *Proc. Am. Phil. Soc.*, *11*.
Cope, E.D. (1876).  *J. Acad. nat. Sci. Philad.*, *8*.
Cope, E.D. (1886).  *Proc. Am. Phil. Soc.*, *23*.
Cope, E.D. (1887).  *Bull. U. S. natn. Mus.* (32).
Cope, E.D. (1892).  *Proc. U. S. natn. Mus.*, *14*.
Coues, E. (1875).  *Wheeler Report*, *5*.
Cristoph, H. (1861).  *Bull. Soc. Nat. Moscow*, *34*.
Cuvier, G.L.C.F.D. (1817).  *Le Regne Animal distribue d'apres son organisation*, *2*.
    Paris, 532 pp.
Cuvier, G.L.C.F.D. (1832).  *Voigt. Thierr.*, *3*.
Daudin, F.M. (1803a).  *Bull. Soc. Philom. Paris*, *3*.
Daudin, F.M. (1803b).  *Histoire Naturelle, Generale et Particuliere des Reptiles.*
    *5, 6, 7 and 8*. Paris.
Deraniyagala, P.E.P. (1951).  *Spolia Zeylanica*, *26*.
Deraniyagala, P.E.P. (1955).  *A Colored Atlas of Some Vertebrates from Ceylon.*
    *3* (Serpentoid Reptilia).  Government Press, Ceylon, 121 pp.
Deuve, P. (1961).  *Bull. Mus. natn. Hist. nat.*, *Paris* (2), *32*.
De Vis, C.W. (1884).  *Proc. Roy. Soc. Queensland*, *1*.
De Vis, C.W. (1905).  *Ann. Queensland Mus.*, *6*.
De Witte, G.-F. (1953).  *Inst. Parcs nat. Congo Belge*, *6*.
De Witte, G.-F. (1959).  *Rev. Zool. Bot. Afr.*, *60*.
Dollo, L. (1886).  *Bull. Mus. r. Hist. nat. Belg.*, *4*.
Duges, A.A.D. (1891).  *La Naturaleza, Mexico*, *1*.
Dumeril, A.M.C., Bibron, G. and Dumeril, A.H.A. (1854).  *Erpetologie Generale ou*
    *Histoire Naturelle Complete des Reptiles.*  *7*.  Paris, 1536 pp.
Dunn, E.R. (1919).  *Proc. biol. Soc. Wash.*, *32*.
Dunn, E.R. (1939).  *Proc. biol. Soc. Wash.*, *52*.
Dunn, E.R. (1942).  *Notulae Nat. Acad. Philad.* (108).
Duvernoy, G.L. (1832).  *Ann. Sci. nat. Paris*, *26*.
Dvigubsky, J.A. (1832).  *Opit. estestv. Istoriy*, *3*.
Eichwald, E. (1831).  *Zoologia Specialis Rossiae et Poloniae.*  *3*.  Vilna.
Emelianov, A.A. (1929).  *Zap. Vladivostok Otd. Russ. Geog. Obsc.*, *20*.
Emelianov, A.A. (1937).  *Bull. Far E. Br. Acad. Sci. U.S.S.R.* (24).
Fitzinger, L.I. (1843).  *Systema Reptilium.*  Fasciculus primus Amblyglossae.
    Vindobonae, 106 pp.
Fitzinger, L.I. (1861).  *Sber. Akad. Wiss. Wien*, *42*.
FitzSimons, V.F.M. (1959).  *Ann. Transvaal Mus.*, *23*.
Fleming, J. (1822).  *The Philosophy of Zoology; or a General View of the Structure,*
    *Functions, and Classification of Animals.*  *1*.  London, 432 pp.
Fraser, D.F. (1964).  *Copeia* (3).
Fritze, A. (1894).  *Zool. Jahrb. Syst.*, *7*.
Garcia, A. (1896).  *Los Ofid. Ven. del Cauca.*  Cali, Colombia.
Garman, S. (1881).  *Bull. Mus. Comp. Zool., Harv.*, *8*.
Garman, S. (1883).  *Mem. Mus. Comp. Zool., Harv.*, *8*.
Garman, S. (1887).  *Proc. Am. Phil. Soc.*, *24*.
Geoffroy Saint Hilaire, E.C.T. (1827).  *Description de l'Egypte Histoire Naturelle.* *1*.
Girard, C. (1854).  *Proc. Acad. nat. Sci. Philad.*, *7*.
Glauert, L. (1948).  *W. Aust. Nat.*, *1*.
Gloyd, H.K. (1935).  *Occ. Pap. Mus. Zool., Univ. Mich.* (322).
Gloyd, H.K. (1936a).  *Occ. Pap. Mus. Zool., Univ. Mich.* (337).
Gloyd, H.K. (1936b).  *Occ. Pap. Mus. Zool., Univ. Mich.* (325).
Gloyd, H.K. (1940).  *Chicago Acad. Sci. spec. pub.* (4).
Gloyd, H.K. (1948).  *Nat. Hist. Misc.* (17).
Gloyd, H.K. (1955).  *Bull. Chicago Acad. Sci.*, *10*.
Gloyd, H.K. (1969).  *Proc. biol. Soc. Wash.*, *82*.

Gloyd, H.K. (1972).   *Proc. biol. Soc. Wash., 85.*
Gloyd, H.K. (1977).   *Proc. biol. Soc. Wash., 90.*
Gloyd, H.K. and Conant, R. (1934).  *Occ. Pap. Mus. Zool., Univ. Mich. (283).*
Gloyd, H.K. and Conant, R. (1943).  *Bull. Chicago Acad. Sci., 7.*
Gloyd, H.K. and Kauffeld, C.F. (1940).  *Bull. Chicago Acad. Sci., 6.*
Gomes, F.J. (1913).   *Ann. Paul. Med. Cirurg. Sao Paulo, 1.*
Gray, J.E. (1830-35).   *Illustrations of Indian Zoology; Chiefly Selected from the Collection of Major-General Hardwicke.*  1 and 2.  London, 263 pls.
Gray, J.E. (1841).  In Sir G. Grey, *Journals of Two Expeditions of Discovery in North-West and Western Australia, During the Years 1837, 38 and 39, Under the Authority of Her Majesty's Government Describing Many Newly Discovered, Important, and Fertile Districts, with Observations on the Moral and Physical Conditions of the Aboriginal Inhabitants &c., &c.*  2.  T. & W. Boone, London.
Gray, J.E. (1842).  *The Zoological Miscellany.*  London.
Gray, J.E. (1846).  In J.L.Stokes, *Discoveries in Australia with an Account of the Coasts and Rivers Explored and Surveyed during the Voyage of H.M.S. Beagle in 1837-1843.*  1.  London, 521 pp.
Gray, J.E. (1849).  *Catalogue of the Specimens of Snakes in the Collection of the British Museum.*  London, 125 pp.
Griffin, L.E. (1909).  *Philipp. J. Sci., 4.*
Griffin, L.E. (1910).  *Philipp. J. Sci., 5.*
Griffin, L.E. (1916).  *Mem. Carnegie Mus., 7.*
Gunther, A.C.L.G. (1858).  *Catalogue of Colubrine Snakes in the Collection of the British Museum.*  London, 281 pp.
Gunther, A.C.L.G. (1859).  *Proc. zool. Soc. Lond.*
Gunther, A.C.L.G. (1862).  *Ann. Mag. nat. Hist.* (3), *9.*
Gunther, A.C.L.G. (1863a). *Ann. Mag. nat. Hist.* (3), *12.*
Gunther, A.C.L.G. (1863b). *Ann. Mag. nat. Hist.* (3), *11.*
Gunther, A.C.L.G. (1864a).  *The Reptiles of British India.*  Ray Society, London, 443 pp.
Gunther, A.C.L.G. (1864b).  *Proc. zool. Soc. Lond.*
Gunther, A.C.L.G. (1866).  *Ann. Mag. nat. Hist.* (3), *18.*
Gunther, A.C.L.G. (1868).  *Ann. Mag. nat. Hist.* (4), *1.*
Gunther, A.C.L.G. (1872a).  *Ann. Mag. nat. Hist.* (4), *9.*
Gunther, A.C.L.G. (1872b).  *Proc. zool. Soc. Lond.*
Gunther, A.C.L.G. (1874).  *Proc. zool. Soc. Lond.*
Gunther, A.C.L.G. (1875).  *Proc. zool. Soc. Lond.*
Gunther, A.C.L.G. (1876).  *J. Mus. Godeffroy, 12.*
Gunther, A.C.L.G. (1878).  *Proc. zool. Soc. Lond.*
Gunther, A.C.L.G. (1881).  In Oates, *Matabeleland and the Victoria Falls.*  London.
Gunther, A.C.L.G. (1888).  *Ann. Mag. nat. Hist.* (6), *1.*
Gunther, A.C.L.G. (1889).  *Ann. Mag. nat. Hist.* (6), *4.*
Gunther, A.C.L.G. (1895).  *Biologia Centrali-Americana.*  Reptilia and Batrachia.  London, 326 pp.
Haacke, W.D. (1975).  *Cimbebasia,* (A), *4.*
Haas, G. (1950).  *Copeia* (1).
Hallowell, E. (1842).  *J. Acad. nat. Sci. Philad., 8.*
Hallowell, E. (1844).  *Proc. Acad. nat. Sci. Philad., 2.*
Hallowell, E. (1845).  *Proc. Acad. nat. Sci. Philad., 2.*
Hallowell, E. (1854).  *Proc. Acad. nat. Sci. Philad., 7.*
Hallowell, E. (1855).  *J. Acad. nat. Sci. Philad.* (2), *3.*
Hallowell, E. (1857).  *Proc. Acad. nat. Sci. Philad., 9.*
Hallowell, E. (1860).  *Proc. Acad. nat. Sci. Philad., 12.*
Hartweg, N. and Oliver, J.A. (1938).  *Occ. Pap. Mus. Zool., Univ. Mich. (390).*
Hewitt, J. (1937).  *A Guide to the Vertebrate Fauna of Eastern Cape Province, 2.*  Cape Town.
Hoge, A.R. (1948).  *Mem. Inst. Butantan, 20.*
Hoge, A.R. (1953).  *Mem. Inst. Butantan, 25.*
Hoge, A.R. (1966).  *Mem. Inst. Butantan, 32.*

Hoge, A.R. and Belluomini, H.E. (1959). *Mem. Inst. Butantan, 28.*
Hoge, A.R. and Romano, S.A.R.W.D.L. (1966). *Mem. Inst. Butantan, 32.*
Holbrook, J.E. (1840). *North American Herpetology, 4.*
Humboldt, F.H.A. von (1833).  In Humboldt and Bonpland, *Rec. Obs. Zool. Anat. Comp.,*
    2.
Jan, G. (1858).  *Rev. Mag. Zool.* (2), *10.*
Jan, G. (1859).  *Rev. Mag. Zool.* (2), *10.*
Jan, G. (1862).  *Archo Zool. Anat. Fisiol., 2.*
Jan, G. (1863).  *Archo Zool. Anat. Fisiol., 2.*
Jan, G. (1872).  In G. Jan and F. Sordelli, *Iconographie Generale des Ophidiens.*  *3.*
    Milan.
Jerdon, T.C. (1854).  *J. Asiat. Soc. Beng., 22.*
Kennicott, R. (1859).  In F.S. Baird, *U.S./Mex. Boundary Surv., 2.*
Kennicott, R. (1860).  *Proc. Acad. nat. Sci. Philad., 12.*
Kennicott, R. (1861).  *Proc. Acad. nat. Sci. Philad., 13.*
Kinghorn, J.R. (1921).  *Rec. Aust. Mus., 13.*
Kinghorn, J.R. (1923).  *Rec. Aust. Mus., 14.*
Kinghorn, J.R. (1939).  *Rec. Aust. Mus., 20.*
Klauber, L.M. (1930).  *Trans. San Diego Soc. nat. Hist., 6.*
Klauber, L.M. (1935).  *Trans. San Diego Soc. nat. Hist., 8.*
Klauber, L.M. (1941).  *Trans. San Diego Soc. nat. Hist., 9.*
Klauber, L.M. (1944).  *Trans. San Diego Soc. nat. Hist., 10.*
Klauber, L.M. (1949).  *Trans. San Diego Soc. nat. Hist., 11.*
Klauber, L.M. (1952).  *Bull. zool. Soc. San Diego* (26).
Klauber, L.M. (1963).  *Trans. San Diego Soc. nat. Hist., 13.*
Klemmer, K. (1963).  In Behringwerk-Mitteilungen, *Die Giftschlangen der Erde.*
    Marburg/Lahn.
Knoeppfler, L.P. and Sochurek, E. (1955).  *Burgenl. Heimathl., 17.*
Kopstein, F. (1932).  *Treubia, 14.*
Kramer, E. (1958).  *Viertl. Naturf. Ges. Zurich, 103.*
Krefft, G. (1863).  *Proc. zool. Soc. Lond.*
Krefft, G. (1864).  *Proc. zool. Soc. Lond.*
Krefft, G. (1866).  *Proc. zool. Soc. Lond.*
Krefft, G. (1869a).  *Proc. zool. Soc. Lond.*
Krefft, G. (1869b).  *The Snakes of Australia; an Illustrated and Descriptive*
    *Catalogue of all the Known Species.*  Government Printer, Sydney, 100 pp.
Lacepede, Count B.G.E. (1789).  *Histoire Naturelle des Quadrupedes Ovipares et des*
    *Serpents. 2.*  Paris, 671 pp.
Lacepede, Count B.G.E. (1804).  *Annls. Mus. Hist. nat. Paris, 4.*
Lacerda, J.B. de (1884).  *Lec. Ven. Serp. Brasil.*
Laidlaw, F.F. (1901).  *Proc. zool. Soc. Lond.*
Lancini, A.R. (1962).  *Publ. Occ. Mus. Cien. nat. Caracas,* zool. (3).
Lataste, F. (1879).  *Bull. Soc. zool. France, Paris, 4.*
Lataste, F. (1887).  *Naturaliste, Paris, 9.*
Latreille, P.A. (1802).  In Sonnini de Manoncourt and Latreille (1802).
Laurent, R.F. (1945).  *Rev. Zool. Bot. Afr., 38.*
Laurent, R.F. (1950a).  *Rev. Zool. Bot. Afr., 43.*
Laurent, R.F. (1950b).  *Mem. Inst. Sci. nat. Belg.* (2), *38.*
Laurent, R.F. (1955).  *Rev. Zool. Bot. Afr., 51.*
Laurent, R.F. (1956a).  *Ann. Mus. r. Congo Belg.* (8), *48.*
Laurent, R.F. (1956b).  *Rev. Zool. Bot. Afr., 53.*
Laurent, R.F. (1958).  *Rev. Zool. Bot. Afr., 58.*
Laurent, R.F. (1960).  *Ann. Mus. r. Congo Belg.* (8), *84.*
Laurenti, J.N. (1768).  *Austriaci Viennensis Specimen Medicum Exhibens Synopsin*
    *Reptilium.*  Vienna, 214 pp.
Lesson, R.P. (1830).  In M.L.I. Duperrey, *Voyage Autour du Monde Execute par Ordre*
    *du Roi, dur la Corvette de La Majeste, La Coquille Pendant les Annees 1822,*
    *1823, 1824 et 1825. 2.*  Arthur Bertrand, Paris.
Lesson, R.P. (1831).  In Ferrussac, *Bull. Sci. nat. Paris, 25.*

Leviton, A.E. and Anderson, S.C. (1967). *Proc. Calif. Acad. Sci., 35.*

Leybold, H. (1873). *Excurs. Pamp. Argent.*

Lichtenstein, H. (1823). *Vers. Doubl. Mus. zool. Berlin.*

Linnaeus, C. (1754). *Mus. Ad. Frid.*

Linnaeus, C. (1758). *Systema Naturae per Regna Tria Naturae, Secundum Classes, Ordines, Genera, Species cum Characteribus Differentiis, Synonymis, Locis.* 10th Edition. *1.* Stockholm, 824 pp.

Linnaeus, C. (1766). *Systema Naturae per Regna Tria Naturae, Secundum Classes, Ordines, Genera, Species cum Characteribus Differentiis, Synonymis, Locis.* 12th Edition. *1.* Holmiae, 1327 pp.

Longman, H.A. (1915). *Mem. Queensland Mus., 3.*

Lonnberg, E. and Andersson, L.G. (1913a). *Ark. Zool., Uppsala, 8.*

Lonnberg, E. and Andersson, L.G. (1913b). *Kungl. Sr. Vet.-Akad. Handl. Stockholm, 52.*

Loveridge, A. (1930). *Proc. New Eng. zool. Club, 11.*

Loveridge, A. (1936). *Proc. biol. Soc. Wash., 49.*

Loveridge, A. (1938). *Proc. biol. Soc. Wash., 51.*

Loveridge, A. (1944). *Bull. Mus. Comp. Zool., Harv., 95.*

Lowe, C.H. and Norris, K. (1954). *Trans. San Diego Soc. nat. Hist., 12.*

Macleay, W. (1878). *Proc. Linn. Soc. N.S.W., 2.*

Macleay, W. (1884). *Proc. Linn. Soc. N.S.W., 9.*

Macleay, W. (1887). *Proc. Linn. Soc. N.S.W (2), 2.*

Maki, M. (1931). *Monograph of the Snakes of Japan.* Dai-ichi Shobo, Tokyo, 240 pp.

Maki, M. (1935). *Trans. nat. Hist. Soc. Formosa, 25.*

Martin, W. (1838). *Proc. zool. Soc. Lond.*

Marx, H. and Rabb, G.B. (1965). *Fieldiana Zool., 44.*

McCoy, F. (1878). *Prodromus of the Zoology of Victoria; or Figures and Descriptions of the Living Species of all Classes of the Victorian Indigenous Animals. 1.* Decade 2. Government Printer, Melbourne.

McDowell, S.B. (1969). *J. Zool., Lond., 159.*

McDowell, S.B. (1970). *J. Zool., Lond., 161.*

Meek, S.E. (1905). *Field Col. Mus. zool. ser., 7.*

Mehely, L. von (1894). *Zool. Anz., Leipzig, 16.*

Mehely, L. von (1911). *Ann. Hist. nat. Hungar.*

Meisner, F. (1820). *Mus. nat. Helv.*

Merrem, B. (1820). *Versuch Eines Systems der Amphibien* (Tentamen Systemis Amphibiorum). Marburg, 191 pp.

Mertens, R. (1927). *Senckenbergiana, 9.*

Mertens, R. (1942). *Beitr. Fauna Peru, 11.*

Mertens, R. (1954). *Zool. Anz., Leipzig, 152.*

Mertens, R. (1956). *Senck. biol. Frankfurt, 37.*

Mertens, R., Darevsky, I.S. and Klemmer, K. (1967). *Senck. biol. Frankfurt, 48.*

Miranda Ribeiro, A. de (1915). *Arch. Mus. Nac. Rio de Janeiro, 17.*

Mitchell, F.J. (1951). *Rec. Sth. Aust. Mus., 9.*

Mocquard, M.F. (1885). *Bull. Soc. Philom. Paris, (7), 10.*

Mocquard, M.F. (1887). *Bull. Soc. Philom. Paris, (7), 11.*

Mocquard, M.F. (1897). *Bull. Sci. Philom. Paris, (8), 9.*

Muller, F. (1885). *Verh. nat. Ges. Basel, 7.*

Muller, F. (1890). *Verh. nat. Ges. Basel, 8.*

Muller, L. (1924). *Mitt. zool. Mus. Berlin, 11.*

Nagai, K. (1928). *Rept. Nat. Hist., Prov. Kagoshima, 3.*

Niceforo Maria, H. (1942). *Rev. Acad. Colombiana Cien. Exact. Fis. Nat., 5.*

Nikolsky, A.M. (1909). *Mitt. Kaukas, Mus. Tiflis, 4.*

Nikolsky, A.M. (1916). *Faune Russie, Rept., 2.*

Oshima, S. (1920). *Annu. Report. Inst. Sci. Govt. Formosa, 8.*

Pallas, P.S. (1776). *Reise vers. Prov. Russ. Reichs, 3.*

Parker, H.W. (1926). *Ann. Mag. nat. Hist. (9), 17.*

Parker, H.W. (1930). *Ann. Mag. nat. Hist. (10), 5.*

Parker, H.W. (1932). *J. Linn. Soc. (Zool.), 38.*

Parker, H.W. (1934). *Ann. Mag. nat. Hist. (10), 14.*

Parker, H.W. (1938). *Ann. Mag. nat. Hist.* (11), 2.
Parker, H.W. (1949). *Zool. verh. Rijksmus. nat. Hist. Leiden, 6.*
Perret, J.L. (1960). *Rev. Suisse zool., Geneve, 67.*
Peters, J.A. (1968). *Proc. Biol. Soc. Wash., 81.*
Peters, W. (1854). *Mber. k. preuss Akad. Wiss.*
Peters, W. (1859). *Mber. k. preuss Akad. Wiss.*
Peters, W. (1861). *Mber. k. preuss Akad. Wiss.*
Peters, W. (1862). *Mber. k. preuss Akad. Wiss.*
Peters, W. (1863). *Mber. k. preuss Akad. Wiss.*
Peters, W. (1864). *Mber. k. preuss Akad. Wiss.*
Peters, W. (1867). *Mber. k. preuss Akad. Wiss.*
Peters, W. (1869). *Mber. k. preuss Akad. Wiss.*
Peters, W. (1871). *Mber. k. preuss Akad. Wiss.*
Peters, W. (1872). *Mber. k. preuss Akad. Wiss.*
Peters, W. (1873). *Mber. k. preuss Akad. Wiss.*
Peters, W. (1877). *Mber. k. preuss Akad. Wiss.*
Peters, W. (1881). *S. B. Ges. Naturf. Freunde Berlin.*
Peters, W. and Doria, E.G. (1878). *Ann. Mus. Civ. Stor. nat. Giacomo Doria, 13.*
Pope, C.H. (1928a). *Am. Mus. Novit.* (320).
Pope, C.H. (1928b). *Am. Mus. Novit.* (325).
Prado, A. (1939). *Mem. Inst. Butantan, 12.*
Pringle, J.A. (1955). *Ann. Natal Mus., 13.*
Radcliffe, C.W. and Maslin, T.P. (1975). *Copeia* (3).
Raffles, T.S. (1822). *Trans. Linn. Soc. Lond., 13.*
Rafinesque, C.S. (1818). *Amer. Mth. Mag. Crit. Rev., 4.*
Reinhardt, J.T. (1837). In Schlegel (1837).
Reinhardt, J.T. (1843). *Daiske Vidensk. Selsk. Skrifth, 10.*
Reinhardt, J.T. (1844). *Calcutta J. nat. Hist., 4.*
Rendahl, H. and Vestergren, G. (1940). *Arkiv. f. Zool., 33A.*
Rosen, P. (1905). *Ann. Mag. nat. Hist.* (7), 15.
Roux, J. (1910). *Abh. Senck. naturf. Ges.* (33).
Roux, J. (1934). *Verh. naturg. Ges. Basel, 45.*
Roze, J.A. (1958). *Acta Biol., Venez., 2.*
Roze, J.A. (1967). *Am. Mus. Novit.* (2287).
Ruppel, E. (1845). *Ver. Mus. Senck., 3.*
Saint Girons, H. (1954). *Bull. Soc. zool. France, Paris, 78.*
Salvin, O. (1860). *Proc. zool. Soc. Lond.*
Sandner Montilla, F. (1952). *Mon. Cien. Inst. Ter. Exp. Lab. "Veros" Ltda.* (21).
Sauvage, H.E. (1877). *Bull. Soc. Philom. Paris* (7), 1.
Savage, J.M. and Cliff, F.S. (1953). *Nat. Hist. Misc.* (119).
Say, T. (1823). In F. James, *Long's Expedition from Pittsburgh to the Rocky Mountains. 1.*
Schinz, H.R. (1833). *Naturgesch. Abh. Rept.*
Schlegel, H. (1837). *Essai dur la Physionomie des Serpents.* Partie descriptive. La Haye, 606 pp.
Schlegel, H. (1841). *Mag. Zool. Rept.* (1-3).
Schlegel, H. (1848). *Vers. zool. Gen. Amsterdam.*
Schlegel, H. (1855). *Vers. Meded. Akad. Wet. Amsterdam, Afd. Nat., 3.*
Schmidt, K.P. (1925a). *Am. Mus. Novit.* (157).
Schmidt, K.P. (1925b). *Am. Mus. Novit.* (175).
Schmidt, K.P. (1928). *Bull. Antiv. Inst. Am., 2.*
Schmidt, K.P. (1930). *Field Mus. Nat. Hist., ser. zool., 17.*
Schmidt, K.P. (1932). *Proc. Calif. Acad. Sci.* (4), 20.
Schmidt, K.P. (1933). *Field Mus. Nat. Hist., ser. zool., 20.*
Schmidt, K.P. (1936a). *Field Mus. Nat. Hist., ser. zool., 20.*
Schmidt, K.P. (1936b). *Proc. biol. Soc. Wash., 9.*
Schmidt, K.P. (1937). *Field Mus. Nat. Hist., ser. zool., 20.*
Schmidt, K.P. (1939). *Field Mus. Nat. Hist., ser. zool., 24.*
Schmidt, K.P. (1952). *Fieldiana Zool., 34.*

Schmidt, K.P. (1953). *Fieldiana Zool.*, *34.*
Schmidt, K.P. (1954). *Fieldiana Zool.*, *34.*
Schmidt, K.P. (1955). *Fieldiana Zool.*, *34.*
Schmidt, K.P. and Schmidt, F.W.J. (1925). *Field Mus. Nat. Hist.*, *ser. zool.*, *12.*
Schmidt, K.P. and Smith, H.M. (1943). *Field Mus. Nat. Hist.*, *ser. zool.*, *29.*
Schmidt, O. (1852). *Abh. naturw. Ver. Hamburg*, *2.*
Schneider, J.G. (1799). *Historiae Amphibiorum Naturalis et Literariae.* Fasciculus primus. Jena, 266 pp.
Schneider, J.G. (1801). *Historiae Amphibiorum Naturalis et Literariae.* Fasciculus secundus. Jena, 374 pp.
Scortecci, G. (1928). *Atti. Soc. Ital. Sci. nat. Milano*, *67.*
Scortecci, G. (1932). *Atti. Soc. Ital. Sci. nat. Milano*, *71.*
Shaw, G. (1794a). *Nat. Misc.*
Shaw, G. (1794b). *Zoo. N. Holl.*
Shaw, G. (1797). *Nat. Misc.*
Shaw, G. (1802a). *General Zoology or Systematic Natural History.* *3.* London, 615 pp.
Shaw, G. (1802b). *Nat. Misc.*, *3.*
Shreve, B. (1934). *Occ. Pap. Boston Soc. nat. Hist.*, *8.*
Sjostedt, Y. (1896). *Zool. Anz.*, *Leipzig*, *19.*
Slater, K.R. (1956). *Mem. natn. Mus. Vict.* (20).
Slevin, J.R. (1934). *Proc. Calif. Acad. Sci.* (4), *21.*
Smith, A. (1829). *Zool. Journ.*, *4.*
Smith, A. (1849). *Illustrations of the Zoology of South Africa.* *3* (Reptiles). London.
Smith, H.M. (1941). *Zoologica*, *26.*
Smith, H.M. (1960). *Trans. Kansas Acad. Sci.*, *62.*
Smith, H.M. and Chrapliwy, P.S. (1958). *Herpetologica*, *13.*
Smith, M.A. (1917). *J. nat. Hist. Soc. Siam*, *2.*
Smith, M.A. (1920). *J. fed. Malay St. Mus.*, *10.*
Smith, M.A. (1925). *Sarawak Mus. J.*, *3.*
Smith, M.A. (1926). *Monograph of the Sea Snakes.* British Museum, London. 130pp.
Smith, M.A. (1930). *Ann. Mag. nat. Hist.* (10), *6.*
Smith, M.A. (1931a). *Proc. zool. Soc. Lond.*
Smith, M.A. (1931b). *Bull. Raffles Mus.* (5).
Smith, M.A. (1935). *Dana Report* (8).
Smith, M.A. (1937). *J. Bombay nat. Hist. Soc.*, *39.*
Smith, M.A. (1938). *Proc. zool. Soc. Lond.*
Smith, M.A. (1940). *Rec. Indian Mus.*, *42.*
Smith, M.A. (1943). *The Fauna of British India, Ceylon and Burma, Including the Whole of the Indo-Chinese Sub-Region.* Reptilia and Amphibia. *3* (Serpentes). Taylor and Francis, London. 583 pp.
Smith, M.A. (1949). *J. Bombay nat. Hist. Soc.*, *48.*
Sonnini de Manoncourt, C.S. and Latreille, P.A. (1801). *Histoire Naturelle des Reptiles, avec Figures Dessinees d'Apres Nature.* *3.* Paris.
Sonnini de Manoncourt, C.S. and Latreille, P.A. (1802). *Histoire Naturelle des Reptiles, avec Figures Dessinees d'Apres Nature.* *4.* Paris. 410 pp.
Steindachner, F. (1867). In *Reise Osterrreichischen Fregatte Novara um Die Erde in Den Jahren 1857, 1858, 1859.* B. von Wullerstorfurbair, Zoologischer Theil, Erster Band, Aus der Kaiserlich-Koniglichen Hof- und Straatsdruckerei, Wien. 98 pp.
Steindachner, F. (1891). *S. B. Akad. Wiss. Wien*, *100.*
Steindachner, F. (1913). *Akad. Anz. Jahrg.*, *12.*
Stejneger, L. (1898). *Journ. Sci. Coll. Tokyo.*
Stejneger, L. (1907). *Bull. U.S. natn. Mus.* (58).
Stemmler, von O. (1969). *Aquaterra*, *6.*
Stemmler, von O. (1970). *Rev. Suisse Zool.*, *77.*
Stemmler, von O. and Sochurek, E. (1969). *Aquaterra*, *6.*
Sternfeld, R. (1913). *Sber. Ges. naturf. Berlin.*
Sternfeld, R. (1917). *Wiss. Ergeb. Zweite Deut. Zent.-Afr. Exped. 1910-11*, *1.*

Sternfeld, R. (1920). *Senckenbergiana*, 2.
Stoliczka, F. (1870). *J. Asiat. Soc. Beng.*, 39.
Storr, G.M. (1964). *W. Aust. Nat.*, 9.
Storr, G.M. (1967). *Jl. R. Soc. West Aust.*, 50.
Strauch, A. (1868). *Trudy Perv. Siezda Russ. Yestestv. Zool.*, 1.
Takahashi, T. (1922). *Japanese Venomous Snakes*.
Tanner, W.W. (1966). *Herpetologica*, 22.
Taylor, E.H. (1919). *Philipp. J. Sci.*, 14.
Taylor, E.H. (1922). *The Snakes of the Philippine Islands*. Manilla.
Taylor, E.H. (1941). *Univ. Kansas Sci. Bull.*, 27.
Taylor, E.H. (1944). *Univ. Kansas Sci. Bull.*, 30.
Taylor, E.H. (1954). *Univ. Kansas Sci. Bull.*, 36.
Theobald, W. (1868). *J. Asiat. Soc. Beng.*, Supp.  88 pp.
Thomson, D.F. (1934). *Proc. zool. Soc. Lond.*
Tornier, G. (1902). *Zool. Jahrb. System.*, 15.
Traill, T.S. (1843). In the English translation of Schlegel (1837).
Troost, R. (1836). *Ann. Lyc. N.Y.*, 3.
Troschel, F.H. (1865). In F. Muller, *Reisen in den Vereinigten Staaten Canada und Mexico*, 3.
Tschudi, J.J. (1837). *Arch. f. Nat.*
Tschudi, J.J. (1845). *Faun. Per. Herp.*
Van Denburgh, J. (1895). *Proc. Calif. Acad. Sci.* (2), 5.
Van Denburgh, J. (1912). *Adv. Diagnoses New Rept., San Francisco.*
Van Denburgh, J. (1920). *Proc. Calif. Acad. Sci.* (4), 10.
Van Denburgh, J. and Slevin, J.R. (1921). *Proc. Calif. Acad. Sci.* (4), 11.
Van Lidth de Jeude, T.W. (1886). *Notes Leyden Mus.*, 8.
Van Lidth de Jeude, T.W. (1887). *Notes Leyden Mus.*, 9.
Wagler, J. (1824). In J. de Spix, *Animalia Nova Sive Species Novae*. Monaco, 75 pp.
Wagler, J.G. (1830). *Naturliches System der Amphibien mit Vorangehender Classification der Saugthiere und Vogel.* Munchen, Stuttgart and Tubingen, 354 pp.
Waite, E.R. and Longman, H.A. (1920). *Rec. Sth. Aust. Mus.*, 1.
Wall, F. (1907). *J. Bombay nat. Hist. Soc.*, 17.
Wall, F. (1908). *J. Bombay nat. Hist. Soc.*, 18.
Wall, F. (1913). *J. Bombay nat. Hist. Soc.*, 22.
Wall, F. and Evans, G.H. (1901). *J. Bombay nat. Hist. Soc.*, 13.
Werner, F. (1895). *Verh. Zool. Bot. Ges. Wien*, 45.
Werner, F. (1897a). *Verh. Zool. Bot. Ges. Wien.*, 47.
Werner, F. (1897b). *Sitzber. Akad. Wiss. Munchen*, 27.
Werner, F. (1898). *Zool. Anz., Leipzig*, 21.
Werner, F. (1901a). *Verh. Zool. Bot. Ges. Wien*, 51.
Werner, F. (1901b). *Abh. Ber. Mus. Dresden*, 9.
Werner, F. (1902). *Verh. Zool Bot. Ges. Wien*, 52.
Werner, F. (1903). *Zool. Anz., Leipzig*, 26.
Werner, F. (1919). *Denkschr. Akad. Wiss. Wien*, 96.
Werner, F. (1922). *Anz. Akad. Wiss. Wien*, 59.
Werner, F. (1927). *Sitzber. Akad. Wiss. Wien*, 135.
Werner, F. (1935). *Sitzber. Akad. Wiss. Wien*, 144.
Werner, F. (1938). *Zool. Anz., Leipzig*, 122.
Wied-Neuwied, Prince M.A.P. (1821). *Reise. Brazil*, 2.
Wied-Neuwied, Prince M.A.P. (1824). *Abbild. Nat. Brazil Lief.*
Wiegmann, A.F.A. (1834). *Nova Acta Acad. Leop.-Carol.*, 17.
Woodbury, A.M. (1929). *Bull. Univ. Utah*, 20.
Worrell, E. (1955). *Proc. Roy. Soc. N.S.W.*
Worrell, E. (1961). *W. Aust. Nat.*, 8.
Worrell, E. (1963a). *Aust. Rept. Park. Rec.* (1).
Worrell, E. (1963b). *Aust. Rept. Park. Rec.* (2).
Zarevsky, S.T. (1917). *Ann. Mus. Zool. Acad. Sci. Petrograd*, 21.
Zweifel, R.G. and Norris, K.S. (1955). *Am. Midl. Nat.*, 54.

# SECTION 2

# *GEOGRAPHICAL DISTRIBUTION*

# PART 1

# *THE AMERICAS*

## CANADA

*Crotalus horridus horridus*      Timber Rattlesnake
*Crotalus viridis viridis*      Prairie Rattlesnake
*Crotalus viridis oreganus*      Northern Pacific Rattlesnake
*Sistrurus catenatus catenatus*      Eastern Massasauga

Literature:  Wright and Wright (1957), Klauber (1972).

## UNITED STATES OF AMERICA

*Micruroides euryxanthus euryxanthus*      Arizona Coral Snake
*Micrurus fulvius fulvius*      Eastern Coral Snake
*Micrurus fulvius tenere*      Texas Coral Snake
*Agkistrodon contortrix contortrix*      Southern Copperhead
*Agkistrodon contortrix laticinctus*      Broad-Banded Copperhead
*Agkistrodon contortrix mokasen*      Northern Copperhead
*Agkistrodon contortrix phaeogaster*      Osage Copperhead
*Agkistrodon contortrix pictigaster*      Trans-Pecos Copperhead
*Agkistrodon piscivorus piscivorus*      Eastern Cottonmouth
*Agkistrodon piscivorus conanti*      Florida Cottonmouth
*Agkistrodon piscivorus leucostoma*      Western Cottonmouth
*Crotalus adamanteus*      Eastern Diamondback Rattlesnake
*Crotalus atrox*      Western Diamondback Rattlesnake
*Crotalus cerastes cerastes*      Mojave Desert Sidewinder
*Crotalus cerastes cercobombus*      Sonoran Desert Sidewinder
*Crotalus cerastes laterorepens*      Colorado Desert Sidewinder
*Crotalus horridus horridus*      Timber Rattlesnake
*Crotalus horridus atricaudatus*      Canebrake Rattlesnake
*Crotalus lepidus lepidus*      Mottled Rock Rattlesnake
*Crotalus lepidus klauberi*      Banded Rock Rattlesnake
*Crotalus mitchelli pyrrhus*      Southwestern Speckled Rattlesnake
*Crotalus mitchelli stephensi*      Panamint Rattlesnake
*Crotalus molossus molossus*      Northern Black-Tailed Rattlesnake
*Crotalus pricei pricei*      Western Twin-Spotted Rattlesnake
*Crotalus ruber ruber*      Red Diamond Rattlesnake

*Crotalus scutulatus scutulatus*     Mojave Rattlesnake
*Crotalus tigris*     Tiger Rattlesnake
*Crotalus viridis viridis*     Prairie Rattlesnake
*Crotalus viridis abyssus*     Grand Canyon Rattlesnake
*Crotalus viridis cerberus*     Arizona Black Rattlesnake
*Crotalus viridis concolor*     Midget-Faced Rattlesnake
*Crotalus viridis helleri*     Southern Pacific Rattlesnake
*Crotalus viridis lutosus*     Great Basin Rattlesnake
*Crotalus viridis nuntius*     Hopi Rattlesnake
*Crotalus viridis oreganus*     Northern Pacific Rattlesnake
*Crotalus willardi willardi*     Arizona Ridge-Nosed Rattlesnake
*Crotalus willardi silus*     West Chihuahua Ridge-Nosed Rattlesnake
*Sistrurus catenatus catenatus*     Eastern Massasauga
*Sistrurus catenatus edwardsi*     Desert Massasauga
*Sistrurus catenatus tergeminus*     Western Massasauga
*Sistrurus miliarius miliarius*     Carolina Pigmy Rattlesnake
*Sistrurus miliarius barbouri*     Dusky Pigmy Rattlesnake
*Sistrurus miliarius streckeri*     Western Pigmy Rattlesnake

Literature:  Wright and Wright (1957), Klauber (1972), Stebbins (1966), Conant
        (1975), Gloyd and Conant (1943), Schmidt (1953).


MEXICO

*Micruroides euryxanthus euryxanthus*     Arizona Coral Snake
*Micruroides euryxanthus australis*     Southern Arizona Coral Snake
*Micruroides euryxanthus neglectus*     Sinaloan Coral Snake
*Micrurus bernardi*     Bernard's Coral Snake
*Micrurus bogerti*     Bogert's Coral Snake
*Micrurus browni browni*     Brown's Coral Snake
*Micrurus browni taylori*     Taylor's Coral Snake
*Micrurus diastema*     Atlantic Coral Snake
*Micrurus distans distans*     Broad-Banded Coral Snake
*Micrurus distans michoacanensis*     Michoacan Coral Snake
*Micrurus distans oliveri*     Oliver's Coral Snake
*Micrurus distans zweifeli*     Zweifel's Coral Snake
*Micrurus elegans elegans*     Elegant Coral Snake
*Micrurus elegans veraepacis*
*Micrurus ephippifer*
*Micrurus fitzingeri*     Fitzinger's Coral Snake
*Micrurus fulvius maculatus*     Spotted Coral Snake
*Micrurus fulvius microgalbineus*
*Micrurus fulvius tenere*     Texas Coral Snake
*Micrurus laticollaris laticollaris*
*Micrurus laticollaris maculirostris*
*Micrurus latifasciatus*
*Micrurus limbatus*
*Micrurus nigrocinctus zunilensis*     Black-Banded Coral Snake
*Micrurus nuchalis*
*Micrurus proximans*
*Pelamis platurus*     Pelagic Sea Snake
*Agkistrodon bilineatus bilineatus*     Cantil
*Agkistrodon bilineatus russeolus*
*Agkistrodon bilineatus taylori*     Taylor's Mocassin
*Bothrops asper*
*Bothrops barbouri*     Barbour's Pit Viper
*Bothrops bicolor*

*Bothrops dunni*     Dunn's Pit Viper
*Bothrops godmanni*     Godman's Pit Viper
*Bothrops hesperus*
*Bothrops melanurus*     Black-Tailed Pit Viper
*Bothrops nasutus*     Hog-Nosed Pit Viper
*Bothrops nigroviridis aurifer*
*Bothrops nummifer nummifer*     Jumping Viper
*Bothrops nummifer mexicanus*     Mexican Jumping Viper
*Bothrops rowleyi*
*Bothrops schlegeli*     Eyelash Viper
*Bothrops sphenophrys*
*Bothrops undulatus*
*Bothrops yucatannicus*     Yucatan Pit Viper
*Crotalus atrox*     Western Diamondback Rattlesnake
*Crotalus basiliscus basiliscus*     Mexican West-Coast Rattlesnake
*Crotalus basiliscus oaxacus*     Oaxacan Rattlesnake
*Crotalus catalinensis*     Santa Catalina Island Rattlesnake
*Crotalus cerastes cercobombus*     Sonoran Desert Sidewinder
*Crotalus cerastes laterorepens*     Colorado Desert Sidewinder
*Crotalus durissus durissus*     Central American Rattlesnake
*Crotalus durissus culminatus*     Northwestern Neotropical Rattlesnake
*Crotalus durissus totonacus*     Totonican Rattlesnake
*Crotalus durissus tzabcan*     Yucatan Neotropical Rattlesnake
*Crotalus enyo enyo*     Lower California Rattlesnake
*Crotalus enyo cerralvensis*     Cerralvo Island Rattlesnake
*Crotalus enyo furvus*     Rosario Rattlesnake
*Crotalus exsul*     Cedros Island Diamond Rattlesnake
*Crotalus intermedius intermedius*     Totalcan Small-Headed Rattlesnake
*Crotalus intermedius gloydi*     Oaxacan Small-Headed Rattlesnake
*Crotalus intermedius omiltemanus*     Omilteman Small-Headed Rattlesnake
*Crotalus lannomi*     Autland Rattlesnake
*Crotalus lepidus lepidus*     Mottled Rock Rattlesnake
*Crotalus lepidus klauberi*     Banded Rock Rattlesnake
*Crotalus lepidus morulus*     Tamaulipan Rock Rattlesnake
*Crotalus mitchelli mitchelli*     San Lucan Speckled Rattlesnake
*Crotalus mitchelli angelensis*     Angel de la Guarda Island Speckled Rattlesnake
*Crotalus mitchelli muertensis*     El Muerto Island Speckled Rattlesnake
*Crotalus mitchelli pyrrhus*     Southwestern Speckled Rattlesnake
*Crotalus molossus molossus*     Northern Black-Tailed Rattlesnake
*Crotalus molossus estebanensis*     San Esteban Island Rattlesnake
*Crotalus molossus nigrescens*     Mexican Black-Tailed Rattlesnake
*Crotalus polystictus*     Mexican Lance-Headed Rattlesnake
*Crotalus pricei pricei*     Western Twin-Spotted Rattlesnake
*Crotalus pricei miquihuanus*     Eastern Twin-Spotted Rattlesnake
*Crotalus pusillus*     Tancitaran Dusky Rattlesnake
*Crotalus ruber ruber*     Red Diamond Rattlesnake
*Crotalus ruber lorenzoensis*     San Lorenzo Sur Island Rattlesnake
*Crotalus ruber lucasensis*     San Lucan Diamond Rattlesnake
*Crotalus scutulatus scutulatus*     Mojave Rattlesnake
*Crotalus scutulatus salvini*     Huamantlan Rattlesnake
*Crotalus stejnegeri*     Long-Tailed Rattlesnake
*Crotalus tigris*     Tiger Rattlesnake
*Crotalus tortugensis*     Tortuga Island Diamond Rattlesnake
*Crotalus triseriatus triseriatus*     Central-Plateau Dusky Rattlesnake
*Crotalus triseriatus aquilus*     Queretaran Dusky Rattlesnake
*Crotalus viridis caliginis*     Coronado Island Rattlesnake
*Crotalus viridis helleri*     Southern Pacific Rattlesnake
*Crotalus willardi willardi*     Arizona Ridge-Nosed Rattlesnake
*Crotalus willardi amabilis*     Del Nido Ridge-Nosed Rattlesnake

*Crotalus willardi meridionalis*     Southern Ridge-Nosed Rattlesnake
*Crotalus willardi silus*     West Chihuahua Ridge-Nosed Rattlesnake
*Sistrurus catenatus edwardsi*     Desert Massasauga
*Sistrurus ravus*     Mexican Pigmy Rattlesnake

Literature:  Alvarez del Toro (1960), Klauber (1972), Smith and Taylor (1945),
         Peters and Orejas-Miranda (1970), Hoge (1966), Schmidt (1933).


## GUATEMALA

*Micrurus browni browni*     Brown's Coral Snake
*Micrurus browni importunus*     Antigua Basin Coral Snake
*Micrurus diastema*     Atlantic Coral Snake
*Micrurus elegans veraepacis*
*Micrurus hippocrepis*
*Micrurus latifasciatus*
*Micrurus nigrocinctus zunilensis*     Black-Banded Coral Snake
*Micrurus stuarti*     Stuart's Coral Snake
*Pelamis platurus*     Pelagic Sea Snake
*Agkistrodon bilineatus bilineatus*     Cantil
*Bothrops asper*
*Bothrops bicolor*
*Bothrops godmanni*     Godman's Pit Viper
*Bothrops nasutus*     Hog-Nosed Pit Viper
*Bothrops nigroviridis aurifer*
*Bothrops nummifer mexicanus*     Mexican Jumping Viper
*Bothrops ophryomegas*
*Bothrops schlegeli*     Eyelash Viper
*Crotalus durissus durissus*     Central American Rattlesnake
*Crotalus durissus tzabcan*     Yucatan Neotropical Rattlesnake

Literature:  Stuart (1963), Peters and Orejas-Miranda (1970), Hoge (1966), Roze
         (1967), Klauber (1972), Schmidt (1933).


## BELIZE

*Micrurus diastema*     Atlantic Coral Snake
*Micrurus hippocrepis*
*Micrurus nigrocinctus divaricatus*
*Agkistrodon bilineatus russeolus*     Cantil
*Bothrops asper*
*Bothrops nasutus*     Hog-Nosed Pit Viper
*Bothrops nummifer mexicanus*     Mexican Jumping Viper
*Bothrops schlegeli*     Eyelash Viper
*Crotalus durissus durissus*     Central American Rattlesnake
*Crotalus durissus tzabcan*     Yucatan Neotropical Rattlesnake

Literature:  Henderson and Hoevers (1975), Klauber (1972), Hoge (1966), Peters and
         Orejas-Miranda (1970), Roze (1967), Schmidt (1933), Schmidt (1941).


## HONDURAS

*Micrurus diastema*     Atlantic Coral Snake
*Micrurus nigrocinctus divaricatus*     Black-Banded Coral Snake
*Micrurus nigrocinctus zunilensis*

*Micrurus ruatanus*
*Pelamis platurus*      Pelagic Sea Snake
*Agkistrodon bilineatus bilineatus*      Cantil
*Bothrops asper*
*Bothrops bicolor*
*Bothrops godmanni*      Godman's Pit Viper
*Bothrops lansbergi annectens*
*Bothrops nasutus*      Hog-Nosed Pit Viper
*Bothrops nigroviridis marchi*
*Bothrops nummifer mexicanus*      Mexican Jumping Viper
*Bothrops ophryomegas*
*Bothrops schlegeli*      Eyelash Viper
*Crotalus durissus durissus*      Central American Rattlesnake

Literature:   Peters and Orejas-Miranda (1970), Roze (1967), Hoge (1966), Klauber
              (1972), Schmidt (1933).


## EL SALVADOR

*Micrurus nigrocinctus zunilensis*      Black-Banded Coral Snake
*Pelamis platurus*      Pelagic Sea Snake
*Agkistrodon bilineatus bilineatus*      Cantil
*Bothrops godmanni*      Godman's Pit Viper
*Bothrops nasutus*      Hog-Nosed Pit Viper
*Bothrops nummifer mexicanus*      Mexican Jumping Viper
*Bothrops nummifer occidduus*
*Bothrops ophryomegas*
*Bothrops schlegeli*      Eyelash Viper
*Crotalus durissus durissus*      Central American Rattlesnake

Literature:   Mertens (1952b), Peters and Orejas-Miranda (1970), Hoge (1966),
              Roze (1967), Klauber (1972), Schmidt (1933).


## NICARAGUA

*Micrurus alleni alleni*      Allen's Coral Snake
*Micrurus mipartitus hertwigi*      Black-Ringed Coral Snake
*Micrurus nigrocinctus babaspul*      Babaspul Coral Snake
*Micrurus nigrocinctus melanocephalus*      Black-Headed Coral Snake
*Micrurus nigrocinctus mosquitensis*
*Pelamis platurus*      Pelagic Sea Snake
*Agkistrodon bilineatus bilineatus*      Cantil
*Bothrops asper*
*Bothrops godmanni*      Godman's Pit Viper
*Bothrops nasutus*      Hog-Nosed Pit Viper
*Bothrops nummifer mexicanus*      Mexican Jumping Viper
*Bothrops ophryomegas*
*Bothrops schlegeli*      Eyelash Viper
*Crotalus durissus durissus*      Central American Rattlesnake

Literature:   Peters and Orejas-Miranda (1970), Klauber (1972), Hoge (1966),
              Roze (1967), Schmidt (1933).

## COSTA RICA

*Micrurus alleni alleni*    Allen's Coral Snake
*Micrurus alleni yatesi*    Yates's Coral Snake
*Micrurus clarki*    Clark's Coral Snake
*Micrurus mipartitus hertwigi*    Black-Ringed Coral Snake
*Micrurus nigrocinctus nigrocinctus*    Black-Banded Coral Snake
*Micrurus nigrocinctus melanocephalus*    Black-Headed Coral Snake
*Micrurus nigrocinctus mosquitensis*
*Pelamis platurus*    Pelagic Sea Snake
*Lachesis muta stenophrys*    Central American Bushmaster
*Agkistrodon bilineatus bilineatus*    Cantil
*Bothrops asper*
*Bothrops godmanni*    Godman's Pit Viper
*Bothrops lateralis*
*Bothrops nasutus*    Hog-Nosed Pit Viper
*Bothrops nigroviridis nigroviridis*
*Bothrops nummifer mexicanus*    Mexican Jumping Viper
*Bothrops ophryomegas*
*Bothrops picadoi*    Picado's Pit Viper
*Bothrops schlegeli*    Eyelash Viper
*Bothrops supraciliaris*
*Crotalus durissus durissus*

Literature:  Peters and Orejas-Miranda (1970), Picado (1931), Taylor (1951),
         Hoge (1966), Roze (1967), Klauber (1972), Schmidt (1933).


## PANAMA

*Micrurus alleni alleni*    Allen's Coral Snake
*Micrurus alleni yatesi*    Yates's Coral Snake
*Micrurus ancoralis jani*    Jan's Coral Snake
*Micrurus clarki*    Clark's Coral Snake
*Micrurus dissoleucus dunni*    Dunn's Coral Snake
*Micrurus mipartitus mipartitus*    Black-Ringed Coral Snake
*Micrurus mipartitus hertwigi*
*Micrurus mipartitus multifasciatus*
*Micrurus nigrocinctus nigrocinctus*    Black-Banded Coral Snake
*Micrurus nigrocinctus coibensis*    Coiban Coral Snake
*Micrurus nigrocinctus mosquitensis*
*Micrurus stewarti*    Stewart's Coral Snake
*Pelamis platurus*    Pelagic Sea Snake
*Lachesis muta stenophrys*    Central American Bushmaster
*Bothrops asper*
*Bothrops godmanni*    Godman's Pit Viper
*Bothrops lateralis*
*Bothrops nasutus*    Hog-Nosed Pit Viper
*Bothrops nigroviridis nigroviridis*
*Bothrops nummifer mexicanus*    Mexican Jumping Viper
*Bothrops ophryomegas*
*Bothrops punctatus*
*Bothrops schlegeli*    Eyelash Viper

Literature:  Schmidt (1933), Roze (1967), Hoge (1966), Peters and Orejas-Miranda
         (1970).

## ARUBA

*Crotalus unicolor*    Aruba Island Rattlesnake

Literature:  Klauber (1972).

## ST. LUCIA

*Bothrops caribbaeus*    St. Lucia Serpent

Literature:  Lazell (1964), Peters and Orejas-Miranda (1970), Hoge (1966).

## MARTINIQUE

*Bothrops lanceolatus*    Fer-de-Lance

Literature:  Lazell (1964), Peters and Orejas-Miranda (1970), Hoge (1966).

## TRINIDAD

*Micrurus lemniscatus diutius*    Large Coral Snake
*Micrurus psyches circinalis*    Small Coral Snake
*Lachesis muta muta*    Bushmaster, Mapepire Zannana
*Bothrops atrox*    Barba Amarilla, Fer-de-Lance, Mapepire

Literature:  Emsley (1977), Harding (in preparation).

## COLOMBIA

*Leptomicrurus narduccii*
*Micrurus ancoralis jani*    Jan's Coral Snake
*Micrurus bocourti sangilensis*    San Gil Coral Snake
*Micrurus clarki*    Clark's Coral Snake
*Micrurus dissoleucus dissoleucus*
*Micrurus dissoleucus melanogenys*
*Micrurus dissoleucus nigrirostris*
*Micrurus dumerili dumerili*    Dumeril's Coral Snake
*Micrurus dumerili antioquiensis*    Antioquian Coral Snake
*Micrurus dumerili carinicauda*    Rough-Tailed Coral Snake
*Micrurus dumerili colombianus*    Santa Marta Rough-Tailed Coral Snake
*Micrurus dumerili transandinus*    Transandian Coral Snake
*Micrurus filiformis filiformis*    Thread-Form Coral Snake
*Micrurus filiformis subtilis*    Slender Coral Snake
*Micrurus hemprichi hemprichi*    Hemprich's Coral Snake
*Micrurus langsdorffi langsdorffi*    Langsdorff's Coral Snake
*Micrurus lemniscatus helleri*    Heller's Coral Snake
*Micrurus mipartitus mipartitus*    Black-Ringed Coral Snake
*Micrurus mipartitus anomalus*
*Micrurus mipartitus decussatus*
*Micrurus nigrocinctus nigrocinctus*    Black-Banded Coral Snake
*Micrurus psyches psyches*

*Micrurus psyches medemi*      Medem's Coral Snake
*Micrurus spixi obscurus*
*Micrurus spurrelli*      Spurrell's Coral Snake
*Micrurus surinamensis surinamensis*      Surinam Coral Snake
*Pelamis platurus*      Pelagic Sea Snake
*Lachesis muta muta*      Bushmaster
*Bothrops asper*
*Bothrops atrox*      Barba Amarilla
*Bothrops brazili*      Brazil's Pit Viper
*Bothrops colombiensis*      Colombian Pit Viper
*Bothrops hyoprorus*
*Bothrops lansbergi lansbergi*      Lansberg's Pit Viper
*Bothrops microphthalmus colombianus*
*Bothrops nasutus*      Hog-Nosed Pit Viper
*Bothrops punctatus*
*Bothrops schlegeli*      Eyelash Viper
*Bothrops xantogrammus*
*Crotalus durissus cumanensis*

Literature:  Hoge (1966), Roze (1967), Schmidt (1955), Peters and Orejas-Miranda
            (1970).


# VENEZUELA

*Leptomicrurus collaris*
*Micrurus dissoleucus dissoleucus*
*Micrurus dumerili carincauda*      Rough-Tailed Coral Snake
*Micrurus hemprichi hemprichi*      Hemprich's Coral Snake
*Micrurus isozonus*
*Micrurus lemniscatus diutius*
*Micrurus lemniscatus helleri*      Heller's Coral Snake
*Micrurus mipartitus anomalus*
*Micrurus mipartitus semipartitus*
*Micrurus psyches psyches*
*Micrurus psyches circinalis*      Circled Coral Snake
*Micrurus spixi obscurus*
*Micrurus surinamensis surinamensis*      Surinam Coral Snake
*Micrurus surinamensis nattereri*      Natterer's Coral Snake
*Lachesis muta muta*      Bushmaster
*Bothrops atrox*      Barba Amarilla
*Bothrops bilineatus bilineatus*
*Bothrops brazili*      Brazil's Pit Viper
*Bothrops colombiensis*      Colombian Pit Viper
*Bothrops hyoprorus*
*Bothrops lansbergi rozei*      Roze's Pit Viper
*Bothrops lichenosus*
*Bothrops medusa*
*Bothrops schlegeli*      Eyelash Viper
*Bothrops venezuelensis*      Venezuelan Pit Viper
*Crotalus durissus cumanensis*
*Crotalus durissus rurima*
*Crotalus vegrandis*      Uracoan Rattlesnake

Literature:  Roze (1966), Roze (1967), Sandner Montilla (1965), Hoge (1966),
            Peters and Orejas-Miranda (1970).

## GUYANA

*Leptomicrurus collaris*
*Micrurus averyi*      Avery's Coral Snake
*Micrurus hemprichi hemprichi*      Hemprich's Coral Snake
*Micrurus lemniscatus lemniscatus*
*Micrurus lemniscatus diutius*
*Micrurus psyches psyches*
*Micrurus surinamensis surinamensis*      Surinam Coral Snake
*Lachesis muta muta*      Bushmaster
*Bothrops atrox*      Barba Amarilla
*Bothrops bilineatus bilineatus*
*Bothrops brazili*      Brazil's Pit Viper
*Crotalus durissus dryinus*

Literature:  Roze (1967), Hoge (1966), Peters and Orejas-Miranda (1970).

## SURINAM

*Leptomicrurus collaris*
*Micrurus hemprichi hemprichi*      Hemprich's Coral Snake
*Micrurus lemniscatus lemniscatus*
*Micrurus lemniscatus diutius*
*Micrurus psyches psyches*
*Micrurus surinamensis surinamensis*      Surinam Coral Snake
*Lachesis muta muta*      Bushmaster
*Bothrops atrox*      Barba Amarilla
*Bothrops bilineatus bilineatus*
*Bothrops brazili*      Brazil's Pit Viper
*Crotalus durissus dryinus*

Literature:  Roze (1967), Hoge (1966), Peters and Orejas-Miranda (1970).

## FRENCH GUIANA

*Leptomicrurus collaris*
*Micrurus hemprichi hemprichi*      Hemprich's Coral Snake
*Micrurus lemniscatus lemniscatus*
*Micrurus lemniscatus diutius*
*Micrurus psyches psyches*
*Micrurus surinamensis surinamensis*      Surinam Coral Snake
*Lachesis muta muta*      Bushmaster
*Bothrops atrox*      Barba Amarilla
*Bothrops bilineatus bilineatus*
*Bothrops brazili*      Brazil's Pit Viper
*Crotalus durissus dryinus*

Literature:  Roze (1967), Hoge (1966), Peters and Orejas-Miranda (1970).

## ECUADOR

*Leptomicrurus narduccii*
*Micrurus ancoralis ancoralis*      Anchor Coral Snake

*Micrurus annellatus annellatus*      Annellated Coral Snake
*Micrurus bocourti bocourti*    Bocourt's Coral Snake
*Micrurus dumerili transandinus*      Transandian Coral Snake
*Micrurus hemprichi ortoni*      Orton's Coral Snake
*Micrurus langsdorffi langsdorffi*      Langsdorff's Coral Snake
*Micrurus langsdorffi ornatissimus*
*Micrurus lemniscatus helleri*      Heller's Coral Snake
*Micrurus mertensi*      Mertens' Coral Snake
*Micrurus mipartitus decussatus*
*Micrurus spixi obscurus*
*Micrurus steindachneri steindachneri*      Steindachner's Coral Snake
*Micrurus steindachneri petersi*      Peters' Coral Snake
*Micrurus surinamensis surinamensis*      Surinam Coral Snake
*Micrurus tschudii olssoni*      Olsson's Coral Snake
*Pelamis platurus*      Pelagic Sea Snake
*Lachesis muta muta*      Bushmaster
*Bothrops albocarinatus*
*Bothrops alticolus*
*Bothrops asper*
*Bothrops atrox*      Barba Amarilla
*Bothrops bilineatus smaragdinus*
*Bothrops castelnaudi*      Castelnaud's Pit Viper
*Bothrops hyoprorus*
*Bothrops lojanus*      Lojan Pit Viper
*Bothrops microphthalmus microphthalmus*
*Bothrops nasutus*      Hog-Nosed Pit Viper
*Bothrops pulcher*
*Bothrops punctatus*
*Bothrops schlegeli*      Eyelash Viper
*Bothrops xantogrammus*

Literature:  Roze (1967), Hoge (1966), Peters and Orejas-Miranda (1970).


PERU

*Leptomicrurus narduccii*
*Micrurus annellatus annellatus*      Annellated Coral Snake
*Micrurus annellatus montanus*      Mountain Ringed Coral Snake
*Micrurus filiformis filiformis*      Thread-Form Coral Snake
*Micrurus hemprichi ortoni*      Orton's Coral Snake
*Micrurus langsdorffi langsdorffi*      Langsdorff's Coral Snake
*Micrurus langsdorffi ornatissimus*
*Micrurus lemniscatus helleri*      Heller's Coral Snake
*Micrurus margaritiferus*
*Micrurus mertensi*      Mertens' Coral Snake
*Micrurus peruvianus*      Peruvian Coral Snake
*Micrurus putumayensis*      Putumayan Coral Snake
*Micrurus spixi obscurus*
*Micrurus tschudii tschudii*      Tschudi's Coral Snake
*Micrurus tschudii olssoni*      Olsson's Coral Snake
*Pelamis platurus*      Pelagic Sea Snake
*Lachesis muta muta*      Bushmaster
*Bothrops andianus*      Andean Pit Viper
*Bothrops atrox*      Barba Amarilla
*Bothrops barnetti*      Barnett's Pit Viper
*Bothrops bilineatus smaragdinus*
*Bothrops castelnaudi*      Castelnaud's Pit Viper

*Bothrops hyoprorus*
*Bothrops microphthalmus microphthalmus*
*Bothrops oligolepis*
*Bothrops peruvianus*      Peruvian Pit Viper
*Bothrops pictus*
*Bothrops pulcher*
*Bothrops roedingeri*      Roedinger's Pit Viper

Literature:  Roze (1967), Hoge (1966), Peters and Orejas-Miranda (1970).


## BRAZIL

*Leptomicrurus collaris*
*Leptomicrurus narduccii*
*Leptomicrurus schmidti*      Schmidt's Thread Coral Snake
*Micrurus albicinctus*      White-Ringed Coral Snake
*Micrurus corallinus*
*Micrurus decoratus*
*Micrurus filiformis filiformis*      Thread-Form Coral Snake
*Micrurus filiformis subtilis*      Slender Coral Snake
*Micrurus frontalis frontalis*
*Micrurus frontalis altirostris*
*Micrurus frontalis brasiliensis*
*Micrurus frontalis pyrrhocryptus*
*Micrurus hemprichi ortoni*      Orton's Coral Snake
*Micrurus ibiboboca*
*Micrurus langsdorffi langsdorffi*      Langsdorff's Coral Snake
*Micrurus lemniscatus lemniscatus*
*Micrurus lemniscatus carvalhoi*      Carvalho's Coral Snake
*Micrurus lemniscatus helleri*      Heller's Coral Snake
*Micrurus spixi spixi*      Spix's Coral Snake
*Micrurus spixi martiusi*      Martius's Coral Snake
*Micrurus surinamensis surinamensis*      Surinam Coral Snake
*Micrurus surinamensis nattereri*      Natterer's Coral Snake
*Lachesis muta muta*      Bushmaster
*Lachesis muta noctivaga*      Atlantic Bushmaster
*Bothrops alternatus*      Urutu Pit Viper
*Bothrops atrox*      Barba Amarilla
*Bothrops bilineatus bilineatus*
*Bothrops bilineatus smaragdinus*
*Bothrops brazili*      Brazil's Pit Viper
*Bothrops castelnaudi*      Castelnaud's Pit Viper
*Bothrops cotiara*
*Bothrops erythromelas*
*Bothrops fonsecai*      Fonseca's Pit Viper
*Bothrops hyoprorus*
*Bothrops inglesiasi*      Inglesias's Pit Viper
*Bothrops insularis*      Jararaca Ilhoa
*Bothrops itapetiningae*
*Bothrops jararaca*      Jararaca
*Bothrops jararacussu*      Jararacussu
*Bothrops leucurus*
*Bothrops marajoensis*
*Bothrops moojeni*
*Bothrops neuwiedi neuwiedi*      Prince Neuwied's Pit Viper
*Bothrops neuwiedi bolivianus*
*Bothrops neuwiedi diporus*

*Bothrops neuwiedi goyazensis*
*Bothrops neuwiedi lutzi*      Lutz's Pit Viper
*Bothrops neuwiedi mattogrossensis*
*Bothrops neuwiedi meridionalis*
*Bothrops neuwiedi paranaensis*
*Bothrops neuwiedi pauloensis*
*Bothrops neuwiedi piauhyensis*
*Bothrops neuwiedi pubescens*
*Bothrops neuwiedi urutu*
*Bothrops pessoai*
*Bothrops pirajai*      Piraja's Pit Viper
*Bothrops pradoi*      Prado's Pit Viper
*Crotalus durissus cascavella*
*Crotalus durissus collilineatus*
*Crotalus durissus marajoensis*
*Crotalus durissus rurima*
*Crotalus durissus terrificus*

Literature:  Hoge (1966), Roze (1967), Peters and Orejas-Miranda (1970), Amaral
            (1979).


## BOLIVIA

*Leptomicrurus narduccii*
*Micrurus annellatus balzani*      Balzan's Coral Snake
*Micrurus annellatus bolivianus*      Bolivian Ringed Coral Snake
*Micrurus annellatus montanus*      Mountain Ringed Coral Snake
*Micrurus frontalis pyrrhocryptus*
*Micrurus hemprichi ortoni*      Orton's Coral Snake
*Micrurus lemniscatus frontifasciatus*
*Micrurus lemniscatus helleri*      Heller's Coral Snake
*Micrurus spixi princeps*
*Micrurus surinamensis surinamensis*      Surinam Coral Snake
*Lachesis muta muta*      Bushmaster
*Bothrops atrox*      Barba Amarilla
*Bothrops bilineatus smaragdinus*
*Bothrops jararacussu*      Jararacussu
*Bothrops microphthalmus microphthalmus*
*Bothrops neuwiedi bolivianus*
*Bothrops oligolepis*
*Bothrops santaecrucis*
*Crotalus durissus terrificus*

Literature:  Roze (1967), Hoge (1966), Peters and Orejas-Miranda (1970).


## PARAGUAY

*Micrurus frontalis frontalis*      Southern Coral Snake
*Micrurus frontalis pyrrhocryptus*
*Bothrops alternatus*      Urutu Pit Viper
*Bothrops jararaca*      Jararaca
*Bothrops jararacussu*      Jararacussu
*Bothrops neuwiedi diporus*
*Crotalus durissus terrificus*

Literature:  Roze (1967), Hoge (1966), Peters and Orejas-Miranda (1970).

URUGUAY

*Micrurus frontalis altirostris*
*Bothrops alternatus*     Urutu Pit Viper
*Bothrops neuwiedi pubescens*
*Crotalus durissus terrificus*

Literature:  Roze (1967), Hoge (1966), Peters and Orejas-Miranda (1970).


ARGENTINA

*Micrurus corallinus*
*Micrurus frontalis frontalis*     Southern Coral Snake
*Micrurus frontalis altirostris*
*Micrurus frontalis mesopotamicus*
*Micrurus frontalis pyrrhocryptus*
*Bothrops alternatus*     Urutu Pit Viper
*Bothrops ammodytoides*     Patagonian Pit Viper
*Bothrops cotiara*
*Bothrops jararaca*     Jararaca
*Bothrops jararacussu*     Jararacussu
*Bothrops neuwiedi diporus*
*Crotalus durissus terrificus*

Literature:  Hoge (1966), Roze (1967), Peters and Orejas-Miranda (1970).

# PART 2

# *EUROPE*

### GREAT BRITAIN

*Vipera berus berus*    Adder, Northern Viper

Literature:  Smith (1973), Appleby (1971), Arnold and Burton (1978), Steward (1971).

### NORWAY

*Vipera berus berus*    Northern Viper, Kyy

Literature:  Arnold and Burton (1978), Steward (1971).

### SWEDEN

*Vipera berus berus*    Northern Viper, Huggorm

Literature:  Arnold and Burton (1978), Steward (1971).

### FINLAND

*Vipera berus berus*    Northern Viper, Kyy

Literature:  Arnold and Burton (1978), Steward (1971).

### DENMARK

*Vipera berus berus*    Northern Viper, Kreuzotter

Literature:  Arnold and Burton (1978), Steward (1971).

## THE NETHERLANDS

*Vipera berus berus*     Adder, Northern Viper

Literature:  Arnold and Burton (1978), Steward (1971).


## BELGIUM

*Vipera berus berus*     Adder, Northern Viper

Literature:  Arnold and Burton (1978), Steward (1971).


## LUXEMBURG

*Vipera berus berus*     Adder, Northern Viper

Literature:  Steward (1971), Arnold and Burton (1978).


## POLAND

*Vipera berus berus*     Northern Viper, Zmija Zygzakowata

Literature:  Steward (1971), Arnold and Burton (1978).


## FRANCE

*Vipera aspis aspis*     Aspic Viper, Vipere aspic
*Vipera aspis zinnikeri*    Gascony Aspic Viper
*Vipera berus berus*     Northern Viper, Vipere Peliade
*Vipera ursinii wettsteini*     French Meadow Viper, Vipere d'Orsini

Literature:  Fretey (1975), Steward (1971), Arnold and Burton (1978).


## GERMANY

*Vipera aspis aspis*     Aspic Viper, Aspis-Otter
*Vipera berus berus*     Northern Viper, Kreuzotter

Literature:  Steward (1971), Arnold and Burton (1978).


## CZECHOSLOVAKIA

*Vipera ammodytes ammodytes*     Western Sand Viper, Zmije ruzkata
*Vipera berus berus*     Northern Viper, Zmije obecna

Literature:  Steward (1971), Arnold and Burton (1978).

## HUNGARY

*Vipera ammodytes ammodytes*    Western Sand Viper
*Vipera berus berus*    Northern Viper
*Vipera ursinii rakosiensis*    Danubian Meadow Viper

Literature:  Steward (1971), Arnold and Burton (1978).


## ROMANIA

*Vipera ammodytes ammodytes*    Western Sand Viper, Vipera-cu-corn
*Vipera ammodytes montandoni*    Transdanubian Sand Viper
*Vipera berus berus*    Northern Viper, Vipera neagra
*Vipera ursinii rakosiensis*    Danubian Meadow Viper, Vipera-de-stepa
*Vipera ursinii renardi*    Steppe Viper

Literature:  Steward (1971), Arnold and Burton (1978).


## BULGARIA

*Vipera ammodytes ammodytes*    Western Sand Viper, Pepeljanka
*Vipera ammodytes montandoni*    Transdanubian Sand Viper
*Vipera berus berus*    Northern Viper, Usojnica
*Vipera berus bosniensis*    Balkan Cross Adder
*Vipera ursinii rakosiensis*    Danubian Meadow Viper, Ostromunucesta usojnica

Literature:  Steward (1971), Arnold and Burton (1978).


## AUSTRIA

*Vipera ammodytes ammodytes*    Western Sand Viper, Sandotter
*Vipera aspis aspis*    Aspic Viper, Aspis-Otter
*Vipera berus berus*    Northern Viper, Kreuzotter
*Vipera ursinii rakosiensis*    Danubian Meadow Viper, Weisenotter

Literature:  Steward (1971), Arnold and Burton (1978).


## SWITZERLAND

*Vipera aspis aspis*    Aspic Viper, Vipere aspic
*Vipera aspis atra*    Alpine Viper
*Vipera berus berus*    Northern Viper, Vipere Peliade

Literature:  Grossenbacher and Brand (1973), Steward (1971), Arnold and Burton
             (1978).

## ITALY

*Vipera ammodytes ammodytes*    Western Sand Viper, Vipera dal corno
*Vipera aspis aspis*    Aspic Viper, Vipera aspide
*Vipera aspis francisciredi*
*Vipera aspis hugyi*    South Italian Aspic Viper
*Vipera aspis montecristi*    Monte Cristo Aspic Viper
*Vipera berus berus*    Northern Viper, Vipera rossa
*Vipera ursinii ursinii*    Italian Meadow Viper

Literature:  Steward (1971), Capocaccia (1968), Arnold and Burton (1978).


## YUGOSLAVIA

*Vipera ammodytes ammodytes*    Western Sand Viper
*Vipera aspis aspis*    Aspic Viper
*Vipera berus berus*    Northern Viper
*Vipera berus bosniensis*    Balkan Cross Adder
*Vipera ursinii macrops*    Karst Viper
*Vipera ursinii rakosiensis*    Danubian Meadow Viper

Literature:  Steward (1971), Arnold and Burton (1978), Pozzi (1966).


## ALBANIA

*Vipera ammodytes meridionalis*    Eastern Sand Viper
*Vipera berus berus*    Northern Viper
*Vipera ursinii macrops*    Karst Viper

Literature:  Steward (1971), Arnold and Burton (1978).


## GREECE

*Vipera ammodytes meridionalis*    Eastern Sand Viper
*Vipera lebetina schweitzeri*    Cyclades Blunt-Nosed Viper

Literature:  Steward (1971), Arnold and Burton (1978).


## CYPRUS

*Vipera lebetina lebetina*    Blunt-Nosed Viper

Literature:  Steward (1971), Arnold and Burton (1978).


## SPAIN

*Vipera berus berus*    Northern Viper, Vibora del Norte
*Vipera berus seoanei*    Iberian Cross Viper
*Vipera latastei latastei*    Snub-Nosed Viper, Vibora comun

Literature:  Steward (1971), Arnold and Burton (1978), Salvador (1974).


## PORTUGAL

*Vipera berus seoanei*     Iberian Cross Viper
*Vipera latastei latastei*     Snub-Nosed Viper

Literature:  Steward (1971), Arnold and Burton (1978).

# PART 3

# *AFRICA*

MOROCCO

*Naja haje haje*   Egyptian Cobra
*Bitis arietans arietans*   Puff Adder
*Cerastes cerastes cerastes*   Sahara Horned Viper
*Cerastes vipera*   Sahara Sand Viper
*Echis carinatus pyramidium*   Saw-Scaled Viper
*Vipera latastei latastei*   Lataste's Viper
*Vipera latastei monticola*   Atlas Mountain Viper
*Vipera lebetina mauritanica*   Sahara Rock Viper

Literature:  Bons and Girot (1962), Saint Girons (1956).


TUNISIA

*Naja haje haje*   Egyptian Cobra
*Cerastes cerastes cerastes*   Sahara Horned Viper
*Cerastes vipera*   Sahara Sand Viper
*Echis carinatus pyramidium*   Saw-Scaled Viper
*Vipera latastei latastei*   Lataste's Viper
*Vipera lebetina deserti*   Desert Viper
*Vipera lebetina mauritanica*   Sahara Rock Viper

Literature:  Bons and Girot (1962), Saint Girons (1956), Dowling, Minton and
             Russell (1970).


ALGERIA

*Naja haje haje*   Egyptian Cobra
*Bitis arietans arietans*   Puff Adder
*Cerastes cerastes cerastes*   Sahara Horned Viper
*Cerastes vipera*   Sahara Sand Viper
*Echis carinatus pyramidium*   Saw-Scaled Viper
*Vipera latastei latastei*   Lataste's Viper

*Vipera lebetina deserti*     Desert Viper
*Vipera lebetina mauritanica*     Sahara Rock Viper

Literature:   Bons and Girot (1962), Saint Girons (1956), Dowling, Minton and
              Russell (1970).


## LIBYA

*Naja haje haje*     Egyptian Cobra
*Cerastes cerastes cerastes*     Sahara Horned Viper
*Cerastes vipera*     Sahara Sand Viper
*Echis carinatus pyramidium*     Saw-Scaled Viper
*Vipera lebetina deserti*     Desert Viper

Literature:   Kramer and Schnurrenberger (1963), Dowling, Minton and Russell (1970).


## EGYPT

*Atractaspis engaddensis*
*Naja haje haje*     Egyptian Cobra
*Naja mossambica pallida*
*Naja nigricollis*     Spitting Cobra
*Walterinnesia aegyptia*     Desert Black Snake
*Cerastes cerastes cerastes*     Sahara Horned Viper
*Cerastes vipera*     Sahara Sand Viper
*Echis carinatus pyramidium*     Saw-Scaled Viper
*Echis coloratus*

Literature:   Marx (1956), Dowling, Minton and Russell (1970).


## MAURITANIA

*Atractaspis microlepidota micropholis*
*Elapsoidea semiannulata moebiusi*
*Naja haje haje*     Egyptian Cobra
*Naja nigricollis*     Spitting Cobra
*Bitis arietans arietans*     Puff Adder
*Cerastes cerastes cerastes*     Sahara Horned Viper
*Cerastes vipera*     Sahara Sand Viper
*Echis carinatus pyramidium*     Saw-Scaled Viper
*Causus maculatus*     West African Night Adder

Literature:   Villiers (1950), Angel and Lhote (1938).


## MALI

*Atractaspis microlepidota micropholis*
*Elapsoidea semiannulata moebiusi*
*Naja haje haje*     Egyptian Cobra
*Naja melanoleuca*     Forest Cobra
*Naja mossambica katiensis*

*Naja nigricollis*    Spitting Cobra
*Bitis arietans arietans*    Puff Adder
*Cerastes cerastes cerastes*    Sahara Horned Viper
*Cerastes vipera*    Sahara Sand Viper
*Echis carinatus pyramidium*    Saw-Scaled Viper
*Causus maculatus*    West African Night Adder

Literature:  Angel and Lhote (1938), Villiers (1965), Dowling, Minton and Russell
             (1970).


## NIGER

*Atractaspis microlepidota micropholis*
*Naja haje haje*    Egyptian Cobra
*Naja melanoleuca*    Forest Cobra
*Naja nigricollis*    Spitting Cobra
*Bitis arietans arietans*    Puff Adder
*Cerastes cerastes cerastes*    Sahara Horned Viper
*Cerastes vipera*    Sahara Sand Viper
*Echis carinatus pyramidium*    Saw-Scaled Viper
*Causus rhombeatus*    Common Night Adder

Literature:  Angel and Lhote (1938), Dowling, Minton and Russell (1970).


## CHAD

*Naja haje haje*    Egyptian Cobra
*Naja melanoleuca*    Forest Cobra
*Echis carinatus pyramidium*    Saw-Scaled Viper
*Causus maculatus*    West African Night Adder
*Causus resimus*    Green Night Adder

Literature:  Angel and Lhote (1938), Roussel and Villiers (1965).


## SUDAN

*Atractaspis irregularis uelensis*
*Atractaspis microlepidota microlepidota*
*Atractaspis microlepidota magrettii*
*Elapsoidea laticincta*
*Naja haje haje*    Egyptian Cobra
*Naja melanoleuca*    Forest Cobra
*Naja mossambica pallida*
*Naja nigricollis*    Spitting Cobra
*Bitis gabonica gabonica*    Gaboon Viper
*Bitis nasicornis*    Rhinoceros Viper
*Echis carinatus pyramidium*    Saw-Scaled Viper
*Causus resimus*    Green Night Adder
*Causus rhombeatus*    Common Night Adder

Literature:  Corkill (1935), Dowling, Minton and Russell (1970).

ETHIOPIA

*Atractaspis irregularis angeli*
*Atractaspis leucomelas*
*Atractaspis microlepidota microlepidota*
*Atractaspis microlepidota magretti*
*Dendroaspis polylepis antinorii*     Antinori's Black Mamba
*Elapsoidea laticincta*
*Naja haje haje*     Egyptian Cobra
*Naja melanoleuca*     Forest Cobra
*Naja mossambica pallida*
*Naja nigricollis*     Spitting Cobra
*Echis carinatus pyramidium*     Saw-Scaled Viper
*Causus resimus*     Green Night Adder
*Causus rhombeatus*     Common Night Adder

Literature:  Dowling, Minton and Russell (1970).


SOMALI REPUBLIC

*Dispholidus typus typus*     Boomslang
*Thelotornis kirtlandi kirtlandi*     Twig Snake
*Atractaspis engdahli*
*Atractaspis leucomelas*
*Atractaspis microlepidota microlepidota*
*Atractaspis scorteccii*
*Dendroaspis polylepis antinorii*     Antinori's Black Mamba
*Naja haje haje*     Egyptian Cobra
*Naja melanoleuca*     Forest Cobra
*Naja mossambica pallida*
*Naja nigricollis*     Spitting Cobra
*Pelamis platurus*     Pelagic Sea Snake
*Bitis arietans somalica*     Somali Puff Adder
*Echis carinatus leakeyi*     Leakey's Saw-Scaled Viper
*Causus resimus*     Green Night Adder
*Causus rhombeatus*     Common Night Adder

Literature:  Parker (1949), Dowling, Minton and Russell (1970).


SENEGAL

*Dendroaspis viridis*     Green Mamba
*Elapsoidea semiannulata moebiusi*
*Naja haje haje*     Egyptian Cobra
*Naja melanoleuca*     Forest Cobra
*Naja nigricollis*     Spitting Cobra
*Bitis arietans arietans*     Puff Adder
*Echis carinatus pyramidium*     Saw-Scaled Viper
*Causus maculatus*     West African Night Adder

Literature:  Hughes (1977), Dowling, Minton and Russell (1970), Cansdale (1961).

## THE GAMBIA

*Dendroaspis viridis*     Green Mamba
*Elapsoidea semiannulata moebiusi*
*Naja melanoleuca*     Forest Cobra
*Naja nigricollis*     Spitting Cobra
*Bitis arietans arietans*     Puff Adder
*Echis carinatus pyramidium*     Saw-Scaled Viper
*Causus maculatus*     West African Night Adder

Literature:  Hughes (1977), Dowling, Minton and Russell (1970), Cansdale (1961).


## GUINEA-BISSAU

*Thelotornis kirtlandi kirtlandi*     Twig Snake
*Atractaspis aterrima*
*Dendroaspis viridis*     Green Mamba
*Elapsoidea semiannulata moebiusi*
*Naja melanoleuca*     Forest Cobra
*Naja nigricollis*     Spitting Cobra
*Atheris squamiger chloroechis*     Western Tree Viper
*Bitis arietans arietans*     Puff Adder
*Bitis gabonica rhinoceros*     West African Gaboon Viper
*Bitis nasicornis*     Rhinoceros Viper
*Causus lichtensteini*     Lichtenstein's Night Adder
*Causus maculatus*     West African Night Adder

Literature:  Hughes (1977), Dowling, Minton and Russell (1970), Cansdale (1961).


## GUINEA

*Thelotornis kirtlandi kirtlandi*     Twig Snake
*Atractaspis aterrima*
*Atractaspis dahomeyensis*
*Atractaspis irregularis irregularis*
*Dendroaspis jamesoni jamesoni*     Jameson's Mamba
*Dendroaspis viridis*     Green Mamba
*Elapsoidea semiannulata moebiusi*
*Naja melanoleuca*     Forest Cobra
*Naja nigricollis*     Spitting Cobra
*Atheris squamiger chloroechis*     Western Tree Viper
*Bitis arietans arietans*     Puff Adder
*Bitis gabonica rhinoceros*     West African Gaboon Viper
*Bitis nasicornis*     Rhinoceros Viper
*Causus lichtensteini*     Lichtenstein's Night Adder
*Causus maculatus*     West African Night Adder

Literature:  Hughes (1977), Dowling, Minton and Russell (1970), Cansdale (1961).


## SIERRA LEONE

*Dispholidus typus typus*     Boomslang
*Thelotornis kirtlandi kirtlandi*     Twig Snake

*Atractaspis irregularis irregularis*
*Dendroaspis viridis*        Green Mamba
*Elapsoidea semiannulata moebiusi*
*Naja melanoleuca*      Forest Cobra
*Naja nigricollis*      Spitting Cobra
*Pseudohaje nigra*      Black Tree Cobra
*Atheris squamiger chloroechis*      Western Tree Viper
*Bitis gabonica rhinoceros*      West African Gaboon Viper
*Bitis nasicornis*      Rhinoceros Viper
*Causus maculatus*      West African Night Adder

Literature:  Menzies (1966), Hughes (1977), Cansdale (1961).

## LIBERIA

*Dispholidus typus typus*      Boomslang
*Thelotornis kirtlandi kirtlandi*      Twig Snake
*Atractaspis irregularis irregularis*
*Dendroaspis jamesoni jamesoni*      Jameson's Mamba
*Dendroaspis viridis*      Green Mamba
*Elapsoidea semiannulata moebiusi*
*Naja melanoleuca*      Forest Cobra
*Pseudohaje nigra*      Black Tree Cobra
*Atheris squamiger chloroechis*      Western Tree Viper
*Bitis gabonica rhinoceros*      West African Gaboon Viper
*Bitis nasicornis*      Rhinoceros Viper
*Causus lichtensteini*      Lichtenstein's Night Adder
*Causus maculatus*      West African Night Adder

Literature:  Briscoe (1949), Hughes (1977), Loveridge (1943), Cansdale (1961).

## IVORY COAST

*Dispholidus typus typus*      Boomslang
*Thelotornis kirtlandi kirtlandi*      Twig Snake
*Atractaspis aterrima*
*Atractaspis corpulenta leucura*
*Atractaspis dahomeyensis*
*Atractaspis irregularis irregularis*
*Dendroaspis jamesoni jamesoni*      Jameson's Mamba
*Dendroaspis viridis*
*Elapsoidea semiannulata moebiusi*
*Naja melanoleuca*      Forest Cobra
*Naja nigricollis*      Spitting Cobra
*Pseudohaje nigra*      Black Tree Cobra
*Atheris squamiger chloroechis*      Western Tree Viper
*Bitis gabonica rhinoceros*      West African Gaboon Viper
*Bitis nasicornis*      Rhinoceros Viper
*Causus maculatus*      West African Night Adder

Literature:  Doucet (1963), Hughes (1977), Cansdale (1961).

## UPPER VOLTA

*Dendroaspis jamesoni jamesoni*      Jameson's Mamba
*Elapsoidea semiannulata moebiusi*
*Naja haje haje*     Egyptian Cobra
*Naja melanoleuca*     Forest Cobra
*Naja nigricollis*     Spitting Cobra
*Causus maculatus*     West African Night Adder

Literature:  Roman (1973), Hughes (1977), Villiers (1965), Cansdale (1961).

## GHANA

*Dispholidus typus typus*     Boomslang
*Thelotornis kirtlandi kirtlandi*     Twig Snake
*Atractaspis aterrima*
*Atractaspis corpulenta leucura*
*Atractaspis dahomeyensis*
*Atractaspis irregularis irregularis*
*Dendroaspis jamesoni jamesoni*     Jameson's Mamba
*Dendroaspis viridis*     Green Mamba
*Elapsoidea semiannulata moebiusi*
*Naja melanoleuca*     Forest Cobra
*Naja mossambica katiensis*
*Naja nigricollis*     Spitting Cobra
*Pseudohaje goldii*     Goldi's Tree Cobra
*Pseudohaje nigra*     Black Tree Cobra
*Atheris squamiger chloroechis*     Western Tree Viper
*Bitis arietans arietans*     Puff Adder
*Bitis gabonica rhinoceros*     West African Gaboon Viper
*Bitis nasicornis*     Rhinoceros Viper
*Echis carinatus ocellatus*     West African Saw-Scaled Viper
*Causus lichtensteini*     Lichtenstein's Night Adder
*Causus maculatus*     West African Night Adder

Literature:  Hughes and Barry (1968), Hughes (1977), Leeson (1950), Cansdale (1961).

## TOGO

*Thelotornis kirtlandi kirtlandi*     Twig Snake
*Atractaspis irregularis irregularis*
*Dendroaspis jamesoni jamesoni*     Jameson's Mamba
*Elapsoidea semiannulata moebiusi*
*Naja melanoleuca*     Forest Cobra
*Pseudohaje goldii*     Goldi's Tree Cobra
*Pseudohaje nigra*     Black Tree Cobra
*Atheris squamiger chloroechis*     Western Tree Viper
*Bitis gabonica rhinoceros*     West African Gaboon Viper
*Bitis nasicornis*     Rhinoceros Viper
*Echis carinatus ocellatus*     West African Saw-Scaled Viper
*Causus maculatus*     West African Night Adder

Literature:  Hughes (1977), Hulselmans, de Roo and De Vree (1970), Hulselmans, de Vree and Van der Straeten (1971), Cansdale (1961).

## BENIN

*Thelotornis kirtlandi kirtlandi*      Twig Snake
*Atractaspis dahomeyensis*
*Atractaspis irregularis irregularis*
*Dendroaspis jamesoni jamesoni*      Jameson's Mamba
*Elapsoidea semiannulata moebiusi*
*Naja melanoleuca*      Forest Cobra
*Pseudohaje goldii*      Goldi's Tree Cobra
*Pseudohaje nigra*      Black Tree Cobra
*Atheris squamiger chloroechis*      Western Tree Viper
*Bitis nasicornis*      Rhinoceros Viper
*Echis carinatus ocellatus*      West African Saw-Scaled Viper
*Causus lichtensteini*      Lichtenstein's Night Adder
*Causus maculatus*      West African Night Adder


Literature:  Hughes (1977), Dowling, Minton and Russell (1970), Cansdale (1961).


## NIGERIA

*Thelotornis kirtlandi kirtlandi*      Twig Snake
*Atractaspis dahomeyensis*
*Atractaspis irregularis irregularis*
*Atractaspis microlepidota micropholis*
*Dendroaspis jamesoni jamesoni*      Jameson's Mamba
*Elapsoidea semiannulata moebiusi*
*Naja haje haje*      Egyptian Cobra
*Naja melanoleuca*      Forest Cobra
*Naja mossambica katiensis*
*Pseudohaje goldii*      Goldi's Tree Cobra
*Pseudohaje nigra*      Black Tree Cobra
*Atheris squamiger chloroechis*      Western Tree Viper
*Bitis gabonica rhinoceros*      West African Gaboon Viper
*Bitis nasicornis*      Rhinoceros Viper
*Echis carinatus ocellatus*      West African Saw-Scaled Viper
*Causus lichtensteini*      Lichtenstein's Night Adder
*Causus maculatus*      West African Night Adder
*Causus resimus*      Green Night Adder
*Causus rhombeatus*      Common Night Adder


Literature:  Hughes (1977), Dowling, Minton and Russell (1970), Cansdale (1961).


## CAMEROUN

*Thelotornis kirtlandi kirtlandi*      Twig Snake
*Atractaspis boulengeri matschiensis*
*Atractaspis coalescens*
*Atractaspis congica congica*
*Atractaspis corpulenta corpulenta*
*Atractaspis dahomeyensis*
*Atractaspis irregularis irregularis*
*Atractaspis irregularis parkeri*
*Atractaspis reticulata reticulata*
*Atractaspis reticulata heterochilus*
*Boulengerina annulata annulata*      Banded Water Cobra

*Elapsoidea semiannulata moebiusi*
*Dendroaspis jamesoni jamesoni*     Jameson's Mamba
*Naja haje haje*     Egyptian Cobra
*Naja melanoleuca*     Forest Cobra
*Paranaja multifasciata anomala*     Burrowing Cobra
*Pseudohaje goldii*     Goldi's Tree Cobra
*Atheris squamiger squamiger*     Green Tree Viper
*Atheris squamiger chloroechis*     Western Tree Viper
*Bitis arietans arietans*     Puff Adder
*Bitis nasicornis*     Rhinoceros Viper
*Echis carinatus ocellatus*     West African Saw-Scaled Viper
*Causus lichtensteini*     Lichtenstein's Night Adder
*Causus maculatus*     West African Night Adder
*Causus resimus*     Green Night Adder
*Causus rhombeatus*     Common Night Adder

Literature:  Mertens (1938), Cansdale (1961), Monard (1951).


## CENTRAL AFRICAN EMPIRE

*Dispholidus typus typus*     Boomslang
*Dendroaspis jamesoni jamesoni*     Jameson's Mamba
*Elapsoidea laticincta*
*Elapsoidea semiannulata moebiusi*
*Naja haje haje*     Egyptian Cobra
*Naja melanoleuca*     Forest Cobra
*Naja nigricollis*     Spitting Cobra
*Pseudohaje goldii*     Goldi's Tree Cobra
*Causus maculatus*     West African Night Adder

Literature:  Dowling, Minton and Russell (1970).


## UGANDA

*Dispholidus typus typus*     Boomslang
*Dispholidus typus kivuensis*
*Thelotornis kirtlandi kirtlandi*     Twig Snake
*Atractaspis aterrima*
*Atractaspis irregularis bipostocularis*
*Atractaspis irregularis uelensis*
*Dendroaspis jamesoni kaimosae*     East African Jameson's Mamba
*Dendroaspis polylepis polylepis*     Black Mamba
*Dendroaspis polylepis antinorii*     Antinori's Black Mamba
*Elapsoidea laticincta*     Sudanese Garter Snake
*Elapsoidea loveridgei colleti*     Collet's Garter Snake
*Elapsoidea loveridgei multicincta*     Ugandan Garter Snake
*Naja haje haje*     Egyptian Cobra
*Naja melanoleuca*     Forest Cobra
*Naja nigricollis*     Spitting Cobra
*Pseudohaje goldii*     Goldi's Tree Cobra
*Atheris hispidus*     Rough-Scaled Tree Viper
*Atheris nitschei nitschei*     Black and Green Tree Viper
*Atheris squamiger squamiger*     Green Tree Viper
*Bitis arietans arietans*     Puff Adder
*Bitis gabonica gabonica*     Gaboon Viper

*Bitis nasicornis*     Rhinoceros Viper
*Echis carinatus leakeyi*     Leakey's Saw-Scaled Viper
*Causus lichtensteini*     Lichtenstein's Night Adder
*Causus resimus*     Green Night Adder
*Causus rhombeatus*     Common Night Adder

Literature:  Pitman (1974), Loveridge (1957).


## KENYA

*Dispholidus typus typus*     Boomslang
*Dispholidus typus kivuensis*
*Thelotornis kirtlandi kirtlandi*     Twig Snake
*Atractaspis bibroni*
*Atractaspis irregularis bipostocularis*
*Atractaspis microlepidota microlepidota*
*Dendroaspis angusticeps*     Eastern Green Mamba
*Dendroaspis polylepis polylepis*     Black Mamba
*Dendroaspis polylepis antinorii*     Antinori's Black Mamba
*Elapsoidea loveridgei loveridgei*     Loveridge's Garter Snake
*Elapsoidea loveridgei multicincta*     Ugandan Garter Snake
*Naja haje haje*     Egyptian Cobra
*Naja melanoleuca*     Forest Cobra
*Naja mossambica pallida*
*Naja nigricollis*     Spitting Cobra
*Pelamis platurus*     Pelagic Sea Snake
*Atheris desaixi*
*Atheris hindii*     Kenyan Mountain Tree Viper
*Atheris hispidus*     Rough-Scaled Tree Viper
*Atheris squamiger squamiger*     Green Tree Viper
*Bitis arietans arietans*     Puff Adder
*Bitis arietans somalica*     Somali Puff Adder
*Bitis nasicornis*     Rhinoceros Viper
*Bitis worthingtoni*     Kenyan Horned Viper
*Echis carinatus leakeyi*     Leakey's Saw-Scaled Viper
*Causus lichtensteini*     Lichtenstein's Night Adder
*Causus resimus*     Green Night Adder
*Causus rhombeatus*     Common Night Adder

Literature:  Pitman (1974), Loveridge (1957).


## RWANDA

*Dispholidus typus typus*     Boomslang
*Dispholidus typus kivuensis*
*Atractaspis aterrima*
*Atractaspis irregularis bipostocularis*
*Dendroaspis jamesoni kaimosae*     East African Jameson's Mamba
*Dendroaspis polylepis polylepis*     Black Mamba
*Elapsoidea loveridgei colleti*     Collet's Garter Snake
*Naja haje haje*     Egyptian Cobra
*Naja melanoleuca*     Forest Cobra
*Naja nigricollis*     Spitting Cobra
*Pseudohaje goldii*     Goldi's Tree Cobra
*Atheris nitschei nitschei*     Black and Green Tree Viper

*Bitis arietans arietans*     Puff Adder
*Bitis nasicornis*     Rhinoceros Viper
*Echis carinatus pyramidium*     Saw-Scaled Viper
*Causus bilineatus*     Lined Night Adder
*Causus resimus*     Green Night Adder


Literature:  Pitman (1974), Loveridge (1957).


## TANZANIA

*Dispholidus typus typus*     Boomslang
*Thelotornis kirtlandi kirtlandi*     Twig Snake
*Thelotornis kirtlandi capensis*     Cape Twig Snake
*Atractaspis aterrima*
*Atractaspis bibroni*
*Atractaspis irregularis bipostocularis*
*Boulengerina annulata stormsi*
*Dendroaspis angusticeps*     Eastern Green Mamba
*Dendroaspis jamesoni kaimosae*     East African Jameson's Mamba
*Dendroaspis polylepis polylepis*     Black Mamba
*Elapsoidea loveridgei loveridgei*     Loveridge's Garter Snake
*Elapsoidea loveridgei multicincta*     Ugandan Garter Snake
*Elapsoidea nigra*
*Elapsoidea semiannulata boulengeri*
*Naja haje haje*     Egyptian Cobra
*Naja melanoleuca*     Forest Cobra
*Naja mossambica mossambica*     Mozambique Cobra
*Naja nigricollis*     Spitting Cobra
*Pelamis platurus*     Pelagic Sea Snake
*Adenorhinos barbouri*     Uzungwe Viper
*Atheris ceratophorus*     Usambara Tree Viper
*Atheris nitschei nitschei*     Black and Green Tree Viper
*Atheris nitschei rungweensis*     Rungwe Tree Viper
*Atheris superciliaris*     Swamp Viper
*Bitis arietans arietans*     Puff Adder
*Bitis gabonica gabonica*     Gaboon Viper
*Causus defilippii*     Snouted Night Adder
*Causus resimus*     Green Night Adder
*Causus rhombeatus*     Common Night Adder


Literature:  Pitman (1974), Loveridge (1957).


## EQUATORIAL GUINEA

*Thelotornis kirtlandi kirtlandi*     Twig Snake
*Atractaspis irregularis irregularis*
*Atractaspis reticulata heterochilus*
*Naja melanoleuca*     Forest Cobra
*Pseudohaje goldii*     Goldi's Tree Cobra
*Atheris squamiger chloroechis*     Western Tree Viper
*Bitis gabonica gabonica*     Gaboon Viper
*Bitis nasicornis*     Rhinoceros Viper


Literature:  Dowling, Minton and Russell (1970).

## GABON

*Thelotornis kirtlandi kirtlandi*      Twig Snake
*Atractaspis aterrima*
*Atractaspis boulengeri boulengeri*
*Atractaspis corpulenta corpulenta*
*Atractaspis irregularis irregularis*
*Atractaspis reticulata heterochilus*
*Boulengerina annulata annulata*      Banded Water Cobra
*Naja melanoleuca*      Forest Cobra
*Pseudohaje goldii*      Goldi's Tree Cobra
*Atheris squamiger chloroechis*      Western Tree Viper
*Bitis gabonica gabonica*      Gaboon Viper
*Bitis nasicornis*      Rhinoceros Viper
*Causus maculatus*      West African Night Adder

Literature:  Dowling, Minton and Russell (1970).


## CONGO

*Thelotornis kirtlandi kirtlandi*      Twig Snake
*Atractaspis boulengeri schultzei*
*Atractaspis corpulenta corpulenta*
*Atractaspis reticulata heterochilus*
*Boulengerina annulata annulata*      Banded Water Cobra
*Boulengerina christyi*      Christy's Water Cobra
*Dendroaspis jamesoni jamesoni*      Jameson's Mamba
*Elapsoidea semiannulata moebiusi*
*Naja melanoleuca*      Forest Cobra
*Naja nigricollis*      Spitting Cobra
*Pseudohaje goldii*      Goldi's Tree Cobra
*Atheris squamiger anisolepis*
*Bitis gabonica gabonica*      Gaboon Viper
*Bitis nasicornis*      Rhinoceros Viper
*Echis carinatus pyramidium*      Saw-Scaled Viper
*Causus rhombeatus*      Common Night Adder

Literature:  Villiers (1966), Laurent (1956), Dowling, Minton and Russell (1970).


## ZAIRE

*Dispholidus typus typus*      Boomslang
*Dispholidus typus punctatus*
*Thelotornis kirtlandi kirtlandi*      Twig Snake
*Thelotornis kirtlandi oatesi*      Oates's Twig Snake
*Atractaspis aterrima*
*Atractaspis battersbyi*
*Atractaspis boulengeri mixta*
*Atractaspis boulengeri schmidti*
*Atractaspis boulengeri vanderbourghti*
*Atractaspis congica congica*
*Atractaspis congica leleupi*
*Atractaspis congica orientalis*
*Atractaspis corpulenta corpulenta*
*Atractaspis corpulenta kivuensis*

*Atractaspis irregularis bipostocularis*
*Atractaspis irregularis parkeri*
*Atractaspis irregularis uelensis*
*Atractaspis reticulata brieni*
*Boulengerina annulata annulata*      Banded Water Cobra
*Boulengerina annulata stormsi*
*Dendroaspis jamesoni jamesoni*    Jameson's Mamba
*Dendroaspis jamesoni kaimosae*
*Dendroaspis polylepis polylepis*    Black Mamba
*Elapsoidea guntheri*    Gunther's Garter Snake
*Elapsoidea laticincta*    Sudanese Garter Snake
*Elapsoidea loveridgei colleti*    Collet's Garter Snake
*Elapsoidea loveridgei multicincta*    Ugandan Garter Snake
*Elapsoidea loveridgei scalaris*
*Elapsoidea semiannulata semiannulata*
*Elapsoidea semiannulata moebiusi*
*Naja haje haje*    Egyptian Cobra
*Naja haje anchietae*    Angolan Cobra
*Naja melanoleuca*    Forest Cobra
*Naja nigricollis*    Spitting Cobra
*Paranaja multifasciata multifasciata*    Burrowing Cobra
*Pseudohaje goldii*    Goldi's Tree Cobra
*Atheris hispidus*    Rough-Scaled Tree Viper
*Atheris katangensis*    Katanga Tree Viper
*Atheris nitschei nitschei*    Black and Green Tree Viper
*Atheris squamiger squamiger*    Green Tree Viper
*Atheris squamiger anisolepis*
*Atheris squamiger robustus*
*Bitis arietans arietans*    Puff Adder
*Bitis gabonica gabonica*    Gaboon Viper
*Bitis nasicornis*    Rhinoceros Viper
*Echis carinatus pyramidium*    Saw-Scaled Viper
*Causus bilineatus*    Lined Night Adder
*Causus defilippii*    Snouted Night Adder
*Causus lichtensteini*    Lichtenstein's Night Adder
*Causus maculatus*    West African Night Adder
*Causus resimus*    Green Night Adder
*Causus rhombeatus*    Common Night Adder

Literature:  Laurent (1956), de Witte (1962), Dowling, Minton and Russell (1970).


ANGOLA

*Dispholidus typus typus*    Boomslang
*Dispholidus typus punctatus*
*Thelotornis kirtlandi kirtlandi*    Twig Snake
*Thelotornis kirtlandi oatesi*    Oates's Twig Snake
*Atractaspis bibroni*
*Atractaspis congica congica*
*Atractaspis irregularis parkeri*
*Aspidelaps lubricus cowlesi*    Cowles's Shield Snake
*Dendroaspis polylepis polylepis*    Black Mamba
*Elapsoidea guntheri*    Gunther's Garter Snake
*Elapsoidea semiannulata semiannulata*    Angolan Garter Snake
*Naja haje anchietae*    Angolan Cobra
*Naja melanoleuca*    Forest Cobra
*Naja mossambica nigricincta*

*Naja nigricollis*      Spitting Cobra
*Pseudohaje goldii*     Goldi's Tree Cobra
*Atheris squamiger squamiger*      Green Tree Viper
*Atheris squamiger anisolepis*
*Bitis arietans arietans*      Puff Adder
*Bitis caudalis caudalis*      Cape Horned Viper
*Bitis gabonica gabonica*      Gaboon Viper
*Bitis heraldica*
*Bitis nasicornis*      Rhinoceros Viper
*Bitis peringueyi*      Peringuey's Viper
*Causus bilineatus*      Lined Night Adder
*Causus lichtensteini*      Lichtenstein's Night Adder
*Causus maculatus*      West African Night Adder
*Causus resimus*      Green Night Adder
*Causus rhombeatus*      Common Night Adder

Literature:  Bogert (1940), Laurent (1964).


ZAMBIA

*Dispholidus typus typus*      Boomslang
*Dispholidus typus kivuensis*
*Dispholidus typus punctatus*
*Thelotornis kirtlandi capensis*      Cape Twig Snake
*Atractaspis bibroni*
*Atractaspis congica orientalis*
*Dendroaspis polylepis polylepis*      Black Mamba
*Elapsoidea guntheri*      Gunther's Garter Snake
*Elapsoidea semiannulata semiannulata*      Angola Garter Snake
*Elapsoidea semiannulata boulengeri*      Boulenger's Garter Snake
*Naja haje anchietae*      Angolan Cobra
*Naja haje annulifera*
*Naja melanoleuca*
*Naja mossambica mossambica*      Mozambique Cobra
*Naja nigricollis*      Spitting Cobra
*Pseudohaje goldii*      Goldi's Tree Cobra
*Atheris nitschei rungweensis*      Rungwe Tree Viper
*Bitis arietans arietans*      Puff Adder
*Bitis gabonica gabonica*      Gaboon Viper
*Causus bilineatus*      Lined Night Adder
*Causus defilippii*      Snouted Night Adder
*Causus rhombeatus*      Common Night Adder

Literature:  Broadley (1971).


MALAWI

*Dispholidus typus typus*      Boomslang
*Thelotornis kirtlandi capensis*      Cape Twig Snake
*Atractaspis bibroni*
*Dendroaspis angusticeps*      Eastern Green Mamba
*Dendroaspis polylepis polylepis*      Black Mamba
*Elapsoidea semiannulata boulengeri*      Boulenger's Garter Snake
*Naja haje annulifera*
*Naja melanoleuca*      Forest Cobra

*Naja mossambica mossambica*     Mozambique Cobra
*Atheris nitschei rungweensis*     Rungwe Tree Viper
*Atheris superciliaris*     Swamp Viper
*Bitis arietans arietans*     Puff Adder
*Causus defilippii*     Snouted Night Adder
*Causus resimus*     Green Night Adder
*Causus rhombeatus*     Common Night Adder

Literature:  Sweeney (1969).


## MOZAMBIQUE

*Dispholidus typus typus*     Boomslang
*Thelotornis kirtlandi capensis*     Cape Twig Snake
*Atractaspis bibroni*
*Aspidelaps scutatus scutatus*     Shield Snake
*Aspidelaps scutatus fulafulus*
*Dendroaspis angusticeps*     Eastern Green Mamba
*Dendroaspis polylepis polylepis*     Black Mamba
*Elapsoidea semiannulata boulengeri*     Boulenger's Garter Snake
*Elapsoidea sundevalli decosteri*
*Elapsoidea sundevalli longicauda*
*Naja haje annulifera*
*Naja melanoleuca*     Forest Cobra
*Naja mossambica mossambica*     Mozambique Cobra
*Pelamis platurus*     Pelagic Sea Snake
*Atheris superciliaris*     Swamp Viper
*Bitis arietans arietans*     Puff Adder
*Bitis gabonica gabonica*     Gaboon Viper
*Causus defilippii*     Snouted Night Adder
*Causus resimus*     Green Night Adder
*Causus rhombeatus*     Common Night Adder

Literature:  Manacas (1956).


## ZIMBABWE-RHODESIA

*Dispholidus typus typus*     Boomslang
*Thelotornis kirtlandi capensis*     Cape Twig Snake
*Thelotornis kirtlandi oatesi*     Oates's Twig Snake
*Atractaspis bibroni*
*Aspidelaps scutatus scutatus*     Shield Snake
*Aspidelaps scutatus fulafulus*
*Dendroaspis angusticeps*     Eastern Green Mamba
*Elapsoidea semiannulata boulengeri*     Boulenger's Garter Snake
*Elapsoidea sundevalli longicauda*
*Hemachatus haemachatus*     Ringhals
*Naja haje anchietae*     Angolan Cobra
*Naja haje annulifera*
*Naja melanoleuca*     Forest Cobra
*Naja mossambica mossambica*     Mozambique Cobra
*Bitis arietans arietans*     Puff Adder
*Bitis atropos atropos*     Berg Adder
*Bitis caudalis caudalis*     Cape Horned Viper
*Bitis gabonica gabonica*     Gaboon Viper

*Causus defilippii*        Snouted Night Adder
*Causus rhombeatus*        Common Night Adder

Literature:  Broadley and Cock (1975).


BOTSWANA

*Dispholidus typus typus*        Boomslang
*Thelotornis kirtlandi capensis*        Cape Twig Snake
*Thelotornis kirtlandi oatesi*        Oates's Twig Snake
*Atractaspis bibroni*
*Aspidelaps scutatus scutatus*        Shield Snake
*Dendroaspis polylepis polylepis*        Black Mamba
*Elapsoidea semiannulata boulengeri*        Boulenger's Garter Snake
*Elapsoidea sundevalli fitzsimonsi*
*Naja haje anchietae*        Angolan Cobra
*Naja haje annulifera*
*Naja mossambica mossambica*        Mozambique Cobra
*Naja nivea*        Cape Cobra
*Bitis arietans arietans*        Puff Adder
*Bitis caudalis caudalis*        Cape Horned Viper
*Causus rhombeatus*        Common Night Adder

Literature:  FitzSimons (1974).


SOUTH AFRICA
(including Namibia)

*Dispholidus typus typus*        Boomslang
*Thelotornis kirtlandi capensis*        Cape Twig Snake
*Atractaspis bibroni*
*Aspidelaps lubricus lubricus*        African Coral Snake
*Aspidelaps lubricus infuscatus*        Western Coral Snake
*Aspidelaps scutatus scutatus*        Shield Snake
*Aspidelaps scutatus intermedius*
*Dendroaspis angusticeps*        Eastern Green Mamba
*Dendroaspis polylepis polylepis*        Black Mamba
*Elapsoidea semiannulata semiannulata*        Angolan Garter Snake
*Elapsoidea semiannulata boulengeri*        Boulenger's Garter Snake
*Elapsoidea sundevalli sundevalli*
*Elapsoidea sundevalli decosteri*
*Elapsoidea sundevalli fitzsimonsi*
*Elapsoidea sundevelli longicauda*
*Elapsoidea sundevalli media*
*Hemachatus haemachatus*        Ringhals
*Naja haje anchietae*        Angolan Cobra
*Naja haje annulifera*
*Naja melanoleuca*        Forest Cobra
*Naja mossambica mossambica*        Mozambique Cobra
*Naja mossambica nigricincta*
*Naja mossambica woodi*
*Naja nivea*        Cape Cobra
*Pseudohaje goldii*        Goldi's Tree Cobra
*Pelamis platurus*        Pelagic Sea Snake
*Bitis arietans arietans*        Puff Adder

*Bitis atropos atropos*     Berg Adder
*Bitis atropos unicolor*     Mountain Adder
*Bitis caudalis caudalis*     Cape Horned Viper
*Bitis caudalis paucisquamata*     Dwarf Adder
*Bitis cornuta cornuta*     Hornsman Adder
*Bitis cornuta albanica*     Eastern Hornsman Adder
*Bitis gabonica gabonica*     Gaboon Viper
*Bitis inornata*     Cape Puff Adder
*Bitis schneideri*     Schneider's Puff Adder
*Bitis xeropaga*
*Causus defilippii*     Snouted Night Adder
*Causus rhombeatus*     Common Night Adder

Literature:  FitzSimons (1974), Visser and Chapman (1978).


## SWAZILAND

*Dispholidus typus typus*     Boomslang
*Atractaspis bibroni*
*Dendroaspis polylepis polylepis*     Black Mamba
*Elapsoidea sundevalli sundevalli*     Natal Garter Snake
*Elapsoidea sundevalli decosteri*
*Hemachatus haemachatus*     Ringhals
*Naja haje annulifera*
*Naja mossambica mossambica*     Mozambique Cobra
*Bitis arietans arietans*     Puff Adder
*Bitis atropos atropos*     Berg Adder

Literature:  FitzSimons (1974).


## LESOTHO

*Dispholidus typus typus*     Boomslang
*Dendroaspis polylepis polylepis*     Black Mamba
*Hemachatus haemachatus*     Ringhals
*Naja nivea*     Cape Cobra
*Bitis arietans arietans*     Puff Adder
*Bitis atropos atropos*     Berg Adder

Literature:  FitzSimons (1974).


## MADAGASCAR

*Pelamis platurus*     Pelagic Sea Snake

Literature:  Guibe (1958).

# PART 4

# *ASIA*

*Naja naja oxiana*    Asian Cobra
*Pelamis platurus*    Pelagic Sea Snake
*Echis carinatus pyramidium*    Saw-Scaled Viper
*Vipera ammodytes transcaucasiana*    Armenian Sand Viper
*Vipera berus berus*    Northern Viper
*Vipera berus sachalinensis*    Sakhalin Island Viper
*Vipera kaznakovi*    Caucasus Viper
*Vipera lebetina obtusa*    West Asian Blunt-Nosed Viper
*Vipera lebetina turanica*    East Asian Blunt-Nosed Viper
*Vipera ursinii renardi*    Steppe Viper
*Vipera xanthina raddei*    Coastal Viper
*Agkistrodon halys halys*    Asian Pit Viper
*Agkistrodon halys caraganus*    Siberian Pit Viper
*Agkistrodon halys caucasicus*
*Agkistrodon halys intermedius*
*Agkistrodon saxatalis*

Literature:  Nikolsky (1916), Terentyev and Chernov (1949).

## MONGOLIA

*Agkistrodon halys halys*    Asian Pit Viper
*Agkistrodon halys intermedius*

Literature:  Dowling, Minton and Russell (1970).

## CHINA

*Rhabdophis nuchalis*
*Rhabdophis subminiatus*    Red-Necked Keelback
*Rhabdophis tigrinus*
*Bungarus fasciatus*    Banded Krait
*Bungarus multicinctus multicinctus*    Many-Banded Krait

*Bungarus multicinctus wanghoatingi*
*Naja naja atra*     Chinese Cobra
*Naja naja kaouthia*     Monacled Cobra
*Ophiophagus hannah*     King Cobra
*Calliophis kelloggi*     Kellogg's Coral Snake
*Calliophis macclellandi macclellandi*     MacClelland's Coral Snake
*Laticauda laticaudata*
*Laticauda semifasciata*
*Emydocephalus ijimae*
*Acalyptophis peroni*
*Hydrophis cyanocinctus*
*Hydrophis gracilis*
*Hydrophis melanocephalus*
*Hydrophis ornatus ornatus*
*Hydrophis parviceps*
*Lapemis hardwicki*     Hardwick's Sea Snake
*Thalassophis viperinus*
*Pelamis platurus*     Pelagic Sea Snake
*Vipera berus berus*     Northern Viper
*Vipera russelli siamensis*     Russell's Viper
*Azemiops feae*     Fea's Viper
*Agkistrodon acutus*     Sharp-Nosed Viper
*Agkistrodon blomhoffi brevicaudus*     Korean Mamushi
*Agkistrodon halys ussuriensis*
*Agkistrodon monticola*
*Agkistrodon saxatalis*
*Agkistrodon strauchi*
*Trimeresurus albolabris*     Green Pit Viper
*Trimeresurus jerdoni jerdoni*     Jerdon's Pit Viper
*Trimeresurus jerdoni xanthomelas*
*Trimeresurus monticola monticola*     Chinese Mountain Viper
*Trimeresurus monticola orientalis*
*Trimeresurus mucrosquamatus*     Chinese Habu
*Trimeresurus stejnegeri stejnegeri*     Chinese Green Tree Viper
*Trimeresurus stejnegeri yunnanensis*

Literature:  Pope (1935), Romer (1977).


TURKEY

*Echis carinatus pyramidium*     Saw-Scaled Viper
*Vipera ammodytes meridionalis*     Eastern Sand Viper
*Vipera berus berus*     Northern Viper
*Vipera kaznakovi*     Caucasus Viper
*Vipera lebetina obtusa*     West Asian Blunt-Nosed Viper
*Vipera ursinii renardi*     Steppe Viper
*Vipera xanthina xanthina*     Coastal Viper
*Vipera xanthina raddei*

Literature:  Steward (1971), Mertens (1952a).

## SYRIA

*Walterinnesia aegyptia*     Desert Black Snake
*Vipera ammodytes meridionalis*     Eastern Sand Viper
*Vipera lebetina obtusa*     West Asian Blunt-Nosed Viper
*Vipera palaestinae*     Palestine Viper


Literature:  Dowling, Minton and Russell (1970).


## LEBANON

*Atractaspis engaddensis*
*Walterinnesia aegyptia*     Desert Black Snake
*Cerastes cerastes gasperettii*     Arabian Horned Viper
*Cerastes vipera*     Sahara Sand Viper
*Echis coloratus*     Saw-Scaled Viper
*Pseudocerastes persicus fieldi*     False Horned Viper
*Vipera bornmulleri*
*Vipera lebetina obtusa*     West Asian Blunt-Nosed Viper
*Vipera palaestinae*     Palestine Viper


Literature:  Dowling, Minton and Russell (1970).


## ISRAEL

*Atractaspis engaddensis*
*Walterinnesia aegyptia*     Desert Black Snake
*Cerastes cerastes gasperettii*     Arabian Horned Viper
*Cerastes vipera*     Sahara Sand Viper
*Echis coloratus*     Saw-Scaled Viper
*Pseudocerastes persicus fieldi*     False Horned Viper
*Vipera bornmulleri*
*Vipera lebetina obtusa*     West Asian Blunt-Nosed Viper
*Vipera palaestinae*     Palestine Viper


Literature:  Mendelssohn (1963), Mendelssohn (1965), Hoofien (1972).


## JORDAN

*Atractaspis engaddensis*
*Naja haje haje*     Egyptian Cobra
*Cerastes cerastes gasperettii*     Arabian Horned Viper
*Echis coloratus*     Saw-Scaled Viper
*Pseudocerastes persicus fieldi*     False Horned Viper
*Vipera bornmulleri*
*Vipera palaestinae*     Palestine Viper


Literature:  Dowling, Minton and Russell (1970).

## IRAQ

*Walterinnesia aegyptia*    Desert Black Snake
*Cerastes cerastes gasperettii*    Arabian Horned Viper
*Echis carinatus pyramidium*    Saw-Scaled Viper
*Pseudocerastes persicus persicus*    False Horned Viper
*Vipera lebetina euphratica*    Central Asian Blunt-Nosed Viper
*Vipera lebetina obtusa*    West Asian Blunt-Nosed Viper


Literature:  Khalaf (1959).


## KUWAIT

*Walterinnesia aegyptia*    Desert Black Snake
*Hydrophis cyanocinctus*
*Hydrophis gracilis*
*Hydrophis lapemoides*
*Hydrophis ornatus ornatus*
*Hydrophis spiralis*
*Lapemis curtus*
*Pelamis platurus*    Pelagic Sea Snake
*Thalassophis viperinus*
*Cerastes cerastes gasperettii*    Arabian Horned Viper
*Echis carinatus pyramidium*    Saw-Scaled Viper
*Pseudocerastes persicus persicus*    False Horned Viper


Literature:  Dowling, Minton and Russell (1970).


## SAUDI ARABIA

*Naja haje arabica*    Arabian Cobra
*Walterinnesia aegyptia*    Desert Black Snake
*Hydrophis cyanocinctus*
*Hydrophis gracilis*
*Hydrophis lapemoides*
*Hydrophis ornatus ornatus*
*Hydrophis spiralis*
*Lapemis curtus*
*Pelamis platurus*    Pelagic Sea Snake
*Thalassophis viperinus*
*Bitis arietans arietans*    Puff Adder
*Cerastes cerastes gasperettii*    Arabian Horned Viper
*Echis carinatus pyramidium*    Saw-Scaled Viper
*Echis coloratus*
*Pseudocerastes persicus persicus*    False Horned Viper


Literature:  Dowling, Minton and Russell (1970).


## YEMEN

*Atractaspis microlepidota andersoni*
*Naja haje arabica*    Arabian Cobra
*Bitis arietans arietans*    Puff Adder

*Echis carinatus pyramidium*     Saw-Scaled Viper
*Echis coloratus*

Literature:  Dowling, Minton and Russell (1970).


## SOUTH YEMEN

*Atractaspis microlepidota andersoni*
*Naja haje arabica*     Arabian Cobra
*Pelamis platurus*     Pelagic Sea Snake
*Bitis arietans arietans*     Puff Adder
*Echis carinatus pyramidium*     Saw-Scaled Viper
*Echis coloratus*

Literature:  Dowling, Minton and Russell (1970).


## UNITED ARAB EMIRATES

*Hydrophis cyanocinctus*
*Hydrophis gracilis*
*Hydrophis lapemoides*
*Hydrophis ornatus ornatus*
*Hydrophis spiralis*
*Lapemis curtus*
*Pelamis platurus*     Pelagic Sea Snake
*Thalassophis viperinus*
*Echis carinatus pyramidium*

Literature:  Leviton and Anderson (1967).


## OMAN

*Hydrophis cyanocinctus*
*Hydrophis gracilis*
*Hydrophis lapemoides*
*Hydrophis ornatus ornatus*
*Hydrophis spiralis*
*Lapemis curtus*
*Pelamis platurus*     Pelagic Sea Snake
*Thalassophis viperinus*
*Echis carinatus pyramidium*

Literature:  Dowling, Minton and Russell (1970).


## IRAN

*Walterinnesia aegyptia*     Desert Black Snake
*Hydrophis cyanocinctus*
*Hydrophis gracilis*
*Hydrophis lapemoides*
*Hydrophis crnatus ornatus*

*Hydrophis spiralis*
*Lapemis curtus*
*Pelamis platurus*      Pelagic Sea Snake
*Thalassophis viperinus*
*Echis carinatus pyramidium*      Saw-Scaled Viper
*Eristocophis macmahoni*      Asian Sand Viper
*Pseudocerastes persicus persicus*      False Horned Viper
*Vipera latifii*
*Vipera lebetina obtusa*      West Asian Blunt-Nosed Viper
*Vipera lebetina turanica*      Central Asian Blunt-Nosed Viper
*Vipera ursinii renardi*      Steppe Viper

Literature:  Anderson (1963).


## AFGHANISTAN

*Naja naja oxiana*      Asian Cobra
*Echis carinatus pyramidium*      Saw-Scaled Viper
*Eristocophis macmahoni*      Asian Sand Viper
*Pseudocerastes persicus persicus*      False Horned Viper
*Vipera lebetina obtusa*      West Asian Blunt-Nosed Viper
*Vipera lebetina turanica*      Central Asian Blunt-Nosed Viper

Literature:  Anderson and Leviton (1969), Clark, Clark, Anderson and Leviton (1969),
             Dowling, Minton and Russell (1970).


## PAKISTAN

*Bungarus caeruleus sindanus*
*Naja naja naja*      Indian Cobra
*Hydrophis cyanocinctus*
*Hydrophis gracilis*
*Hydrophis lapemoides*
*Hydrophis ornatus ornatus*
*Hydrophis spiralis*
*Pelamis platurus*      Pelagic Sea Snake
*Thalassophis viperinus*
*Echis carinatus sochureki*      Saw-Scaled Viper
*Eristocophis macmahoni*      Asian Sand Viper
*Pseudocerastes persicus persicus*      False Horned Viper
*Vipera lebetina obtusa*      West Asian Blunt-Nosed Viper
*Vipera lebetina turanica*      Central Asian Blunt-Nosed Viper
*Vipera russelli russelli*      Russell's Viper
*Agkistrodon himalayanus*      Himalayan Pit Viper

Literature:  Minton (1966), Smith (1943).


## INDIA

*Rhabdophis himalayanus*      Himalayan Keelback
*Rhabdophis subminiatus*      Red-Necked Keelback
*Bungarus bungaroides*
*Bungarus caeruleus caeruleus*      Indian Krait

*Bungarus caeruleus sindanus*
*Bungarus fasciatus*     Banded Krait
*Bungarus lividus*
*Bungarus niger*
*Bungarus walli*     Wall's Krait
*Naja naja naja*     Indian Cobra
*Naja naja kaouthia*     Monacled Cobra
*Naja naja oxiana*     Asian Cobra
*Ophiophagus hannah*     King Cobra
*Calliophis beddomei*     Beddome's Coral Snake
*Calliophis bibroni*     Bibron's Coral Snake
*Calliophis macclellandi macclellandi*     MacClelland's Coral Snake
*Calliophis melanurus melanurus*
*Calliophis nigrescens*
*Laticauda colubrina*
*Disteira stokesi*
*Enhydrina schistosa*
*Hydrophis caerulescens*
*Hydrophis cantoris*
*Hydrophis cyanocinctus*
*Hydrophis fasciatus fasciatus*
*Hydrophis gracilis*
*Hydrophis lapemoides*
*Hydrophis mamillaris*
*Hydrophis nigrocinctus*
*Hydrophis obscurus*
*Hydrophis ornatus ornatus*
*Hydrophis spiralis*
*Hydrophis stricticollis*
*Kerilia jerdoni jerdoni*
*Lapemis curtus*
*Lapemis hardwicki*
*Pelamis platurus*     Pelagic Sea Snake
*Thalassophis viperinus*
*Echis carinatus carinatus*     Saw-Scaled Viper
*Echis carinatus sochureki*     Sochurek's Saw-Scaled Viper
*Vipera lebetina turanica*     Central Asian Blunt-Nosed Viper
*Vipera russelli russelli*     Russell's Viper
*Agkistrodon himalayanus*     Himalayan Pit Viper
*Hypnale hypnale*
*Trimeresurus albolabris*     Green Pit Viper
*Trimeresurus erythrurus*
*Trimeresurus gramineus*
*Trimeresurus huttoni*
*Trimeresurus jerdoni jerdoni*     Jerdon's Pit Viper
*Trimeresurus macrolepis*
*Trimeresurus malabaricus*
*Trimeresurus monticola monticola*     Chinese Mountain Viper
*Trimeresurus mucrosquamatus*     Chinese Habu
*Trimeresurus popeorum*     Pope's Pit Viper
*Trimeresurus purpureomaculatus purpureomaculatus*     Shore Pit Viper
*Trimeresurus stejnegeri yunnanensis*
*Trimeresurus strigatus*

Literature:  Smith (1943), Deoras (1970), Whitaker (1978).

## SRI LANKA

*Balanophis ceylonensis*    Flower Krait
*Bungarus caeruleus caeruleus*    Indian Krait
*Bungarus ceylonicus ceylonicus*    Sri Lanka Krait
*Bungarus ceylonicus karavala*
*Naja naja naja*    Indian Cobra
*Calliophis melanurus sinhaleyus*
*Laticauda colubrina*
*Laticauda laticaudata*
*Disteira stokesi*
*Enhydrina schistosa*
*Hydrophis bituberculata*
*Hydrophis caerulescens*
*Hydrophis cantoris*
*Hydrophis cyanocinctus*
*Hydrophis fasciatus fasciatus*
*Hydrophis gracilis*
*Hydrophis lapemoides*
*Hydrophis mamillaris*
*Hydrophis nigrocinctus*
*Hydrophis obscurus*
*Hydrophis ornatus ornatus*
*Hydrophis spiralis*
*Hydrophis stricticollis*
*Kerilia jerdoni jerdoni*
*Lapemis hardwicki*
*Pelamis platurus*    Pelagic Sea Snake
*Thalassophis viperinus*
*Echis carinatus sinhaleyus*    Saw-Scaled Viper
*Vipera russelli pulchella*    Russell's Viper
*Hypnale hypnale*
*Hypnale nepa*
*Hypnale walli*
*Trimeresurus trigonocephalus*    Sri Lanka Pit Viper

Literature:  Wall (1921), Smith (1943), Deraniyagala (1955).

## NEPAL

*Naja naja kaouthia*    Monacled Cobra
*Calliophis macclellandi univirgatus*
*Agkistrodon himalayanus*    Himalayan Pit Viper
*Trimeresurus albolabris*    Green Pit Viper
*Trimeresurus monticola monticola*    Chinese Mountain Viper
*Trimeresurus stejnegeri yunnanensis*

Literature:  Swan and Leviton (1962).

## BHUTAN

*Rhabdophis himalayanus*    Himalayan Keelback
*Rhabdophis subminiatus*    Red-Necked Keelback

Literature:  Smith (1943).

## BANGLADESH

*Rhabdophis himalayanus*     Himalayan Keelback
*Rhabdophis subminiatus*     Red-Necked Keelback
*Bungarus caeruleus caeruleus*     Indian Krait
*Naja naja naja*     Indian Cobra
*Naja naja kaouthia*     Monacled Cobra
*Ophiophagus hannah*     King Cobra
*Echis carinatus sochureki*     Sochurek's Saw-Scaled Viper
*Vipera russelli russelli*     Russell's Viper
*Trimeresurus erythrurus*
*Trimeresurus mucrosquamatus*     Chinese Habu

Literature:  Smith (1943).

## BURMA

*Rhabdophis himalayanus*     Himalayan Keelback
*Rhabdophis nigrocinctus*
*Rhabdophis nuchalis*
*Rhabdophis subminiatus*     Red-Necked Keelback
*Bungarus bungaroides*
*Bungarus fasciatus*     Banded Krait
*Bungarus magnimaculatus*
*Bungarus multicinctus wanghoatingi*
*Naja naja kaouthia*     Monacled Cobra
*Ophiophagus hannah*     King Cobra
*Calliophis macclellandi macclellandi*     MacClelland's Coral Snake
*Calliophis maculiceps maculiceps*
*Laticauda colubrina*
*Enhydrina schistosa*
*Hydrophis caerulescens*
*Hydrophis cantoris*
*Hydrophis fasciatus fasciatus*
*Hydrophis gracilis*
*Hydrophis nigrocinctus*
*Hydrophis obscurus*
*Hydrophis ornatus ornatus*
*Hydrophis spiralis*
*Hydrophis stricticollis*
*Kerilia jerdoni jerdoni*
*Lapemis hardwicki*
*Pelamis platurus*     Pelagic Sea Snake
*Thalassophis viperinus*
*Vipera russelli siamensis*     Russell's Viper
*Azemiops feae*     Fea's Viper
*Trimeresurus albolabris*     Green Pit Viper
*Trimeresurus erythrurus*
*Trimeresurus jerdoni jerdoni*     Jerdon's Pit Viper
*Trimeresurus kaulbacki*
*Trimeresurus monticola monticola*     Chinese Mountain Viper
*Trimeresurus popeorum*     Pope's Pit Viper
*Trimeresurus purpureomaculatus purpureomaculatus*     Shore Pit Viper
*Trimeresurus stejnegeri yunnanensis*

Literature:  Smith (1943).

## THAILAND

*Rhabdophis chrysargus*
*Rhabdophis subminiatus*        Red-Necked Keelback
*Rhabdophis tigrinus*
*Bungarus candidus*
*Bungarus fasciatus*      Banded Krait
*Bungarus flaviceps flaviceps*      Red-Headed Krait
*Naja naja kaouthia*        Monacled Cobra
*Ophiophagus hannah*      King Cobra
*Calliophis maculiceps maculiceps*
*Calliophis maculiceps hughi*
*Calliophis maculiceps smithi*
*Maticora bivirgata flaviceps*
*Maticora intestinalis lineata*
*Laticauda colubrina*
*Aipysurus eydouxi*
*Enhydrina schistosa*
*Hydrophis brooki*
*Hydrophis caerulescens*
*Hydrophis cyanocinctus*
*Hydrophis fasciatus fasciatus*
*Hydrophis fasciatus atriceps*
*Hydrophis gracilis*
*Hydrophis klossi*
*Hydrophis ornatus ornatus*
*Hydrophis torquatus diadema*
*Kerilia jerdoni siamensis*
*Lapemis harwicki*
*Pelamis platurus*      Pelagic Sea Snake
*Thalassophis anomalus*
*Thalassophis viperinus*
*Vipera russelli siamensis*      Russell's Viper
*Agkistrodon rhodostoma*      Malayan Pit Viper
*Trimeresurus albolabris*      Green Pit Viper
*Trimeresurus kanburiensis*
*Trimeresurus monticola meridionalis*
*Trimeresurus popeorum*      Pope's Pit Viper
*Trimeresurus puniceus*

Literature: Taylor (1965), Smith (1943).

## MALAYSIA
### (including North Borneo)

*Rhabdophis chrysargus*
*Rhabdophis subminiatus*        Red-Necked Keelback
*Bungarus candidus*
*Bungarus fasciatus*      Banded Krait
*Bungarus flaviceps flaviceps*      Red-Headed Krait
*Bungarus flaviceps baluensis*
*Naja naja miolepis*
*Naja naja sputatrix*
*Ophiophagus hannah*      King Cobra
*Calliophis gracilis*
*Calliophis maculiceps maculiceps*
*Maticora bivirgata flaviceps*

*Maticora intestinalis everetti*
*Maticora intestinalis lineata*
*Laticauda colubrina*
*Aipysurus eydouxi*
*Disteira stokesi*
*Enhydrina schistosa*
*Hydrophis brooki*
*Hydrophis caerulescens*
*Hydrophis cyanocinctus*
*Hydrophis fasciatus fasciatus*
*Hydrophis gracilis*
*Hydrophis klossi*
*Hydrophis melanosoma*
*Hydrophis ornatus ornatus*
*Hydrophis spiralis*
*Hydrophis torquatus torquatus*
*Hydrophis torquatus aagaardi*
*Kerilia jerdoni jerdoni*
*Kolpophis annandalei*
*Lapemis hardwicki*
*Pelamis platurus*      Pelagic Sea Snake
*Thalassophis anomalus*
*Thalassophis viperinus*
*Agkistrodon rhodostoma*      Malayan Pit Viper
*Trimeresurus albolabris*      Green Pit Viper
*Trimeresurus chaseni*
*Trimeresurus convictus*
*Trimeresurus monticola meridionalis*
*Trimeresurus popeorum*      Pope's Pit Viper
*Trimeresurus puniceus*
*Trimeresurus purpureomaculatus purpureomaculatus*      Shore Pit Viper
*Trimeresurus sumatranus sumatranus*      Sumatran Pit Viper
*Trimeresurus sumatranus malcolmi*
*Trimeresurus wagleri*      Wagler's Temple Viper

Literature:  Tweedie (in preparation), Haile (1958), Grandison (1978).


INDONESIA
(including Irian Jaya)

*Rhabdophis chrysargoides*
*Rhabdophis murudensis*
*Rhabdophis subminiatus*      Red-Necked Keelback
*Bungarus candidus*
*Bungarus fasciatus*      Banded Krait
*Bungarus flaviceps flaviceps*      Red-Headed Krait
*Bungarus javanicus*      Javan Krait
*Naja naja miolepis*
*Naja naja sputatrix*
*Naja naja sumatrana*      Sumatran Cobra
*Ophiophagus hannah*      King Cobra
*Calliophis gracilis*
*Maticora bivirgata bivirgata*
*Maticora bivirgata flaviceps*
*Maticora bivirgata tetrataenia*
*Maticora intestinalis intestinalis*
*Maticora intestinalis lineata*

*Maticora intestinalis nigrotaeniatus*
*Laticauda colubrina*
*Laticauda laticaudata*
*Laticauda schistorhynchus*
*Acanthophis antarcticus antarcticus*      Death Adder
*Aspidomorphus schlegeli*
*Micropechis ikaheka*      New Guinea Small-Eyed Snake
*Toxicocalamus grandis*
*Toxicocalamus loriae*
*Toxicocalamus presussi*
*Toxicocalamus stanleyanus*
*Parahydrophis mertoni*
*Aipysurus apraefrontalis*
*Aipysurus duboisi*
*Aipysurus eydouxi*
*Aipysurus foliosquamata*
*Aipysurus fuscus*
*Aipysurus laevis*
*Emydocephalus annulatus*
*Enhydrina schistosa*
*Hydrophis belcheri*
*Hydrophis brooki*
*Hydrophis caerulescens*
*Hydrophis cyanocinctus*
*Hydrophis fasciatus fasciatus*
*Hydrophis fasciatus atriceps*
*Hydrophis gracilis*
*Hydrophis klossi*
*Hydrophis melanosoma*
*Hydrophis ornatus ornatus*
*Hydrophis ornatus ocellatus*
*Hydrophis pacificus*
*Hydrophis spiralis*
*Hydrophis torquatus torquatus*
*Kerilia jerdoni jerdoni*
*Kolpophis annandalei*
*Lapemis hardwicki*
*Pelamis platurus*      Pelagic Sea Snake
*Thalassophis anomalus*
*Thalassophis viperinus*
*Vipera russelli limitis*      Russell's Viper
*Agkistrodon rhodostoma*      Malayan Pit Viper
*Trimeresurus albolabris*      Green Pit Viper
*Trimeresurus hageni*
*Trimeresurus popeorum*      Pope's Pit Viper
*Trimeresurus puniceus*
*Trimeresurus purpureomaculatus purpureomaculatus*      Shore Pit Viper
*Trimeresurus sumatranus sumatranus*
*Trimeresurus wagleri*      Wagler's Temple Viper

Literature:  Smith (1926), de Rooij (1917), Slater (1968), de Haas (1950),
             Loveridge (1945).


## LAOS

*Rhabdophis subminiatus*      Red-Necked Keelback
*Bungarus fasciatus*      Banded Krait

*Bungarus multicinctus wanghoatingi*
*Ophiophagus hannah*    King Cobra
*Calliophis kelloggi*    Kellogg's Coral Snake
*Calliophis maculiceps michaelis*
*Agkistrodon rhodostoma*    Malayan Pit Viper
*Trimeresurus albolabris*    Green Pit Viper
*Trimeresurus monticola meridionalis*

Literature:  Bourret (1936).


## KAMPUCHEA

*Rhabdophis chrysargus*
*Rhabdophis subminiatus*    Red-Necked Keelback
*Bungarus fasciatus*    Banded Krait
*Bungarus flaviceps flaviceps*    Red-Headed Krait
*Ophiophagus hannah*    King Cobra
*Calliophis maculiceps atrofrontalis*
*Maticora bivirgata flaviceps*
*Laticauda colubrina*
*Aipysurus eydouxi*
*Enhydrina schistosa*
*Hydrophis brooki*
*Hydrophis caerulescens*
*Hydrophis cyanocinctus*
*Hydrophis fasciatus fasciatus*
*Hydrophis fasciatus atriceps*
*Hydrophis gracilis*
*Hydrophis klossi*
*Hydrophis ornatus ornatus*
*Hydrophis torquatus diadema*
*Kerilia jerdoni siamensis*
*Lapemis hardwicki*
*Pelamis platurus*    Pelagic Sea Snake
*Thalassophis anomalus*
*Thalassophis viperinus*
*Agkistrodon rhodostoma*    Malayan Pit Viper
*Trimeresurus albolabris*    Green Pit Viper
*Trimeresurus monticola meridionalis*

Literature:  Bourret (1936).


## VIETNAM

*Rhabdophis callichroma*
*Rhabdophis nuchalis*
*Rhabdophis subminiatus*    Red-Necked Keelback
*Rhabdophis tigrinus*
*Bungarus candidus*
*Bungarus fasciatus*    Banded Krait
*Naja naja atra*    Chinese Cobra
*Naja naja kaouthia*    Monacled Cobra
*Ophiophagus hannah*    King Cobra
*Calliophis macclellandi macclellandi*    MacClelland's Coral Snake
*Calliophis maculiceps atrofrontalis*

*Aipysurus eydouxi*
*Enhydrina schistosa*
*Hydrophis brooki*
*Hydrophis cyanocinctus*
*Hydrophis fasciatus fasciatus*
*Hydrophis fasciatus atriceps*
*Hydrophis gracilis*
*Hydrophis ornatus ornatus*
*Kerilia jerdoni siamensis*
*Kolpophis annandalei*
*Lapemis hardwicki*
*Pelamis platurus*        Pelagic Sea Snake
*Thalassophis viperinus*
*Agkistrodon acutus*        Sharp-Nosed Viper
*Agkistrodon rhodostoma*        Malayan Pit Viper
*Trimeresurus albolabris*        Pope's Pit Viper
*Trimeresurus cornutus*
*Trimeresurus jerdoni bourreti*
*Trimeresurus monticola meridionalis*
*Trimeresurus mucrosquamatus*        Chinese Habu
*Trimeresurus tonkinensis*

Literature:  Bourret (1936).


THE PHILIPPINES

*Rhabdophis auriculatus*
*Rhabdophis spilogaster*
*Naja naja miolepis*
*Naja naja philippinensis*        Philippine Cobra
*Naja naja samarensis*
*Ophiophagus hannah*        King Cobra
*Calliophis calligaster calligaster*
*Calliophis calligaster gemianulis*
*Calliophis calligaster mcclungi*
*Maticora intestinalis bilineata*
*Maticora intestinalis philippina*        Philippine Coral Snake
*Maticora intestinalis suluensis*
*Laticauda colubrina*
*Laticauda laticaudata*
*Laticauda semifasciata*
*Hydrophis belcheri*
*Hydrophis cyanocinctus*
*Hydrophis fasciatus fasciatus*
*Hydrophis fasciatus atriceps*
*Hydrophis inornatus*
*Hydrophis semperi*
*Hydrophis spiralis*
*Lapemis hardwicki*
*Pelamis platurus*        Pelagic Sea Snake
*Trimeresurus flavomaculatus flavomaculatus*
*Trimeresurus flavomaculatus helieus*
*Trimeresurus flavomaculatus mcgregori*
*Trimeresurus schultzei*
*Trimeresurus wagleri*        Wagler's Pit Viper

Literature:  Taylor (1922), Leviton (1961).

ANDAMAN AND NICOBAR ISLANDS

*Naja naja sagittifera*
*Laticauda colubrina*
*Enhydrina schistosa*
*Hydrophis caerulescens*
*Hydrophis cantoris*
*Hydrophis fasciatus fasciatus*
*Hydrophis gracilis*
*Hydrophis nigrocinctus*
*Hydrophis obscurus*
*Hydrophis ornatus ornatus*
*Hydrophis spiralis*
*Hydrophis stricticollis*
*Kerilia jerdoni jerdoni*
*Lapemis hardwicki*
*Pelamis platurus*      Pelagic Sea Snake
*Thalassophis viperinus*
*Trimeresurus cantori*
*Trimeresurus labialis*
*Trimeresurus purpureomaculatus andersoni*


Literature:  Smith (1943).



TAIWAN

*Rhabdophis subminiatus*      Red-Necked Keelback
*Rhabdophis swinhonis*
*Rhabdophis tigrinus*
*Bungarus multicinctus multicinctus*      Many-Banded Krait
*Naja naja atra*      Chinese Cobra
*Calliophis japonicus sauteri*
*Calliophis macclellandi swinhoei*
*Laticauda colubrina*
*Laticauda laticaudata*
*Laticauda semifasciata*
*Emydocephalus ijimae*
*Acalyptophis peroni*
*Hydrophis cyanocinctus*
*Hydrophis gracilis*
*Hydrophis melanocephalus*
*Hydrophis ornatus ornatus*
*Lapemis hardwicki*
*Pelamis platurus*      Pelagic Sea Snake
*Thalassophis viperinus*
*Vipera russelli formosensis*      Russell's Viper
*Agkistrodon acutus*      Sharp-Nosed Viper
*Agkistrodon blomhoffi brevicaudus*      Korean Mamushi
*Trimeresurus albolabris*      Green Pit Viper
*Trimeresurus gracilis*
*Trimeresurus monticola makazayazaya*
*Trimeresurus mucrosquamatus*      Chinese Habu
*Trimeresurus stejnegeri formosensis*
*Trimeresurus stejnegeri kodairai*

Literature:  Kuntz (1963), Smith (1926).

KOREA

*Rhabdophis tigrinus*
*Pelamis platurus*      Pelagic Sea Snake
*Agkistrodon blomhoffi brevicaudus*      Korean Mamushi
*Agkistrodon caliginosus*
*Agkistrodon saxatalis*

Literature:  Stejneger (1907).


JAPAN

*Rhabdophis tigrinus*
*Laticauda colubrina*
*Laticauda laticaudata*
*Laticauda semifasciata*
*Pelamis platurus*      Pelagic Sea Snake
*Emydocephalus ijimae*
*Hydrophis cyanocinctus*
*Hydrophis melanocephalus*
*Lapemis hardwicki*
*Thalassophis viperinus*
*Agkistrodon blomhoffi blomhoffi*      Japanese Mamushi

Literature:  Stejneger (1907), Maki (1931).


RYUKYU ISLANDS

*Calliophis japonicus japonicus*
*Calliophis japonicus boettgeri*
*Calliophis macclellandi iwasakii*
*Laticauda colubrina*
*Laticauda laticaudata*
*Laticauda semifasciata*
*Emydocephalus ijimae*
*Hydrophis cyanocinctus*
*Hydrophis melanocephalus*
*Lapemis hardwicki*
*Pelamis platurus*
*Thalassophis viperinus*
*Agkistrodon blomhoffi affinis*
*Trimeresurus elegans*      Sakishima Habu
*Trimeresurus flavoviridis flavoviridis*      Okinawa Habu
*Trimeresurus flavoviridis tinkhami*
*Trimeresurus okinavensis*      Himehabu
*Trimeresurus tokarensis*

Literature:  Stejneger (1907), Maki (1931).

# PART 5

# AUSTRALASIA AND THE
# PACIFIC ISLANDS

AUSTRALIA

*Laticauda colubrina*
*Laticauda laticaudata*
*Acanthophis antarcticus antarcticus*      Death Adder
*Acanthophis antarcticus laevis*
*Acanthophis pyrrhus*
*Austrelaps superbus*      Australian Copperhead
*Brachyurophis woodjonesi*
*Cacophis harriettae*      White Crowned Snake
*Cacophis kreffti*      Dwarf Crowned Snake
*Cacophis squamulosus*      Golden Crowned Snake
*Cryptophis nigrescens*
*Cryptophis pallidiceps*      Australian Small-Eyed Snake
*Demansia atra*
*Demansia olivacea*      Spotted-Headed Snake
*Demansia psammophis*      Yellow-Faced Whip Snake
*Demansia torquatus*      Collared Whip Snake
*Denisonia devisi*      De Vis' Banded Snake
*Denisonia fasciata*      Rosen's Snake
*Denisonia maculata*      Ornamental Snake
*Denisonia punctata*      Little Spotted Snake
*Drysdalia coronata*      Crowned Snake
*Drysdalia coronoides*      White-Lipped Snake
*Drysdalia mastersi*      Masters' Snake
*Echiopsis curta*      Desert Snake
*Elapognathus minor*      Little Brown Snake
*Furina diadema*      Red-Naped Snake
*Glyphodon barnardi*      Barnard's Snake
*Glyphodon dunmalli*      Dunmall's Snake
*Glyphodon tristis*      Brown-Headed Snake
*Hemiaspis daemelii*      Gray Snake
*Hemiaspis signata*      Black-Bellied Marsh Snake
*Hoplocephalus bitorquatus*      Pale-Headed Snake
*Hoplocephalus bungaroides*      Broad-Headed Snake
*Hoplocephalus stephensi*      Yellow-Banded Snake
*Neelaps bimaculata*      Black-Naped Burrowing Snake
*Neelaps calonotus*      Western Black-Striped Snake

*Notechis ater ater*      Southern Tiger Snake
*Notechis ater humphreysi*      King Island Tiger Snake
*Notechis ater niger*      Kangaroo Island Tiger Snake
*Notechis ater serventyi*      Chappell Island Tiger Snake
*Notechis scutatus scutatus*      Common Tiger Snake
*Notechis scutatus occidentalis*      Western Tiger Snake
*Oxyuranus scutellatus scutellatus*      Taipan
*Pseudechis australis*      Mulga Snake
*Pseudechis colletti*      Collett's Snake
*Pseudechis guttatus*      Spotted Black Snake
*Pseudechis porphyriacus*      Red-Bellied Black Snake
*Pseudonaja affinis*
*Pseudonaja guttata*      Spotted Brown Snake
*Pseudonaja ingrami*      Ingram's Brown Snake
*Pseudonaja modesta*      Ringed Brown Snake
*Pseudonaja nuchalis*      Western Brown Snake
*Pseudonaja textilis*      Eastern Brown Snake
*Rhinoplocephalus bicolor*      Muller's Snake
*Simoselaps australis*      Australian Coral Snake
*Simoselaps bertholdi*      Desert Banded Snake
*Simoselaps fasciolatus*      Narrow-Banded Snake
*Simoselaps incinctus*
*Simoselaps semifasciata*      Half-Girdled Snake
*Simoselaps warro*      Black-Naped Burrowing Snake
*Suta suta*      Mallee Snake
*Tropidechis carinata*      Rough-Scaled Snake
*Unechis brevicaudus*      Short-Tailed Snake
*Unechis carpentariae*      Carpentaria Whip Snake
*Unechis flagellum*      Little Whip Snake
*Unechis gouldi*      Black-Headed Snake
*Unechis monachus*
*Unechis nigrostriatus*      Black-Striped Snake
*Vermicella annulata*      Bandy-Bandy
*Vermicella multifasciata*      Many-Ringed Bandy-Bandy
*Ephalophis greyi*
*Parahydrophis mertoni*
*Hydrelaps darwiniensis*
*Aipysurus duboisi*
*Aipysurus eydouxi*
*Aipysurus laevis*
*Aipysurus tenuis*
*Acalyptophis peroni*
*Disteira kingi*
*Disteira major*
*Disteira stokesi*
*Enhydrina schistosa*
*Hydrophis elegans*
*Hydrophis fasciatus fasciatus*
*Hydrophis fasciatus atriceps*
*Hydrophis gracilis*
*Hydrophis inornatus*
*Hydrophis ornatus ornatus*
*Hydrophis pacificus*
*Lapemis hardwicki*
*Pelamis platurus*      Pelagic Sea Snake

Literature:  Cogger (in press), Gow and Swanson (1977), Worrell (1963),
              Campbell (1976).

## NEW ZEALAND

*Pelamis platurus*     Pelagic Sea Snake

Literature:  Dowling, Minton and Russell (1970).


## PAPUA NEW GUINEA

*Parapistocalamus hedigeri*     Hediger's Snake
*Laticauda colubrina*
*Laticauda laticaudata*
*Laticauda schistorhynchus*
*Acanthophis antarcticus antarcticus*     Death Adder
*Aspidomorphus lineaticollis*
*Aspidomorphus muelleri*
*Aspidomorphus schlegeli*
*Demansia atra*
*Glyphodon tristis*     Brown-Headed Snake
*Micropechis ikaheka*     New Guinea Small-Eyed Snake
*Oxyuranus scutellatus cani*     New Guinea Taipan
*Pseudechis papuanus*     Papuan Black Snake
*Toxicocalamus buergersi*
*Toxicocalamus holopelturus*
*Toxicocalamus longissimus*
*Toxicocalamus loriae*
*Toxicocalamus misimae*
*Toxicocalamus preussi*
*Toxicocalamus spilolepidotus*
*Toxicocalamus stanleyanus*
*Unechis boschmai*
*Parahydrophis mertoni*
*Aipysurus duboisi*
*Aipysurus eydouxi*
*Aipysurus fuscus*
*Aipysurus laevis*
*Enhydrina schistosa*
*Hydrophis fasciatus fasciatus*
*Hydrophis fasciatus atriceps*
*Hydrophis ornatus ornatus*
*Hydrophis ornatus ocellatus*
*Hydrophis pacificus*
*Lapemis hardwicki*
*Pelamis platurus*     Pelagic Sea Snake

Literature:  Slater (1968), Worrell (1963), Smith (1926), Campbell (1976).


## FIJI ISLANDS

*Laticauda colubrina*
*Laticauda laticaudata*
*Laticauda schistorhynchus*
*Ogmodon vitianus*
*Aipysurus duboisi*
*Aipysurus laevis*
*Emydocephalus annulatus*
*Hydrophis belcheri*

*Hydrophis gracilis*
*Pelamis platurus*     Pelagic Sea Snake

Literature:  Smith (1926), Dowling, Minton and Russell (1970).


## SOLOMON ISLANDS

*Parapistocalamus hedigeri*     Hediger's Snake
*Laticauda colubrina*
*Laticauda crockeri*
*Laticauda laticaudata*
*Laticauda schistorhynchus*
*Loveridgelaps elapoides*     Banded Small-Eyed Snake
*Salomonelaps par*
*Aipysurus duboisi*
*Aipysurus laevis*
*Emydocephalus annulatus*
*Hydrophis belcheri*
*Hydrophis gracilis*
*Pelamis platurus*     Pelagic Sea Snake

Literature:  Loveridge (1945), Williams and Parker (1964).


## MELANESIA

*Laticauda colubrina*
*Laticauda laticaudata*
*Laticauda schistorhynchus*
*Aipysurus duboisi*
*Aipysurus laevis*
*Emydocephalus annulatus*
*Hydrophis belcheri*
*Hydrophis gracilis*
*Pelamis platurus*     Pelagic Sea Snake

Literature:  Smith (1926), Dunson (1975).


## POLYNESIA

*Laticauda colubrina*
*Laticauda laticaudata*
*Laticauda schistorhynchus*
*Pelamis platurus*     Pelagic Sea Snake

Literature:  Smith (1926), Dunson (1975).

# BIBLIOGRAPHY

# BIBLIOGRAPHY

Alvarez del Toro, M. (1960) *Los Reptiles de Chiapas*. Instituto Zoologico del
Estado, Tuxtla Gutierrez, Chiapas, Mexico.

Amaral, A. do (1979) *Brazilian Snakes: A Color Iconography*. 2nd ed. Sao Paulo.

Anderson, S.C. (1963) Amphibians and reptiles from Iran. *Proc. Calif. Acad. Sci.*
(4), *31*, 417-498.

Anderson, S.C. and Leviton, A.E. (1969) Amphibians and reptiles collected by the
Street Expedition to Afghanistan, 1965. *Proc. Calif. Acad. Sci.* (4), *37*, 25-56.

Angel, F. and Lhote, H. (1938) Reptiles et amphibiens du Sahara central et du
Soudan. *Bull. Com. Et. hist. scient. A.O.F.*, *21*, 345-384.

Appleby, L.G. (1971) *British Snakes*. John Baker, London.

Arnold, E.N. and Burton, J.A. (1978) *A Field Guide to the Reptiles and Amphibians
of Britain and Europe*. Collins, London.

Bogert, C.M. (1940) Herpetological results of the Vernay Angola Expedition, with
notes on African reptiles in other collections. Part I. Snakes, including an
arrangement of African Colubridae. *Bull. Am. Mus. nat. Hist.*, *77*, 1-107.

Bons, J. and Girot, B. (1962) Cle Illustree des reptiles du Maroc. *Trav. Inst.
Sci. Cherifien, ser. zool.* (26), 1-62.

Bourret, R. (1936) *Les Serpents de l'Indochine*. 2 vols. H. Basuyau, Toulouse.

Briscoe, M.S. (1949) Notes on snakes collected in Liberia. *Copeia* (1), 16-18.

Broadley, D.G. (1968) The venomous snakes of Central and South Africa. In:
W. Bucherl, E.E. Buckley and V. Deulofeu (eds.), *Venomous Animals and Their
Venoms*, vol. 1. Academic Press, New York and London, pp. 403-435.

Broadley, D.G. (1971) The reptiles and amphibians of Zambia. *Puku* (6), 1-143.

Broadley, D.G. and Cock, E.V. (1975) *Snakes of Rhodesia*. Longman Rhodesia,
Salisbury.

Campbell, C.H. (1976) *Snake Bite, Snake Venoms and Venomous Snakes of Australia
and New Guinea. An Annotated Bibliography*. Service Publication (13), School
of Public Health and Tropical Medicine, University of Sydney, Canberra.

Cansdale, G.S. (1961) *West African Snakes*. Longman, London.

Capocaccia, L. (1968) *Anfibi e Rettili*. Mondadori, Milan.

Clark, R.J., Clark, E.D., Anderson, S.C. and Leviton, A.E. (1969) Report on a
collection of amphibians and reptiles from Afghanistan. *Proc. Calif. Acad.
Sci.* (4), *36*, 279-316.

Cogger, H.G. (in press) *Reptiles and Amphibians of Australia*. 2nd ed. A.H. & A.W.
Reed, Sydney, Wellington and London.

Conant, R. (1975) *A Field Guide to Reptiles and Amphibians of Eastern and Central
North America*. 2nd ed. Houghton Mifflin Co., Boston.

Corkill, N.L. (1935). Notes on Sudan snakes. *Publ. Sudan Gvt. Mus. (Nat. Hist.)*,
*3*, 1-40.

De Haas, C.J.P. (1950)  Checklist of the snakes of the Indo-Australian Archipelago. *Treubia, 20,* 511-625.

Deoras, P.J. (1970)  *Snakes of India.*  National Book Trust, Delhi.

Deraniyagala, P.E.P. (1955)  *A Colored Atlas of Some Vertebrates From Ceylon.* Vol. 3 (Serpentoid Reptilia).  Government Press, Ceylon.

De Rooij, N. (1917)  *The Reptiles of the Indo-Australian Archipelago.*  Vol. 2 (Ophidia).  E.J. Brill, Leiden.

De Witte, G.-F. (1962)  Genera des serpents du Congo et du Ruanda-Urundi.  *Ann. Mus. r. Afr. Cent.* (8), *104,* 1-203.

Doucet, J. (1963).  Les serpents de la Republique de cote d'Ivoire.  *Acta Tropica, 20,* 201-340.

Dowling, H.G., Minton, S.A. and Russell, F.E. (eds.) (1970)  *Poisonous Snakes of the World.*  Department of the Navy, Bureau of Medicine and Surgery.  United States Government Printing Office, Washington, D.C.

Dunson, W.A. (ed.) (1975)  *The Biology of Sea Snakes.*  University Park Press, Baltimore, Tokyo and London.

Emsley, M.G. (1977).  Snakes, and Trinidad and Tobago.  *Bull. Maryland Herp. Soc., 13,* 201-304.

FitzSimons, V.F.M. (1974)  *A Field Guide to the Snakes of Southern Africa.*  2nd ed. Collins, London.

Fretey, J. (1975)  *Guide des Reptiles et Batraciens de France.*  Hatier, Paris.

Gloyd, H.K. and Conant, R. (1943)  A synopsis of the American forms of *Agkistrodon* (copperheads and moccasins).  *Bull. Chicago Acad. Sci., 7,* 147-170.

Gow, G.F. and Swanson, S. (1977)  *Snakes and Lizards of Australia.*  Angus and Robertson, London.

Grandison, A.G.C. (1978)  Snakes of West Malaysia and Singapore.  *Ann. Naturhistor. Mus. Wien, 81,* 283-303.

Grossenbacher, K. and Brand, M. (1973)  *Schlussel zur Bestimmung der Amphibien und Reptilien der Schweiz.*  Naturhistorisches Museum, Bern.

Guibe, J. (1958)  Les serpents de Madagascar.  *Mem. Inst. Sci. Madagascar, 12,* 189-260.

Haile, N.S. (1958)  The snakes of Borneo with a key to the species.  *Sarawak Mus. J., 8,* 743-771.

Harding, K.A. (in preparation)  *Reptiles and Amphibians of Trinidad and Tobago.*

Henderson, R.W. and Hoevers, L.G. (1975)  A checklist and key to the amphibians and reptiles of Belize, Central America.  *Milwaukee Pub. Mus. Contr. Biol. Geol., 5,* 1-63.

Hoge, A.R. (1966)  Preliminary account on neotropical Crotalinae (Serpentes, Viperidae).  *Mem. Inst. Butantan, 32,* 109-184.

Hoge, A.R. and Romano, S.A.R.W.D.L. (1971).  Neotropical pit vipers, sea snakes, and coral snakes.  In: W. Bucherl and E.E. Buckley (eds.), *Venomous Animals and Their Venoms,* vol. 2.  Academic Press, New York and London, pp. 211-293.

Hoofien, J.H. (1972)  A taxonomic list of the reptiles of Israel and its administered areas according to the status on May 31st, 1972.  Department of Zoology, Tel-Aviv University.

Hughes, B. (1977)  Latitudinal clines and ecogeography of the West African night adder, *Causus maculatus* (Hallowell, 1842), Serpentes, Viperidae.  *Bull, I.F. A.N., 39,* 358-384.

Hughes, B. and Barry, D.H. (1968).  The snakes of Ghana: a checklist and key.  *Bull. I.F.A.N., 31,* 1004-1041.

Hulselmans, J.L.J. de Roo, A. and de Vree, F. (1970)  Contribution a l'herpetologie de la Republique du Togo. 1. Liste preliminaire des serpents recoltes par la premiere Mission Zoologique Belge au Togo.  *Rev. Zool. Bot. Afr., 81,* 193-196.

Hulselmans, J.L.J., de Vree, F. and Van der Straeten, E. (1971)  Contribution a l'herpetologie de la Republique du Togo. 3. Liste preliminaire des serpents recoltes par la troisieme Mission Zoologique Belge au Togo.  *Rev. Zool. Bot. Afr., 83,* 47-49.

Khalaf, K.T. (1959)  *Reptiles of Iraq with Some Notes on the Amphibians.*  Ministry of Education, Baghdad.

Klauber, L.M. (1972) *Rattlesnakes. Their Habits, Life Histories, and Influence on Mankind.* 2 vols. 2nd ed. University of California Press, Berkeley and Los Angeles.

Klemmer, K. (1963) Liste der rezenten giftschlangen Elapidae, Hydrophiidae, Viperidae und Crotalidae. In Behringwerk-Mitteilungen, *Die Giftschlangen der Erde.* Marburg/Lahn, pp. 255–464.

Klemmer, K. (1968) Classification and distribution of European, North African, and North and West Asiatic venomous snakes. In: W. Bucherl, E.E. Buckley and V. Deulofeu (eds.), *Venomous Animals and Their Venoms*, vol. 1. Academic Press, New York and London, pp. 309–325.

Kramer, E. and Schnurrenberger, H. (1963) Systematik, verbreitung und okologie der Libyschen schlangen. *Rev. Suisse Zool.*, *70*, 453–568.

Kuntz, R.E. (1963) *Snakes of Taiwan.* U.S. Navy Medical Research Unit (2), Taipei, Taiwan.

Laurent, R.F. (1956) Contribution a l'herpetologie de la region des Grands Lacs de l'Afrique Central. Parts 1–3. *Ann. Mus. r. Congo Belg.* (8), *48*, 1–390.

Laurent, R.F. (1964) Reptiles et amphibiens de l'Angola. *Pub. Culturais Mus. Dundo* (67), 1–165.

Lazell, J.D. (1964) The Lesser Antillean representatives of *Bothrops* and *Constrictor.* *Bull. Mus. Comp. Zool., Harv.*, *132*, 245–273.

Leeson, F. (1959) *Identification of Snakes of the Gold Coast.* The Crown Agents for the Colonies, London.

Leviton, A.E. (1961) Keys to the dangerously venomous terrestrial snakes of the Philippine Islands. *Silliman Jour.*, *8*, 98–106.

Leviton, A.E. (1968) The venomous terrestrial snakes of East Asia, India, Malaya and Indonesia. In: W. Bucherl, E.E. Buckley and V. Deulofeu (eds.), *Venomous Animals and Their Venoms*, vol. 1. Academic Press, New York and London, pp. 529–576.

Leviton, A.E. and Anderson, S.C. (1967) Survey of the reptiles of the Sheikhdom of Abu Dhabi, Arabian Peninsula. Part II. Systematic account of the collection of reptiles made in the Sheikhdom of Abu Dhabi by John Gasperetti. *Proc. Calif. Acad. Sci.* (4), *35*, 157–192.

Loveridge, A. (1943) Report on the Smithsonian-Firestone Expedition's collection of reptiles and amphibians from Liberia. *Proc. U.S. natn. Mus.*, *91*, 113–140.

Loveridge, A. (1945) *Reptiles of the Pacific World.* MacMillan Co., New York.

Loveridge, A. (1957) Check list of the reptiles and amphibians of East Africa (Uganda; Kenya; Tanganyika; Zanzibar). *Bull. Mus. Comp. Zool., Harv.*, *117*, 153–362.

Maki, M. (1931) *A Monograph on Snakes of Japan.* Dai-ichi Shobo, Tokyo.

Manacas, S. (1956) Ofidios de Mocambique. *Mem. Junta Invest. Ultram*, *8*, 135–160.

Marx, H. (1956) Keys to the lizards and snakes of Egypt. U.S. Navy Research Report, Cairo.

Mendelssohn, H. (1963) On the biology of the venomous snakes of Israel. Part I. *Israel Jour. Zool.*, *12*, 143–170.

Mendelssohn, H. (1965) On the biology of the venomous snakes of Israel. Part II. *Israel Jour. Zool.*, *14*, 185–212.

Menzies, J.I. (1966) The snakes of Sierra Leone. *Copeia* (2), 169–179.

Mertens, R. (1938) Herpetologische ergebuisse einer reise nach Kamerum. *Abh. Senckenberg. Ges.*, *442*, 1–52.

Mertens, R. (1952a) Amphibien und reptilien aus der Tuerkei. *Rev. Fac. Sci. Univ. Istanbul* (1), 41–75.

Mertens, R. (1952b) Die amphibien und reptilien von El Salvador, auf grund der seisen von R. Mertens und A. Zilch. *Abh. Senckenberg. Ges.*, *487*, 1–120.

Minton, S.A. (1966) A contribution to the herpetology of West Pakistan. *Bull. Am. Mus. nat. Hist*, *134*, 27–184.

Monard, A. (1951) Reptiles et batraciens. In: Resultats de la Mission Zoologique Suisse du Cameroun. *Mem. I.F.A.N.*, *1*, 123–185.

Nikolsky, A.M. (1916) *Faune de la Russie. Reptiles.* Vol. 2. Petrograd.

Parker, H.W. (1949) The snakes of Somaliland and the Sokotra Islands. *Zool. Verh.*

*Rijksmus nat. Hist., Leiden* (6), 1-115.

Peters, J.A. and Orejas-Miranda, B. (1970) Catalogue of the neotropical Squamata. Part I (Snakes). *Bull. U.S. natn. Mus.* (297), 1-347.

Picado, C. (1931) *Serpientes Venenosas de Costa Rica.* Imprenta Alsina, San Jose.

Pitman, C.R.S. (1974) *A Guide to the Snakes of Uganda.* 2nd ed. Wheldon and Wesley, Codicote.

Pope, C.H. (1935) The reptiles of China. *Nat. Hist. Cent. Asia* (Am. Mus. nat. Hist.), *10*, 1-604.

Pozzi, A. (1966) Geonomia catalogo ragionato degli anfibi e dei rettili della Jugoslavia. *Natura, 57*, 5-55.

Roman, B. (1973) Viperides et Elapides de Haute-Volta. *Notes Docs. Voltaiq., 6*, 1-49.

Romer, J.D. (1977) *Illustrated Guide to the Venomous Snakes of Hong Kong.* 6th (updated) imp. J.R. Lee, Government Printer.

Roussel, M.-R. and Villiers, A. (1965) Serpents du Mayo-Kebbi (Chad). *Bull. I.F. A.N., 27*, 1522-1533.

Roze, J.A. (1966) *La Taxonomia y Zoogeografia de los Ofidios de Venezuela.* Universidad Central de Venezuela, Caracas.

Roze, J.A. (1967) A check list of the New World venomous coral snakes (Elapidae), with descriptions of new forms. *Am. Mus. Novit.* (2287), 1-60.

Saint Girons, H. (1956) Les serpents du Maroc. *Var. Scient. Soc. Sci. Nat. Psyc. Maroc, 8*, 1-29.

Salvador, A. (1974) *Guia de los Anfibios y Reptiles Espanoles.* Instituto Nacional para la Conservacion de la Naturaleza.

Sandner Montilla, F. (1965) *Manual de los Serpientes Ponzonosas de Venezuela.* Caracas.

Schmidt, K.P. (1933) Preliminary account of the coral snakes of Central America and Mexico. *Field Mus. Nat. Hist., ser. zool., 20*, 29-40.

Schmidt, K.P. (1941) The amphibians and reptiles of British Honduras. *Field Mus. Nat. Hist., ser. zool., 22*, 475-510.

Schmidt, K.P. (1953) *A Check List of North American Amphibians and Reptiles.* 6th ed. American Society of Ichthyologists and Herpetologists.

Schmidt, K.P. (1955) Coral snakes of the genus *Micrurus* in Colombia. *Fieldiana Zool., 34*, 337-359.

Slater, K.R. (1968) *A Guide to the Dangerous Snakes of Papua.* 2nd ed. Government Printer, Port Moresby.

Smith, H.M., Smith, R.B. and Sawin, H.L. (1977) A summary of snake classification (Reptilia, Serpentes). *J. Herp., 11*, 115-121.

Smith, H.M. and Taylor, E.H. (1945) An annotated checklist and key to the snakes of Mexico. *Bull. U.S. natn. Mus.* (187), 1-239.

Smith, M.A. (1926) *A Monograph of the Sea Snakes.* British Museum, London.

Smith, M.A. (1943) *The Fauna of British India, Ceylon and Burma, Including the Whole of the Indo-Chinese Sub-Region. Reptilia and Amphibia.* Vol. 3 (Serpentes). Taylor and Francis, London.

Smith, M.A. (1973) *The British Amphibians and Reptiles.* 5th ed. Collins, London.

Stebbins, R.C. (1966) *A Field Guide to Western Reptiles and Amphibians.* Houghton Mifflin Co., Boston.

Stejneger, L. (1907) Herpetology of Japan and adjacent territory. *Bull. U.S. natn. Mus.* (58), 1-577.

Steward, J.W. (1971) *The Snakes of Europe.* David and Charles, Newton Abbot.

Stuart, L.C. (1963) A checklist of the herpetofauna of Guatemala. *Misc. Pub. Mus. zool., Univ. Mich.* (122), 1-150.

Swan, L.W. and Leviton, A.E. (1962) The herpetology of Nepal: a history, checklist and zoogeographical analysis of the herpetofauna. *Proc. Calif. Acad. Sci.* (4), *32*, 103-147.

Sweeney, R.C.H. (1969) *The Snakes of Nyasaland.* Asher & Co., Amsterdam.

Taylor, E.H. (1922) *The Snakes of the Philippine Islands.* Manila.

Taylor, E.H. (1951) A brief review of the snakes of Costa Rica. *Kansas Univ. Sci. Bull., 34*, 3-88.

Taylor, E.H. (1965)  The serpents of Thailand and adjacent waters. *Kansas Univ. Sci. Bull.*, *45*, 609–1096.

Terentyev, P.V. and Chernov, S.A. (1949)  *Opredelitel Presmykayushchikhsya i Zemnovodnykh.*  Moscow.

Tweedie, M. (in preparation).  *The Snakes of Malaya.*  3rd ed.

Visser, J. and Chapman, D.S. (1978)  *Snakes and Snakebite. Venomous Snakes and the Management of Snakebite in South Africa.*  Purnell and Sons, Cape Town.

Villiers, A. (1950)  Contribution a l'etude du peuplement de la Mauritanie. Ophidiens.  *Bull. I.F.A.N.*, *12*, 984–998.

Villiers, A. (1965)  Sepents recoltes au Mali et en Haute-Volta par le Dr. Lamontellerie.  *Bull. I.F.A.N.*, *27*, 1192–1195.

Villiers, A. (1966)  Contribution a la faune de Congo (Brazzaville) Mission A. Villiers et A. Descarpentries. XLII. Reptiles Ophidiens.  *Bull. I.F.A.N.*, *28*, 1720–1760.

Wall, F. (1921)  *The Snakes of Ceylon.*  Colombo Museum, Ceylon.

Whitaker, R. (1978)  *Common Indian Snakes. A Field Guide.*  MacMillan and Co., India.

Williams, E.E. and Parker, F. (1964).  The snake genus *Parapistocalamus* on Bougainville, Solomon Islands (Serpentes, Elapidae).  *Senckenberg. Biol.*, *45*, 543–552.

Worrell, E. (1963)  *Dangerous Snakes of Australia and New Guinea.*  5th ed.  Angus and Robertson, Sydney.

Wright, A.H. and Wright, A.A. (1957)  *Handbook of Snakes of the United States and Canada.*  2 vols.  Cornell University Press, New York.

# *INDEXES*

# AUTHOR INDEX

Alcock, A.  51, *77*
Alvarez del Toro, M.  92, *149*
Amaral, A. do  17, 25, 59, 60, 62, 64, 66, *77*, 100, *149*
Anderson, J.A.  53, *77*
Anderson, J.D.  70, *77*
Anderson, S.C.  50, *82*, 131, 132, *149*, *151*
Andersson, L.G.  4, 40, *82*
Angel, F.  12, *77*, 110, 111, *149*
Appleby, L.G.  103, *149*
Arnold, E.N.  103, 104, 105, 106, 107, *149*
Ashe, J.  47, *77*

Baird, S.F.  21, 65, 68, 71, *77*
Barbour, T.  19, 25, 63, *77*
Barrio, A.  21, *77*
Barry, D.H.  115, *150*
Bavay, A.  40, *77*
Beauvois, P. de  56, 57, 65, *77*
Beddome, R.H.  73, *77*
Bedriaga, J.  58, *77*
Belluomini, H.E.  60, *81*
Berthold, A.A.  64, *77*
Bianconi, J.J.  9, *77*
Bibron, G.  19, 20, 23, 24, 30, 32, 34, 36, 41, 49, 51, 59, 60, 63, *79*
Bleeker, P.  26, *77*
Blyth, E.  2, 8, 72, *77*
Bocage, J.V.B. de  40, 10, 11, 12, 49, *77*
Bocourt, M.-F.  59, 62, 63, *77*
Boettger, P.  11, 50, 52, 54, *77*
Bogert, C.M.  9, 12, 48, 64, *78*, 122, *149*
Boie, F.  2, 13, 26, 58, 74, *78*
Boie, H.  2, 33, 56, *78*
Bonaparte, C.L.J.L.  54, *78*
Bons, J.  109, 110, *149*
Bosca, E.  53, *78*

Boulenger, C.A.  2, 5, 7, 9, 11, 12, 13, 14, 18, 23, 25, 26, 29, 31, 32, 33, 34, 35, 36, 37, 38, 40, 41, 43, 47, 49, 51, 52, 54, 55, 60, 63, 74, *78*
Bourret, R.  1, 74, 75, *78*, 139, 140, *149*
Brand, M.  105, *150*
Briscoe, M.S.  114, *149*
Broadley, D.G.  ix, 9, 11, *78*, 122, 124, *149*
Brongersma, L.D.  38, *78*
Brown, B.C.  21, *78*
Buchholz, W.  9, *78*
Burger, W.L.  22, 39, 56, *78*
Burton, J.A.  103, 104, 105, 106, 107, *149*

Campbell, C.H.  144, 145, *149*
Campbell, J.A.  60, *78*
Cansdale, G.S.  112, 113, 114, 115, 116, 117, *149*
Cantor, T.E.  7, 8, 13, 14, 26, 72, 74, *78*
Capocaccia, L.  106, *149*
Chapman, D.S.  125, *153*
Chernov, S.A.  53, *78*, 127, *153*
Chrapliwy, P.S.  24, *84*
Clark, E.D.  132, *149*
Clark, R.J.  132, *149*
Cliff, F.S.  65, 67, *78*, *83*
Cochran, D.M.  16, *78*
Cock, E.V.  124, *149*
Cogger, H.G.  144, *149*
Conant, R.  57, *80*, 90, *149*, *150*
Cope, E.D.  18, 19, 20, 21, 22, 47, 56, 62, 64, 65, 67, 68, 71, *78*
Corkill, N.L.  111, *149*
Coues, E.  70, *79*
Cristoph, H.  54, *79*
Cuvier, G.L.C.F.D.  25, 33, *79*

Darevsky, I.S.  53, *82*

157

# SUBJECT INDEX

161

Suchitepequez  22, 24, 25
Suchumi District  52
Sudan  5, 10, 12, 13, 49, 55, 111
Sudest  29
Sudost-Frankreich  54
Suishako  16
Sulawesi  1, 7, 13, 14, 26, 75
Sulu Archipelago  26
Sumatra  7, 8, 13, 14, 15, 26, 41, 42,
         43, 44, 45, 58, 72, 73, 74,
         75
Sumba  72
Sumbawa  13, 72
Sungii River  75
Sunderbunds  43
Surat  31
Surinam  17, 21, 22, 24, 25, 56, 59,
         66, 97
*Suta*  37
   *suta*  37, 144
Swan River  32
Swaziland  3, 10, 11, 12, 125
Sweden  52, 103
Switzerland  52, 105
Sydney  30
Synonymies  ix
Syria  14, 51, 53, 129
Szechwan  55, 58, 73, 74

Tabasco  20, 63
Taboga Island  23
Taihoku  74
Taipan  144
   New Guinea  145
Taiwan  2, 8, 13, 15, 16, 41, 42, 43,
        45, 53, 56, 57, 72, 73, 74,
        141
Takara shima  75
Talara  59
Tamaulipas  21, 56, 66, 67, 71
Tampico  21, 66
Tancitaro  68
Tanganyika  47, 48
Tangola-Tangola  18
Tangolunda  18
Tanner Trail  70
Tanzania  3, 5, 9, 10, 11, 12, 13, 47,
         48, 49, 55, 119
Tao Island  16
Taoshan  58
Tapanatepec  24
Tapurucuara  17
Tasmania  32, 34
Taylor's Mocassin  90
Teapa  63
Tehuantepec  24
Tengyueh  75
Tennessee  57, 58, 71
Territorio Federal do Roraima  66

Territory of New Guinea  38
Territory of Papua  37, 38
Tete  12
Texas  17, 21, 57, 58, 65, 67, 71
Thailand  1, 2, 7, 8, 13, 14, 16, 26, 54,
         58, 72, 74, 136
*Thalassophis*  45
   *anomalus*  45, 136, 137, 138, 139
   *viperinus*  45, 128, 130, 131, 132,
         133, 134, 135, 136, 137, 138,
         139, 140, 141, 142
*Thamnocenchris aurifer*
*Thelotornis*  3
   *capensis*  3
   *kirtlandi*
      *capensis*  3, 119, 122, 123
      *kirtlandi*  3, 112, 113, 114, 115,
            116, 117, 118, 119, 120, 121
      *oatesi*  3, 120, 121, 123
Tibet  2, 55, 73
Tiflis  52
Tiger Snake
   Chappell Island  144
   Common  144
   Kangaroo Island  144
   King Island  144
   Southern  144
   Western  144
Timor  72
Timor Sea  40
Tindharia  8
Togo  2, 5, 9, 11, 12, 14, 48, 49, 55,
      115
Togoland  11
Tokuchimura  15
Tome Assu  59
*Tomogaster eydouxi*  40
*Tomyris oxiana*  30
Tong-King  1
Tonkin  55
Torara Group  75
Toricelli Mountains  37
Tortuga Island  69
*Toxicocalamus*  37-38
   *buergersi*  37, 145
   *grandis*  37, 138
   *holopelturus*  37, 145
   *longissimus*  37, 145
   *loriae*  38, 138, 145
   *misimae*  38, 145
   *preussi*  38, 138, 145
   *spilolepidotus*  38, 145
   *stanleyanus*  38, 138, 145
Tranquebar  41
Transcaspia  13
Transcaucasia  52, 53, 57
Transkei  48
Transvaal  3, 9, 11, 12, 49, 55
Trebinj  52